A Luminous Future

Growing up in Transylvania in the Shadow of Communism

Teodor Flonta

DeProverbio.com

First published in 2012 by DeProverbio.com
www.deproverbio.com

For Matteo.
With your birth you gave me the *voice* to begin, with your first steps the will to continue, and with your first words the strength to finish this story.

Contents

The *Duba*

Lupoaia, Transylvania. February 13, 1951.

Sometime after midnight, a black, windowless van, with its lights extinguished, stopped in front of our house. Four men hurried out. Two of them entered the courtyard and headed straight for the door, while the other two jumped over the fence; one stationed himself beside the back window of our bedroom, on the garden side, and the other at the front window, overlooking the road. When they were all in position, the first man tried the door handle. He turned to the second man, shook his head and peered through the window. Too dark to see inside, he shook his head again. The second man took a step forward and knocked on the door three times.

"Flonta Pavel, open up," he commanded.

They waited for half a minute. The man knocked louder.

"Flonta Pavel, we know you are in there."

I was asleep in the same room as my young parents. The loud knocks on the door woke me up and, as if having a bad dream, I started crying. Mama rushed over and took me in her arms. In the dark I saw the shadow of my father grabbing clothes, opening the window and closing it again.

"They're everywhere," he whispered.

"God help us," Mama crossed herself.

"Open immediately, otherwise we'll break down the door. We know you are in there, Flonta Pavel. We want to talk to you."

My father nodded to Mama. She put me on the bed and went to open the door. Terrified at being left alone, I started crying again. My father took me in his arms and tried to calm me down. For a moment I felt safer against his rough work-worn, familiar skin, which smelled of straw, cow dung and *pălinca*, the potent plum brandy he distilled. Mama, barefoot and dishevelled in her thick hemp shirt and petticoat, opened the door and two plain clothes men burst into the house. The first took hold of her arm and dragged her into the room, while the second pushed her from behind. Mama started crying, which made me scream all the more. Then the first Securitate man yelled so loudly that I froze and stopped crying. The darkness made him look huge.

"Get some light, woman, and mind the boy," he ordered. Then he turned to my father and, in a calmer voice, said: "You are coming with us."

Just like that. "You are coming with us" was a new phrase repeated thousands and thousands of times all over the country, mainly in the dead of night. It was synonymous with torture, pain, and even death. After hearing those words, some – the newly-created enemies of the people – never came back.

Mama lit the lamp and took me in her arms. The first Securitate man had big hands and big teeth, whiter than sugar cubes. He leered menacingly at Mama with eyes black as charcoal in the low light of the small crowded room.

"Why?" my father asked.

"You are a *chiabur*," the man said curtly.

Chiabur meant rich peasant or, in the new language of the regime, 'enemy of the people'. A few months earlier, my father had been declared a *chiabur* because he had a *cazan*, a small distillery, where he employed two people for two or three months a year. He knew that to argue with these men would only aggravate his situation. Since the previous spring, rumours had circulated in the villages around Lupoaia that the Securitate dragged people from their beds at night and took them to town in the dreaded *duba*, the black windowless van. Now those rumours had become reality and he could do nothing to save himself.

"May I get dressed?" he asked, accepting his fate.

"Hurry up," barked the first Securitate man, who seemed to be in charge.

"Where are you taking him?" Mama cried.

"It's no business of yours."

Mama's sobs grew louder.

"Shut up, woman," the man yelled.

Mama screamed, taking him by surprise. "Where are you taking him? He hasn't done anything wrong!"

The Securitate man jumped at her and slapped her so hard that she fell onto the bed. As she fell, she lost her grip on me. I rolled over the doona and slammed my forehead against the hard wall. I wanted to cry but no sound came out of me.

"Shut up, you devil's bitch! You want to wake the whole neighbourhood?"

The Securitate wanted to do a clean job, unseen and unheard. The Party that wanted to create the new man didn't want to be seen using old fascist methods.

But that was not the way to treat a determined woman. Mama screamed harder. "Help! They are killing us! They are taking Pavelea away!"

The first man grabbed a pillow and smothered her face. As she struggled, he shouted at my father, "Tell her to stop! Tell her!"

The second man, his bulk creating ominous shadows in the crowded room, shoved my father towards the bed, where Mama was suffocating. "Tell her!" he shouted. "You want more trouble?"

With a trembling voice and tears in his eyes, my father tried to calm Mama down. "Nuţa, don't worry darling, I'll come back today, you'll see. Be a good girl."

The Securitate man let go of Mama. She threw the pillow at him. Her shouts were louder than before. "Tell them you didn't do anything wrong! Tell them to leave us alone!"

The first man kicked her hard in the stomach. She groaned, crouched down to the ground, writhing in pain, buried her face in her knees and stayed in that position to defend herself from the beast. He kept kicking her again and again, hatred shining in his eyes.

My father threw himself between the man's boot and Mama's body. "Stop it! Assassin! You'll kill her!" he yelled, grabbing the man's foot.

They subdued my father and tied his hands behind his back. All the while he was crying out Mama's name. I couldn't understand what was happening to my parents. I only knew that when someone did bad things, punishment followed. But Mama had not done anything bad to anybody. How could these people be so cruel? I had seen that kind of hatred in Ghiona's eyes, when he beat his wife and chased her naked in the courtyard with a knife in his hand. But everybody knew that he was a crazy man beyond repair after coming home from the Russian front.

My father yelled at me to go and get my grandparents. I climbed out of bed fast, slipped between the second Securitate man's hands, and raced through the night to my grandparents' house. Grandma Saveta came running behind me, followed by Grandpa Toderea. I wanted to be a *zmeu* – the demon capable of stealing the moon and the sun from the sky – or some other creature, powerful enough to blow these ugly Securitate men into little pieces. I wanted to save my parents. When we arrived, the men were pushing my father into the *duba*. Mama was lying in a pool of blood, with her head against the foot of the bed. Her now crooked nose and badly bruised lips were covered in blood, which was still trickling down her chin onto her neck and shirt. One hand was on the floor, palm opened up and fingers curled, the other pressing on her belly. Her underskirt was soaked in blood. When Grandma saw her, she began to wring her old bony hands, until the paper-thin skin turned white for lack of blood. Then she started to chant that terrible melody for the dead, intoned when the funeral cart starts moving from the courtyard to the cemetery. Grandpa, mumbling and sighing, his distraught eyes fixed on his daughter, asked Grandma to help him lift Mama onto the bed.

As soon as they heard the *duba* leaving, the women from the neighbourhood came in. They already knew what had happened: they had seen my father being taken away. Ana, a neighbour, went back to her house and returned with chicken broth for Mama; the smell made my mouth water. Norca ran down Hurupa to Moaşa Stela's house and they both came dishevelled and puffing. Mama did not talk to anyone. Moaşa Stela, the midwife, asked Grandma for clean clothes and, when they changed Mama into a crisp white petticoat, Grandpa took me into the other room. When we returned, there was silence in the small room where Mama lay in bed. Grandma crouched on the floor, her face in her hands, her body rocking back and forth. Grandpa helped her get up. Her face was shattered and her hands were trembling. She said something to Grandpa.

"Not even the unborn are safe. What has the world come to? May God protect us," he replied, gazing at the ceiling.

The women stared at him and then they looked at me without saying a word. They stayed with us throughout the night and came back every now and then during the day.

Modru, our next door neighbour, went up to Râturi late in the afternoon to see if my father was coming home on the train from Oradea. He wasn't. Were these Securitate men, whom I wanted to blow into little pieces, going to kill my father? I heard the women on our porch talking about this. People coming from the Tinca market had said that was what the Securitate did to the *chiaburs* taken away in a *duba*, in the middle of the night. Was I going to be like my cousin Viorica, whose father died on the Russian front? Auntie Puica, her mother, remarried and left her to be raised by her grandparents. People started calling her the orphan; and some children didn't want to play with her anymore.

I didn't want my father to die. I didn't want Mama to marry again. I didn't want to be called the orphan and have children not want to play with me anymore. I asked Mama about this and she assured me that my father was going to return. No doubt about that at all. He must have missed the train. Sometimes these things happen. She cried when she told me this. Then she wiped her face with her hands and said that I was her precious treasure, behaving so bravely with the Securitate people. Grandma and Grandpa told her they were so proud of me. The next day, they told me, my father was going to come home with the evening train.

I waited and waited for evening to come. I went into the garden and down to Valea Ştefani and there sat on a mound, from where I could see the Râturi and beyond, as far as Holod, waiting for my father to come; but he never did. I started crying, because I did not know whom to believe anymore: Mama and my grandparents or the people coming from the Tinca market who said that the *chiaburs*, taken away in a *duba* in the middle of the night, were killed by the Securitate. I cried because I couldn't become a *zmeu*, or some big, ugly creature and blow the Securitate people into tiny pieces and free my father from their clutches.

The End of the World

Hobart, Tasmania. October 4, 2005.

More than fifty years have passed since I witnessed my father's arrest – the first of many. I've since left Romania, lived in Italy, and ultimately settled in Australia. No matter where I've been, though, those scenes have continued to play in my head, over and over again – more so after my father's death.

I am now 59 years old. I normally feel older; but today is the exception, as I sit in a pristine hospital, waiting for my first grandson to be born. In this clean waiting room I find myself thinking of how different my birth in Lupoaia was. Mama's words echo in my ears, telling me about the freezing cold, the pure white snow reaching the windowsills and the wolves howling in the forest. What I remember most vividly this afternoon, though, is her prophesy about my future. In her dreams she saw the Fates who wove my destiny and determined the course of my life. I can still see her frown and the wrinkles on her forehead, when she told me I was going to spend my last days so far away, that it seemed to her the end of the world; that in my old age I would be surrounded by little children with beautiful, bright eyes and eager faces, who spoke words, unlike anything she'd ever heard and yet, had features resembling my ancestors'. Here I am, cold shivers going down my spine, astonished at the accuracy of her tale, remembering with alarm that both my grandfathers died at the age of 59.

Memories of my father grip me. He is the reason I find myself in this place. His pain. His love. His struggle to give me an education. Perhaps his dreams of escaping his condition through me. We want our children to do better than us in life, to have what we don't. I wish he could be here today, to be the first to see a fourth generation of our family. He would have liked it so much, secretly harbouring the wish that, one day, some of us would return to Lupoaia, to live in the house he built for us. But he died fifteen years ago, a few months after the fall of Communism. He had lived alone for a long time, Mama having died in 1973, just one month before my first son was born in Milan.

He was planning to visit me in 1989 but, when Communism fell, his visa application stalled in Belgrade, because Australia did not have consular offices in Romania. When he finally got the visa, he decided to stay in Romania to recover his land from the collective. He was never able to get the papers. I did that after his death; but a few months later, the government passed a law against foreigners owning Romanian land. By then, I was technically a foreigner, so the regime undid what I had done. The following year I was put on a list, with five relatives, to claim my father's land – land that had always belonged to him, because he had never signed it off to the collective. They took it from him, anyway.

When the Lupoaia collective was dismantled, the cattle were distributed to the villagers. When my father went to claim his, there was only one cow left, so old and skinny that nobody wanted her. He walked her out of the collective stables and paraded her through the village, all the way home, making heads turn. I cannot imagine what went through his mind in those moments. Did he see, in this unwanted cow's condition, a similarity to his own? Was he trying to make a point? I remember one of his favourite sayings, that the world was a big place and there was enough space for everybody. I believe his own experiences with Communism, which had violently invaded his space, reinforced his conviction that everybody deserved a fair chance in life, even a skinny old cow.

Although my father was 70 when Communism fell, he made plans for the future. All of them included me. He wanted to build something with me; but I know that, in his heart, he wanted to look after me again, as he had done until I left Romania in 1972, on the eve of my 26th birthday.

On Friday 10th August, 1990, he harvested all day in the fields, under the scorching sun. Once home, he sat on the bench outside his porch. Some neighbours joined him and he brought a bottle of *pălinca* to share with them, before he retired for the night. On Saturday morning, he did not come out as usual to feed the cow. The neighbours forced the door open and found him dead, still dressed in his work clothes. Burst neck artery, a doctor said. He died unexpectedly and quickly on that August 10th, which is known as the night of the shooting stars. Many events of his life were like that – unexpected, quick and unwarranted. If he could speak to me, he would say that his sudden death had spared him the loneliness of the sick, in a sick country, and that he was happy enough to have been allowed the satisfaction of seeing the regime of his torturers crumble. That gave him the chance to hope, to dream again. Even if that period of his life was cut short, it righted some of the wrongs of the past. Then, with a big grin on his face that always reached his deep, crinkly eyes, he would say that he had completed his mission on earth – he had survived a regime that wanted him dead, recovered the land stolen from him and had ultimately died in the house he built. Lastly, he would wink and remind me not to forget the icing on the cake – his cow. He was a practical man but he understood symbolism.

I never thought I would live long enough to see Communism crumble. In spite of all his tribulations, my father was an optimist and often said to me that a regime that talked to people as if they were stupid or blind, always telling lies, did not have a future. No amount of rifles and bayonets could stop people from rising against it eventually. He was sure the end would come sooner, rather than later. I am glad he lived to see that end.

My Italian wife, Ariella, and I arrived in Lupoaia three days after my father's funeral. On our way home through the village, indignant acquaintances whispered to me that my uncle Gligorea had told everybody that my father's house now belonged to him.

He was the new landlord, as he put it. A Bucharest resident, he had already given the keys of the house to a neighbour who would look after it in his absence. Exhausted by the long trip from Australia and overwhelmed by the loss of my father, the last member of my family, I felt emotionally shattered. More so, as Ariella started sobbing uncontrollably beside me. Uncle Gligorea behaved as if I did not exist. I felt like a prodigal son returning from far away lands, only to find out that my father had died and his mean brother was chasing me away. I was a foreigner to my uncle, just as I had always been to the Communist regime. He knew that, under the Communist law, I couldn't inherit anything from my parents, and that, when I left Romania, I had been forced to sign a renunciation of any claims of that nature. He knew. He had been their darling from an early age. As a young turner, in an Arad factory, he was recruited by the Communists and sent to university to become a devoted and trustworthy engineer – one on whom they could count. While they spoiled him with a scholarship and paid vacations, he failed to pass his last project and spent most of his life as a sub-engineer. My father went out of his way to encourage him to get his engineering degree; but once in the workforce, Gligorea was more attracted to alcohol and women. My father gave up in the end and often joked about Communism failing when it came to our family – one brother was declared an enemy of the people and scheduled to be liquidated but survived; and the other, the chosen one, was pushed towards glory but failed to grasp it.

Neighbours came to greet us and offer condolences; some helped Ariella and me carry our luggage into my old room, passing by the uncle, who had placed his fat belly in the middle of the staircase, his beady eyes watching everybody as they walked past. After a while, feeling the hostility of the neighbours, my uncle and his sour-faced wife left the house. Later, on our way to the cemetery, villagers told us they had taken shelter with Auntie Puica in the Valley.

The morning after, he returned at the head of a group of relatives, his fat belly wobbling beneath his crumpled cotton vest, as he squared his shoulders and raised his double chin. I was washing in a basin at the entrance, when they all came in. No one bothered to greet me. Three cousins I had not seen for years and Auntie Puica stood behind the uncle and his wife, while he declared:

"Nephew, we have to talk."

I was taken aback, not only by the tone of his voice but also by the unfriendliness of my cousins, none of whom showed the slightest intention of shaking hands with me, let alone embracing me or expressing any sort of condolence.

I understood instantly. For all of them my father was dead, buried and forgotten. He did not count anymore; his property did. They wanted only one thing – to know who was getting what. That realization brought on a boundless feeling of sadness. My father's desperate words kept resounding in my ears. "They are like vultures," he said to me on one occasion. "They can't wait to see me dead and share the spoils. Don't let that happen. This is the only thing I am asking of you. Look after my house and land, once I am gone." I felt like crying.

The night before, I had found a fortnight-old note from the Beiuş tribunal in a table drawer. My father was fighting with my cousin Viorica, now standing shamelessly behind our fat uncle, to have her return things she had borrowed from our house: 2 benches, 3 chairs, Mama's sewing machine. He was also complaining that she had stolen soap and oats from the attic, while her husband, Dolea, had stolen 2 barrels, an axe, a big file and a plane. He had seen all these things at their place and they refused to return them. Now I understood better his request for me to look after his house. The terrible sadness of his words, echoing in my ears, made it even more imperative. Despite being harassed by the Communists, he had won many battles against them, the most important of which was staying alive. It was difficult, but at least, in those battles, it was easy to identify the enemy; but you can't defend yourself against greedy relatives, especially when you are living alone. He had needed help from the courts and now I was overwhelmed with shame for these cousins' actions. They were pursuing him even in his death, dancing on his grave and revelling in the hard work his rough hands had performed year after year. How could they be so heartless? Are people everywhere like that? What made my relatives so blind to other people's pain, so lacking in compassion? My father had told me stories of his youth, when he worked for his uncle for no pay at all. His father did the same. They helped each other and none of them would dare disrespect the other party. What made these relatives of mine, standing in front of me, overwhelming me in number and staring at me in insolence, cross the line of everything I deemed decent? Was it something diabolical in their genes? In our family genes? Was it the forty-five years of Communism? Had it reached so deep into their souls that no trace of respect for life and death was left?

"Anything in particular?" I asked.

"About the house and the land," the uncle said without flinching, his sausage-like fingers twitching, as if unable to wait to grasp my father's property.

I dried myself and put on a shirt Ariella offered me. I was thinking fast. I couldn't allow them to make a mockery of my father's memory any further. I couldn't surrender my father's last wish to these people.

"Alright," I said, "Come into the living room, one by one. I will start with you, Uncle."

"No, we'll talk all together." My uncle curled his lip, like an animal ready for a fight.

I wasn't going to be intimidated.

"Well," I said shaking my head, "my father has only been in the ground for three days and I am not going to have a circus over his grave. You are welcome to go in there and talk all together, as long as you wish. When you finish, let me know if you want to talk to me individually."

I took Ariella by the hand and left the house. We walked up the road under the gaze of neighbours who had seen my relatives enter the house. Some asked me what they wanted. I told them and they shook their heads. "Shame on them, your father's body is still warm. How can they do this to him?"

After half an hour, a neighbour came running with the news

that they had left and were going to Auntie Puica's house. By the evening, rumours spread that she was going to a witch to put a curse on me.

In the days that followed, I went about dealing with the succession, the uncertain inheritance laws and a notary who wanted to be paid in dollars. I also had to deal again with my uncle, who had visited the notary to tell him I was a foreigner and had no right to my father's property. The notary showed him the door and exacted more dollars from me for the service.

I couldn't leave without trying to rescue my father's *cazan*. It was such an important part of his life. On the one hand, the *cazan* was his damnation – he was declared an enemy of the people for owning it; but on the other, it was his salvation – it allowed him to buy back his wheat and other produce, that had been punitively taken from him by the Communist regime. So, I went to the Wine and Spirits Company in Oradea to claim it. At first they wouldn't listen to me, hiding behind the vague excuse of 'unclear legislation on the matter.' When I threatened them with legal action, they offered to sell the *cazan* to me; that way they could justify its disappearance from their inventory, they said. I was in a hurry and bought it back for seven hundred dollars, thus making my little contribution to the widespread corruption of the place. I was certain my father would have approved of my action, though; and that was the most important thing for me.

While I was able to obtain most of my family property stolen by the State, I didn't get any of the items my relatives had filched from my father. I would have liked to, for his sake. Instead, I decided it wasn't worth it. My father was a fighter but he knew when to stop and would have understood my decision. Nonetheless, I must confess that, during the three weeks I spent in Lupoaia, I was afraid that something might happen to Ariella and me. So, to my shame and unbeknown to my wife, I found my father's axe and hid it under the bed, just in case my relatives decided to go beyond witches and curses.

There is no going back for me now. I told my sons that my

father's last wish was for me to look after his house and land; but that they were not bound by that wish.

At this moment, with my first grandson about to be born, my own wish was for him to see my father's house, to see where some of his roots lie. I believe that would make him stronger and perhaps wiser. I would gladly give up my own right to go there again if I knew that he would see my Transylvania. As for me, I am content with the memories which, good or bad, I treasure.

I have my father's life condensed into 70 pages, written in his longhand. He used the old orthography, the one from before the war – it was his way of rejecting Communist reforms, aimed at making our language look more Russian. There are his tapes too – he recorded them in my office at the university in 1984, when he visited me. I also have several tapes, recorded by people during my visits back to the village, in the 1970s and 1980s. I smuggled them out of the country, sometimes bribing customs officers. To make my godfather, Gavrila, the Council Secretary, Vidu, Micula, Uncle Ionica and Spirea speak freely, I got them drunk. We taped their stories during the night, with no lights on; and they whispered, when too critical of the regime. I suddenly realised the importance of these words, fragments of the lives of ordinary people, during extraordinary times. I am the only link between them and my grandson. If I don't tell my father's story, his written sheets of paper are dead leaves on the ground. If I don't give them new life, the tapes, recorded for me by him and others, are like thoughts never uttered, never heard. I decided, right then and there, that I had to write this story. For my new grandson, for future grandchildren, and for anybody interested in learning how a wicked regime trampled brutally on innocent people's lives.

My flood of memories was interrupted by my son who emerged from the maternity ward, arms raised, fists clenched:

"*È fatta*. It's done," he exclaimed, a big grin on his face.

"Is it a boy?" I heard myself asking.

"Of course," he said, reproachfully.

I regretted asking; but I remembered my parents describing Grandpa Teodorea's joy when I was born. I was a first grandson for him, just as mine was for me, waiting to be admired. When we entered the room he was sucking his knuckles: peaceful, clean and safe. What a beautiful, pure creature! I was floating on an ocean of joy. I caressed his hand with my finger and he seemed to smile. In that moment, I was sure that we made a connection with our Transylvanian ancestors, somewhere up there in the universe, and they were smiling back at us.

Stork and Cabbage

I wonder what my grandson will be told, when he asks where he came from. He'll perhaps raise his head from his digital world, with its Internet games, fake dinosaurs and fighting robots, to listen to the story of my world, which was made up of real animals, of real people who suffered a great deal, and of dreams that never came true. He will certainly be mesmerized to hear how my parents tried to convince me that a stork brought me to them, in her bill, and placed me under a cabbage in our garden. Well, I soon discovered that there were no cabbages in our garden in frosty January, the month of my birth; so my parents changed the story a bit. The stork had apparently landed on our roof and dropped me down the chimney into the house. That seemed acceptable, until I found out what a chimney was and that we did not have one. Could I have been dropped through the narrow pipe that connected our stove to the roof? It looked too small even for a newborn baby to pass through. Did my parents refrain from lighting the fire on that cold day? How did they know the stork was coming? Did storks talk?

My questions seemed to unsettle my parents, because, one day, they sat me at the table and, with an air of capitulation, said they had to tell me the truth because I was a big boy now. Yes, I was brought to them by the stork because that's the stork's job, to bring babies to young parents. When this particular stork came, she circled high over the house until my father saw her. The man who saw the stork and her bundle first was the father of the child.

That's how it worked for everybody in Lupoaia. My father had to call Mama because storks would never give a child to a man. The moment the stork saw Mama, she began her descent. Her mid-air circling became smaller and smaller, until she was close enough to drop me safely into Mama's loving arms. The question, as to whether I was dressed or naked, was soon put to rest. I was dressed and carefully tied like all the babies in Lupoaia – wrapped like cabbage rolls, with hands and feet nowhere to be seen.

So I had all my questions answered. Happy now?

I was happy until Dorel, my cousin, was born. All the women of the family and neighbourhood were there. Although children were not allowed in the house, my great-auntie Milica called me in and gave me a slice of bread with sunflower oil and sugar, her warm hands ruffling my hair as I sat down to tuck in. She often did that because she liked me. I sat on the little stool she used when she cut the pumpkins to boil for the pigs, at the bottom of the corridor. I heard Auntie Veica yell in a way I had never heard before; and then Moaşa Stela shouted, "Push, push!" I asked myself what was there to push in a room full of women in which you hardly could move. My curiosity was raised, so I looked around furtively and tiptoed towards the door, which was ajar so the women could look inside. As they watched inside the room, sighing and praying, they turned their heads and covered their faces. None of them were paying any attention to me.

Suddenly the women gasped and crossed themselves, as they did in church. My mouth opened as I saw the midwife, her hands covered in blood, lifting my cousin Dorel from the bed and showing him to everybody. He was dripping melted lard and shedding some sort of pig bladder from his face and body, with not so much as a hair on his head. The midwife handed him to my Grandma Saveta, who never missed a birth or funeral.

Auntie Veica looked tired, sweat streaming down her gaunt face; but she smiled, I don't know if at Dorel or at Moaşa Stela. Then the midwife tied something, which looked like a sausage, to his belly and two women washed him in a bread trough. No trace of any stork. Only then, did my parents start telling me the real

story of my birth; and how Mama chased everybody away from
the birthing room, including Moaşa Stela.

I was born at home. Our house was small, like all peasants' houses
in Lupoaia. From the muddy courtyard you opened a little gate
and entered a narrow veranda, which ran along the length of the
house. The main door led to a narrow corridor and accessed the
two rooms, one on the left and one on the right. At the end of
the corridor, there was a small larder. All bulky goods were kept
under the thatched roof in the attic, accessible through a manhole
in the corridor's ceiling.

The room on the left served as a kitchen, living room and
dormitory and was called the small room. Although it was the
same size, the room on the right was called the big room and it
was used only for sleeping, if all the family members couldn't
fit into the small room. Our small room had two high beds, each
wider than a single but smaller than a double, and sleeping two. In
emergency situations, a third person squeezed in between the two
with his head at their feet. The beds had thick mattresses, filled with
straw, and coarse sheets, made of hemp. No matter what season,
a high, feather-down doona covered the mattress and three big
square-shaped embroidered cushions lay on top of each mattress.

At the foot of the bed, there was a cast iron stove with two
hooks nailed into the ceiling boards above. The hooks held a 2m
long stick, draped with sausages and bacon in winter and garlands
of peppers, garlic and onions in autumn. Opposite the stove was
a kitchen cupboard. All the furniture inside was made by my
father and all the linen by my mother, Grandma Saveta and my
late Grandma Maria.

After we passed the stork and cabbage phase, I often asked my
parents about my real birth. For a while, it became my bedtime
story and I relished it. Mama was nineteen when she gave birth to
me. She was a good-looking young woman, but was rather skinny,
so she did not conform to the concept of peasant-beauty, which
was robust so as to be good for work in the fields, with rosy red
cheeks. She had a paler face, brown thin hair, brown chestnut eyes

and a nose that was slightly bent, which gave her face character. Almost as tall as my father, she had a calming effect on him and was generous to a fault. Her determination was strong for a woman of that era – she resisted her father's wish for her to marry somebody else, which was rare in those days.

Mama had been in labour for two days in the big room of the house; and was exhausted, as pushing became increasingly difficult. Her brain was playing tricks on her, telling her to give up one moment and to bring me into the world the next. She wanted to prove the Oradea doctors wrong. They had said she would never get pregnant in the first place, let alone give birth. My parents never told me what the doctors found wrong with Mama. Lying down in the high bed, on the thick straw mattress in her coarse, white underskirt, her hair unkempt and the colour spent in her cheeks, she was now fighting hard to give birth to me. Gradually she became deaf to the midwife's pleas to push, to her mother Saveta's wails, to her young sisters-in-law's chants, and to the old Doanda's expert incantations against evil entering the birthing room. Mama seemed to slide into a hazy unknown world, where life and death embraced each other and pain did not matter anymore. The village women, who were scurrying around her constantly, moved her onto the thick hemp rag on the floor. She had woven it herself on the family loom, washed it for two days with hot lye from oak ashes and kept it on the line for days, to be bleached by the frost.

In a brief moment of lucidity, when everything seemed to be lost, Mama drew on her last reserves of strength and determination. In an act unheard of in the village, she ordered all the women out of the room, telling them to be quiet, and then summoned my father Pavelea. She told him to lift her to her knees and grabbed him tightly by the wrists, gritted her teeth and set her jaw with fierce determination. A mighty, wild, desperate scream reverberated throughout the little village of Lupoaia and could be heard in the night over the surrounding hills and valleys, before an eerie silence once again settled over the frosty, snow-coated land.

Then there I was, all red and puffy, ready to be dropped to my waist into a wooden bucket with tepid water, and be cleansed. My muffled cry brought the women rushing back into the room.

This was the moment Grandpa Teodorea was waiting for to open the oak barrel of *pălinca*, the strong plum brandy that he had made the year before in his own *cazan*, or copper distillery, built by a Hungarian metal beater in Salonta.

Now 57 years old, he had declined since the loss of his wife, Maria, the previous year. He had not been himself since and, when he opened the barrel, his once strong hands were not as steady as they used to be. His thick fingers, chapped and battered by hard work in the fields, failed to grip the flagon properly and he spilled some of the *pălinca* on the ground. "Too much excitement is not good for an old man," he thought; and he was indeed excited to meet his grandson. He had lived for this moment.

He was so desperate to have a grandson that his pint-sized neighbour, Scurtu, teased him that he was going to have a granddaughter instead. He dared Grandpa to bet on his moustache but Grandpa did not want to lose twice – his moustache and not having a grandson. "That wretched Scurtu, who is laughing now?" Grandpa thought. A smile crept over his kind, weatherbeaten face. His first grandson. So peaceful and unaware of the cold outside and of the troubles of the world.

I was fascinated when my father told me about Grandpa's enthusiasm for my birth. He always began by telling me in a grave voice that I was born late at night, perhaps close to midnight. The wolves looked like dark lumps on the white snow at the edge of the forest, howling at the fiery moon in the sky above them, saluting my coming into the world. The chill in the air was freezing the drip running from Modru's hooked nose onto his upper lip, as he was ordered by my Grandpa to go and fetch the gypsies. Modru looked upon Grandpa Teodorea as a father figure. He lived next door with his mother, who had married at thirteen and been abandoned by her husband at sixteen.

My Grandpa gave Modru two bottles of *pălinca*, one for each pocket of his rugged coat, and hurried him off to Dumbrava, the outskirts of the village, to fetch the three gypsy brothers with their violins and drum. There was to be a celebration, unprecedented in Lupoaia. At the sight of the *pălinca* bottles wrapped in white damask handkerchiefs embroidered with red, yellow and blue flowers, the gypsies forgot about sleep. They invited Modru into their hut. The stench of rotten carcasses and urine wafting from inside made Modru retch; he decided to wait outside. He had heard that the gypsies ate crows they found dead on the fields and in the forest; that's why they smelled different from other people. The gypsies threw on their worn out buttonless military jackets, ran dirty fingers through their ragged, long hair, put on their military boots and pulled down their black sheep leather *cușmas* over their ears and forehead. Lanky Zambil and tiny Corcodel emerged with their battered violins, while robust Ciotu went down on his knees to drag his drum, almost as big as a cart wheel, from under the bed.

After gulping more *pălinca* they began playing loudly, excitedly circling Modru, getting closer and closer, only to move away in a sort of dance that seemed to have been rehearsed for weeks. The music and the dancing lasted throughout the entire journey to Grandpa Teodorea's house. Modru was twirling with them, clapping hands, blowing piercing whistles, interspersed with war-cries and shouts of joy, an art perfected over the centuries by the young men of Lupoaia.

Sleepy, yet curious, faces peered from windows and doors, as the procession whirled through the village. Youngsters, with their breeches half undone and worn shirts untucked, joined Modru and his wild band, singing, shouting and performing poor imitations of local folk-dances. Even some women and children got up and, scantily dressed, followed the band to find out where it was heading. This was such an unusual event for them. Although the gypsies had lived next door for decades, there was no memory of such a fracas in that part of the village.

The bottles were soon empty. New provisions were gathered at Pecica's, my Grandma Saveta's brother. Grandpa Teodorea, who had heard the gypsy-band approach, arrived with more *pălinca* in a flagon, which was carried on his shoulders by Micula, the neighbour, with whom Grandpa had fought in the First World War.

As the gypsies got more and more drunk, the drum got louder and louder until it could be heard in the surrounding villages of Holod, Hodiş and Forosig. Many people from those villages were wondering what could have happened so late on a Tuesday night in Lupoaia, where barely anything ever happened, to deserve a party lasting well into the early hours of Wednesday morning.

Grandpa Teodorea had come to life again and was clapping his hands following the rhythm of the music. He was even trying to imitate the young people's dancing.

"Show them, Teodorea, show them," Micula incited him.

Grandpa was happy that I was a boy, because he saw me taking my father's place in that house, just as my father was taking his. He saw his name continuing in Lupoaia, long after his death. And what about those silly doctors from Oradea? My birth was difficult but so were many things in life. The important thing was that, in spite of everything, I had made it. In his own way, he had made it with me.

My Father Had a Dream

Mama couldn't rest all night for the cacophony of violins, drums and people coming in and out of the house; and now my father, who was in his own euphoric world, both for the joy of having a son and for the *pălinca* he had drunk, wanted everybody to follow his orders. He lined up all the family members, waving a rugged finger wildly in the air and pointing randomly at anyone who crossed his path.

"You are not a soldier anymore, Pavelea," Grandpa teased him.

"Grandpa is right," Mama lowered her voice, trying to calm him down, "we will do this later, Pavelea."

"Later is too late," my father decreed, hiccupping as he took another swig.

I was tightly wrapped in a white feather-down cushion, in the cot my father had made. He organized a gift-bearing procession to my cradle as he had seen in the capital. After all, he had dreamt about having a son, especially one who could match the intelligence and the knowledge of his superiors in the army. Perhaps his son would become an architect, like those Italians he worked for in Bucharest, before being drafted into military service.

"What do they have that we don't?" he was saying to the nodding neighbours, between glasses of *pălinca*. "My son will not sweat all day long in the fields, come rain or shine, if I can help it."

My father had blue eyes, a mane of chestnut hair that thinned on top in his later years, a wide forehead and regular facial features.

Of course, he was anything but regular to me. He was my hero. I remember his strong, thick fingers, worn by physical work in his youth. I also remember that he was always busy, either working or defending himself from the Communists. A patient man, with a hearty laugh and a sense of humour, he had to become a thinker and a survivor.

When I was born he was only 25; but had learned a lot in his short life. For as long as he could remember, he had worked hard for his uncle, his father and other people. Before military service, he had worked in Bucharest and done well. That experience opened his eyes to how knowledge could take people places. He discovered how easy it was for him to learn new things, to adapt to new situations and get along with people. For the first time, he regretted having paid so little attention at school. Now it was too late for him, he thought. Then he remembered how his grandpa Pavelea had learned to read and write at about his age. Pavelea came to Lupoaia from Duşeşti for a marriage, arranged by his father and Mӑriuţa's father, in the Ceica tavern during the Wednesday cattle market; he worked for the teacher and the priest and, in exchange, they taught him how to write letters and numbers in the mud and in the ashes. That's why he got the job of forester in Lupoaia. My father understood that a little knowledge brought Grandpa Pavelea prosperity.

The newborn boy will have to go much further, thought my father through his alcoholic fog, and get a real education. The circle of ignorance that had subjugated the family for centuries would have to be broken. Under the curious gaze of the neighbours, he instructed the older men of the family – my two grandfathers – to bring me one book each – an ABC and a grade one maths book – as well as a sum of money. Both named Teodor, but known in the village respectively as Teodorea and Toderea, they placed the gifts on my body. To demonstrate the importance of the male lineage in the family, the sum given by the paternal grandfather had to be greater than that of the maternal grandfather.

Grandmother Maria had died the year before but Grandmother Saveta brought an exercise book and a fistful of banknotes.

My father made me a wooden school bag. He had worked on it for many weeks before I was born; and even painted it blue, in the hope that I would be a male heir. He tucked pencils inside the school bag. He had also made an abacus, which he had learned how to fashion whilst working for the Italians.

My aunties, Puica and Raluca, brought other exercise books and pencils: gifts to fulfil my father's dreams of getting me started young.

Here I was, not yet one day old, as squashed and dazed as any other newborn, and ready for school.

The gypsies, playing with renewed vigour, circled my little cot.

And I was crying my heart out, outraged at the noise and perplexed at the faces that hovered a few inches above me.

Although tired and full of *pălinca*, Grandpa Teodorea decided to take me to the Council himself, to register my birth. He encouraged the gypsies to play and demanded that Mama get me ready for the trip. When she hesitated, the set of his jaw and his defiant eyes challenged her: "Do you have anything against that?"

Mama handed me to Grandpa. "Hold him this way," she said, demonstrating the cradling technique and making sure he did not hurt me.

Zambil and Corcodel, their military jackets undone, were playing their fiddles louder, bending and straightening up, their bodies drawing half circles. Ciotu was balancing the huge drum on his belly while he danced to the rhythm, unleashing sharp whistles.

The ever-growing crowd of drunken men repeatedly toasted my health and wiped their mouths with the backs of their hands; but their words were now slurred and incoherent. The women scolded their husbands for drinking too much; and the husbands shouted insults at their wives for spoiling such a good party.

My father, more sober than Grandpa, took me from his arms and carried me all the way to the Council. The icy air only increased my Grandpa's exuberance. He slipped in the muddy snow, smearing his shirt and trousers with swathes of mud and dung; but that did not stop him from enjoying the congratulations he received along the way. In a loud voice he commanded the gypsies to drink up. He declared them beasts but, in the next breath, ordered them to play louder still. Many villagers came out onto their porches, and remarked on how beautiful I was, before spitting on me to exorcise the evil eye.

At the Council, the young Secretary awaited our party at the door.

"What a beautiful boy, Uncle Teodorea!" he exclaimed, bending over me. Grandpa planted the bottle of *pălinca* firmly in his hands.

"Yes, sir," Grandpa raised his finger in the air, "and he is going to bear my name, Teodor. Yes. Te-o-dor."

My father nodded.

"So, he was born last night... on the 15th."

"What night?" Grandpa barked. "My grandson brought the light into my life... He can't be registered as being born during the night... He had to put up a fight to come out! He is a fighter, a fine boy he is. He is going to be called Te-o-dor, like me. You know why? His father, this one here, is Pavel. I am Teodor, my father was Pavel... and now the boy is Te-o-dor. He is going to be somebody... I tell you... somebody."

Grandpa had begun to repeat himself. The *pălinca* blurred his speech, but he remained clear in his demands.

"We have to register the date of January 15th," mumbled the Secretary, embarrassed at the scene Grandpa was making.

"No, no. Yesterday was dark. My grandson starts his life with light in his heart."

"But Uncle...," the Secretary mumbled.

"No buts, young man, the 16th. You register my grandson on the 16th. Play up, you beasts... and drink!" he urged the gypsies, passing them the bottle. The music drowned out the Secretary. He did as he was told and downed the rest of the *pălinca*, as a reward. My grandpa's word was final.

So Teodor I was, with an official birth certificate stating that I was born on January 16th. Grandpa Teodorea, without knowing it, robbed me of the illustrious company of names born on 15th, like

Martin Luther King, Aristotle Onassis, Molière and Eminescu, the greatest Romanian poet of all time.

The Three Fates and the Evil Eye

On the third day, the sun rose over the muddy tracks and frosty fields surrounding Lupoaia; and the men sobered up to a degree. The women, busier than ever, scurried from house to house, kitchen to kitchen, to fry lard and sausages, cook a hen, make *pancove* – puffy, holeless doughnuts – cheese and plum jam buns and walnut rolls. They placed the food on a table in the corridor and pulled the table to the door, blocking the entrance to the room I shared with Mama. A bottle of *pălinca* and three glasses stood in the middle of the table, just in case. This was done to prevent the strong-willed guests from entering, before they tasted the alluring offerings.

On a smaller table in my room, covered by a white cloth, the women had placed a coin, a round loaf of bread, a plate with freshly-ground and sifted white flour and a bundle of hemp. That third night, the fifth night and the seventh night, three mysterious dark-faced sisters, untouched by man, were expected to visit me. They were the Fates that came, unseen and silent, to tailor my destiny by spinning my thread of life from the hemp bundle. Two of them were dressed in white robes and one in black. The eldest spun the thread, the second made it into a bundle and the third, who was dressed in the black robe and had one leg shorter than the other, cut the thread with a sickle, thus determining how long I should live. The Fates did not touch the food, leaving it for the people to feast on, after the baptism; but sometimes they left traces of their visit in the flour. Only the mother could see them at work in her dreams. She alone saw the destiny they foretold for her baby and she could tell no one about it, except her child.

Grandma Saveta swore she had heard the Fates whispering during the night. She had found their traces in the flour the morning following their visits, because she was the first to enter my room. She made sure Mama woke up with her face turned to the wall, so that she would remember her dreams about the Fates' work and my earthly destiny. If she had woken with her face towards the window, her dreams would have flown away and my destiny would have remained unknown. A mother, who did not see her baby's future in her dreams, was not a happy woman. She would grieve over her lack of dreams, feeling guilty and inconsolable, hiding tears of sorrow because, in their absence, the magic moment of giving birth was the only thing she could share with her child.

Mama told me later about her dreams during those three nights. They were hazy and she couldn't make much sense of blurry images of other worlds. Every night she argued with the Fates, urging them to spin a better destiny for me, a life among my own people, close to my forebears' graves and to the forest they loved; but the ghostly creatures were mute and blind and, even worse, implacable. In the face of such stony countenances, a mother could do nothing but cry out her despair and hand her child over to the unknown.

In her dreams, on the third night, she saw me growing up until the two of us were like brother and sister; and then she suddenly saw her child – a man – trapped inside a flying cage, in the shape of the cranes she often saw in the autumnal skies of Lupoaia, being whisked away from the land of his ancestors at lightning speed. My path meandered under ominous skies and entered into white foamy multi-shaped clouds, that resembled flocks of sheep on Dumbrava's pastures; and then it veered across immense expanses of stormy waters that made one's head spin and stretched further than the eye could see. She saw me fighting battles on my own, sustaining victories and losses without help or consolation from family, longing for the hills of Lupoaia. She saw me longing for the house with the thatched roof, the waterhole under the window, the walnut tree with its fruit aplenty in prosperous years and the mulberry trees – one white and one black. She couldn't see herself in those dreams; and she knew, in her heart, that our earthly ties would be severed forever, that I would not be at her bedside, in her final hours on this earth, to mourn the loss of a mother who had fought so hard to bring me into the world.

On the fifth night, she saw me returning to my father's home and, finding nobody, wandering through the cemetery among weeds taller than crosses. A man, and yet crying like a baby, I was desperately searching for Mama beneath my feet, looking for answers as to why I incessantly scoured this earth, from one end to the other, as if haunted by a terrible curse.

On the seventh night, she saw me somewhere at the end of the world, so far away that none of my kin had trodden there before. A frail white-haired man waiting to die, I was surrounded by children who spoke words, unlike anything she'd ever heard, and yet had features resembling those of great-grandpa Pavelea and his Măriuța, of my grandparents Teodorea and Maria, Toderea and Saveta, and of my father and herself.

And then she saw nothing. Like dreams that end abruptly and vanish, no matter how hard you try to keep them alive.

Only one thing was left to be done: baptism on the eighth day.

The snow was knee deep. The temperature, inside our little village church, was as icy as outside. Although the water for my immersion had been heated in a nearby house, it had quickly cooled.

Father Milea blessed the water, his face solemn and unsmiling, before anointing me with the sacred oil on my forehead, chest, back, ears, on my hands and feet. My naked body shivered in the frigid air. Facing East, he raised me above his head, then immersed me three times, so that no part of my body was untouched by the holy water, not even a tiny piece of skin the size of a pinhead, through which evil spirits could be lured.

I was now an Orthodox Christian, cleansed of all my sins; but the blessings continued with the Holy Chrism, a special mixture blessed by the Romanian Patriarch, including olive oil, fragrant spices and essences boiled together every year on Holy Thursday. At the Constantinople Patriarchate, there is a list of fifty-seven substances that can be used in the Holy Chrism. As this operation is still swathed in mystery, I will never know how many spices were used in mine.

After the anointment, I circled the baptismal font and the table on which the Bible lay three times, in the arms of my godfather, Gavrila, as the priest sang a hymn. It took the form of a *hora*, a popular dance that signified the joy of the Church in receiving me as a new member. The priest then washed away the Holy Chrism to protect it from desecration. Some hairs off the top of my head were cut, leaving the form of a cross to mark my complete deliverance into the power of God.

Everybody was cold, moving their toes inside their shoes to keep them from freezing. Yet, after an initial cry when I hit the water, I was such a good boy during the ceremony. And no wonder: I was blue and motionless.

Grandma Saveta began rubbing my little body frantically, but with no response. No one was sure if I was still breathing. Mama and my father were crying. Grandpa Teodorea asked himself why God allowed an innocent baby, the source of so much joy to him and his family, to be punished for the ignorance of a church full of adults.

They rushed me over the road to Traian's house and placed me in a bucket, on the hot stove. I had to thaw.

Old Doanda threw three red embers from the burning stove into a cup filled with water and, while the embers were still sputtering, cut into the water with the blade of a knife, muttering centuries-old incantations, to exorcise the evil spirits that might have penetrated me through some pores of my skin, left untouched by the holy water.

But fate is a wonderful thing, when it works in your favour. Within the hour, the blue of my skin started to change into a more human colour and my breathing returned to normal.

The women were jubilant and talkative, as they slowly began to disperse from the stove and give me a little more space. Being more God-fearing than the men, they gave thanks to God, throwing their hands up in the air and mumbling prayers.

Relieved, the men sighed and decided that the child was ready for a wetting with *pălinca*. Serving as obliging intermediaries, they drank until dawn.

The family kept a close watch on me over the next few days. When it became clear that the danger had passed and I would survive, Mama, who had cried her eyes out and looked twice her age, had candles burned in forty churches the following Sunday.

The Valley of the Wolves and a Parade of Invaders

The night I was born, my great uncle Moanea, the village forester, shot a wolf. The villagers roasted it in the fire and fed the meat to the dogs. He had inherited the job and the only gun in Lupoaia from his father, my great-grandpa Pavelea. The villagers felt vulnerable to wolves in winter and begged for his help, using great quantities of *pălinca* to bribe him. They lit bonfires throughout the night, to keep the wolves from their cattle and sheep and waited for them armed with pitchforks, axes and hooks with metal tips, heated in the fire to inflict more damage.

The bonfires were more spectacle than protection, as the wolves kept coming to the edge of the forest at dusk, sitting on their haunches, watching the bonfires and the men tending them. The two camps, men and beasts, studied each other, trying to outwit one another. The cunning wolves had become so dangerous and so daring that Pupuleu, whose house was closest to the forest's edge, almost lost his life one night. He was relieving himself, behind the pile of straw in his garden, when a wolf crept up. Only Pupuleu's *buhai*, a long sheepskin coat with an inner wool lining, saved him. The wolf ripped it from his back and tore it to pieces. Pupuleu's cries for help and the dogs' relentless barking made the wolf abandon its prey. The dogs feigned an attack, but when the wolf stopped and bared its teeth, they fled behind their masters, yelping like puppies.

Many men favoured these night rituals because they gave them the pretext to drink. They drank, not only to enjoy themselves, but also to escape the miseries of their hard lives. The women had no choice but to accept this situation. When the danger of wolf attacks dwindled, however, and the *pălinca* nights decreased, the men were forced to return to the grim reality of their lives. Sometimes, in their anger and frustration, they abused and mistreated the women. All the remaining winter long, wives were punished for what they said and for what they did not say. Some were seen with black eyes or bruises darkening their faces.

Moanea retired soon after he shot the wolf. The new forester was from Duşeşti, the village across the forest to the Northeast. He was a much younger man, tall and arrogant, who rode a white horse. His broad shoulders and well-built body made him perfect for the job; but he had a cruel sneer that sat constantly on his face. Sly and cunning like the wolves, he made the horse move so slowly that, from a distance, the animal became one with the snow and his body could easily be mistaken for a bush or a roadside tree. No firewood poacher could escape his clutches; and he was notorious for his preference for young women. He hid in the bushes and let them make their bundle, salivating as he watched their breasts bounce and their hips sway with their exertion. Then he jumped out with his gun pointed at them and his trousers undone. He made the most attractive young woman in the group sit down and wait while he wrote fines for the others, which he never handed out, but kept in his brown leather side bag. He let the rest go and forced himself on the remaining woman. Ironically, some women made their way into the forest more often than before, using more firewood than ever, by lighting the fire in the big room of the house where nobody slept.

The villagers hated the new forester and did not ask him for help. The husbands, whose wives had been subjected to the forester's treatment, whether willingly or unwillingly, soon vowed to drive their pitchforks through his heart and bury him half alive, deep in the snow, to be found by the wolves in spring.

Lupoaia means valley of the wolves, although the bigger half is situated on a hill connected to the valley by Hurupa, a slippery path too narrow for the carts to pass. Hurupa is flanked, on the left, by a bushy ravine, home for lizards, the occasional snake and squirrels, and on the right, by a steep slope which, during the heavy rains of spring, frequently erodes in landslides. Hurupa forms a triangle with the Colnic deviation to the right, used only for carts, and the Râturi road, which leads to the Hodişel creek and then to Holod. Our house is located at the tip of that triangle, where the Râturi road meets Hurupa. From there, the main road ascends to Dumbrava and then disappears into the forest, which separates Lupoaia from Ceica. These two main sections of the village are unimaginatively called the Valley and the Hill. Some say that the name of Lupoaia doesn't come from the animals raging through its forests, but from a different sort of wolves... human ones. The soldiers of the Ottoman Empire, on their way to Vienna, burned and pillaged the area, using the valleys of the forests to slaughter the local people with unimaginable savagery and barbarity, surpassing even Dracula's gruesome deeds.

Seated on benches outside their porches during the milder seasons, rubbing their work-worn hands, the older men of the village recounted stories of heroism and defeat that transported the young ones into a world of mystery and treachery, barbarity and bravery. During the long winter nights, between glasses of *pălinca*, they gathered the young men near the stove, to tell them about the plight of Horia, Cloşca and Crişan, who led the revolt against the Hungarians in 1784, demanding equal rights for the Romanians with the other minorities. Although the Romanians were by far the most numerous ethnic group of the Austro-Hungarian Empire, only the gypsies were treated worse. This was a matter of indignation among the peasants, who were forced to work for the landlords and couldn't move freely from one job to another.

When the story reached the point where the three leaders were condemned to death, everybody had something to say and cursed the weak side of the Romanian soul, inclined more to accept serfdom than to fight for freedom. They admired Crişan who did not give the authorities the satisfaction of torturing him, as he hanged himself in jail with the strings of his *opinci*, peasant shoes made from cow skin, the night before his execution. When the young were told that thousands of peasants were brought to Alba Iulia by force to see Horia and Cloşca being tortured on the wheel, they all pledged that they would rise up against the Hungarian authorities, as Avram Iancu, the mountain lawyer of peasant stock, tried to do fifty years later. He took up the cause of the oppressed Romanian minority and made Emperor Franz Joseph, already dissatisfied with his Hungarian officials, visit Transylvania to assess the situation for himself. As often happens with high dignitaries, the Emperor listened more to the Hungarian authorities than to the flood of petitions he received from the Romanian peasants; he made only a few minor concessions. As soon as he left, Avram Iancu was arrested. The prison years – and the harsh treatment there – devastated his mind. His idealism was confronted with the harsh reality of politics. His failure to achieve a better life for his people left him feeling impotent and distraught. When he was released from prison, he retired to the mountains of his childhood and spent his days playing the flute, roaming from manor to manor across the forest, and scrounging an occasional meal from compassionate hosts.

Sometimes the elders talked about the Dacians, the proud inhabitants of that part of Transylvania, conquered by the Romans in the first century AD, after two wars. They derived their name from a word meaning wolf's head, which the courageous and inventive Dacian warriors waved in battle with a dragon's tail attached. The air passing through the hollow head made haunting wails that terrified the enemy. After their defeat by Emperor Trajan's army in 106 AD, King Decebal's soldiers listened to their leader's last, powerful speech and then committed suicide, just as their king did. To avoid the humiliating capture by the Romans, Decebal, whose name means as strong as ten, slashed his own throat. His head and right arm were brought to Trajan, who considered this victory so important that he ordered the erection of Trajan's Column, which depicts scenes from the battle against the Dacians. Rome took an amazing haul of riches from Dacia, including 165 tons of pure gold and 330 tons of silver. As thanks for these riches and the capture of 100,000 young male slaves, Rome declared 123 days of celebration.

The Roman heritage is seen at its best in the surnames of Lupoaia, most of which end in 'a' rather than the more common 'escu' or 'ovici'. Galea, Lupşa, Popa, Zigrea, Burca, Berdea, Horga and Flonta: even the local variants of first names are sweetened to sound Roman and, as such, to protect our identity, threatened often by Hungarians, Serbs, Bulgarians and Russians. So, in Lupoaia, Teodor, the official name in documents, is converted into Teodorea, as in the case of my paternal Grandfather, or Toderea, as in the case of my maternal Grandfather – it also has a shortened version, Dolea. Pavel is Pavelea, Ion is Ioanea, Nistor becomes Nistorea, Dumitru is Mitrea and Petru is Petrea. A few common names of families in Lupoaia, ending in consonants, were assumed as a result of a more recent empire, the Austro-Hungarian, which annexed my region after the defeat of the Turks. Andor, Lazăr, Buciuman, Bochiş, Cioloş are some common examples.

A hundred years later, in the final stages of World War II, it seemed that more humiliation and oppression would be inflicted. In a few weeks the Russians had done as much damage as the Ottomans and the Austro-Hungarians did in years. It became clear that each occupier learned from their predecessors how to squeeze the peasants harder, leaving them without vigour or hope. Any attempt at rebellion was destined to end up like the valiant efforts of Horia, Cloşca and Crişan and of the poor, ill-fated Avram Iancu.

The new ideas the Russians brought with them alarmed the villagers and confused them more than the *pălinca*, which they drank in great quantities. While the confusion created by the *pălinca* was temporary, passing with the next day's sobering up, the confusion created by the invaders lingered like puss oozing from a festering wound that never healed.

A Luminous Future

Nobody could make sense of the news coming from the Ceica, Oradea and other nearby markets. By the time it reached Lupoaia, one thing was clear to everybody: the news was bad. Despite being the minority in the pro-Russian government of Petru Groza, the Communists controlled it and, strangely enough, the US and Great Britain recognized this government. New elections were held in November 1946. The Communists organized them and won with a big majority, by appropriating the opposition's figures. They followed Stalin's dictum which stated that it was not important who voted for whom, but who counted the votes.

Returning soldiers, who had managed to escape the massacre on the Russian front, described what they had seen in Russia; but the villagers put their bad reports in the war basket. War meant destruction and death. War was not the news they wanted to hear anymore; and that was the end of it.

My father assumed the worst. The words of his Captain, who had returned safely from the Russian front, rang in his ears. The Russian occupation meant disaster and poverty for everybody. Hard days lay ahead. Whatever happened, my father thought, it was his duty to aspire to a better life. Governments came and went, regimes changed and then disappeared, to be replaced by new ones. He had seen the pro-Hitler fascists disappear and now others were coming forward, who would disappear too. What could the Communists do to him? After all, he was not interested in politics. And yet, in spite of his efforts to maintain normality, these thoughts and the burden of work made him edgy.

Mama was having her own problems in raising me. No matter how hard she tried to induce me to nurse, I did not want her milk. I readily accepted the breast of Barbura, Scurtu's daughter, who had given birth to Lucia a couple of weeks before I was born. Mama was distressed and every time I cried, she felt guilty. She hung her head, confused and hurt by my rejection. One day I started crying before dawn and went on for hours. They did not know how to quieten me and rocking the cradle made things worse. I screamed and howled like a red-faced monster. Maybe I had colic, or maybe memories of my icy baptism still lingered. In desperation, Mama begged my father to help her to do something about me. And he did: he gave the cradle such a push that it turned over, with me underneath. I stopped crying instantly.

We all laughed, when they recounted the event to me years later; but I could see my father's remorse all over his face. I did not suffer any injuries or scratches, because I was swaddled in a feather-down cushion, tied with strings like a mummy. That was the way to keep babies, no matter what season, until they were at least one year old. Grandma Saveta explained later that this was done to prevent babies from developing crooked legs.

1947 brought major changes. The king, who had been coerced into siding with the Russians by Communists in 1944, was forced to abdicate. There were rumours that he took with him cars, famous paintings by El Greco, and wagons full of precious treasures, just as his father had done a few years earlier. This was a cause of some consternation among the villagers. Not because he left with possessions they could only dream of, but because how could a country go on without a king? This was unthinkable at a time when the villages were crawling with clean-shaven people from the city who spied on everybody, asked uncomfortable questions and insisted that the villagers join the Workers' Party, in exchange for promises of a new life and a luminous future. These concepts were of little interest to those who had heard it all before from the fascists, or 'legionnaires' as they liked to be called. The Workers' Party activists were playing the same old tune; but, at least, the legionnaires had brought cheap corn, potatoes and beans in times of need. The activists, whom you would not trust enough to invite into your home to share a glass of *pălinca*, carried pistols and made promises and intimidating threats.

The elections were rigged, to look as if the Communists had won, although nobody in the village admitted voting for them. The New Order was coming from the East, the activists were bragging, from where Comrade Stalin resided. Stalin, the man of steel, was the only one capable of ensuring that everybody in the newly-proclaimed People's Republic would have a luminous future. Yes, the People's Republic belonged to the people, to every one of them in the village, they were told. Gone were the days of monarchy where one man dictated to everybody. Now there was only the dictatorship of the proletariat. We would be our own dictators, the activists constantly repeated – yourselves and ourselves, all of us together, with Comrade Stalin at the helm. He was the greatest genius of mankind, the father of all people, who was never wrong and could never be wrong.

The villagers had heard things like this just a few years before, when the head of the legionnaires was said to be the one chosen by God, the one who was going to take the destiny of the people into his hands, to create the new man with a luminous future. The peasants were puzzled. These were the very same promises, only the background colour was different – green for the Legionnaires and red for the Communists. Every peasant knew that black sheep and white sheep gave the same white milk. There was no difference. The colour did not matter. Even a simpleton could understand that. Who chose this Stalin anyway? Why should he dictate in Romania when he had a huge country of his own, a country he governed so badly? Wasn't that enough for him? Didn't he see what had happened to Hitler? How could a peasant trust Stalin and his Russians? Everybody knew what happened to Sbârlea, only three years before, when the Russian army arrived in the village.

A squad of Russians had marched into Sbârlea's courtyard one morning, cutting imposing and menacing figures in spite of their dirty, patched-up uniforms. They divided into teams, one going to the stable, and another to the hen house, while their Commandant and a soldier went into the house. They found Sbârlea scared, but trying desperately to hide it, while Maria, his young wife, hid in the attic. The soldier dragged the terrified woman down the ladder, while the tall, dark and authoritative Commandant shouted orders in Russian. He yelled at Sbârlea and pushed him to the corner of the room, to be held at gunpoint by the soldier. The Commandant got busy with Maria, embracing and kissing her as she whimpered in terror, wide-open eyes and entire body shaking. Sbârlea, red in the face, stepped forward to intervene but the soldier trained his gun on him. The Commandant smiled maliciously at Sbârlea, and said something in Russian, while Maria struggled to free herself. She was soon overcome by the Commandant's power, pushed onto the bed, and raped before her husband's eyes. Sbârlea couldn't bear it anymore and, taking the soldier by surprise, jumped on the Commandant. They struggled for a short while. Maria ran outside, crying hysterically, with her clothes hanging about her in shreds. Sbârlea was shot dead in his own house. When some villagers came out onto the porch of their houses, the Russians left hastily with Sbârlea's cow and hens. They took them to Holod where they had their provisional headquarters and kitchen. That was only the start because, for the duration of their stay, the Russians systematically plundered the surrounding villages. No animal and no woman they sighted, no matter what age, was safe. The peasants started hiding their cattle, daughters and wives in the valleys of the forest or in the fields outside the village. Despite their precautions, many other women became victims of the Russian soldiers. Maria was no comfort to any of them, as the shock of being raped, while her husband was killed, drove her mad. She had to be restrained, as many a night she woke up screaming, tore off her clothes and ran out of the house to the courtyard and onto the road, pulling her once beautiful, lustrous hair and scratching her suddenly-lined and aged face, before being committed to the Oradea madhouse.

All these people coming to Lupoaia were speaking in the name of Stalin, in the name of Russia, now called by another name – some sort of Union. Too many words... and many of them made no sense: proletariat, luminous future, new man, new order, genius of mankind, father of all people. It was like the tower of Babel, when people wanted to reach God with a ladder rather than with their hearts. These Communist activists were speaking in incomprehensible tongues, using words that peasants did not know. When a man didn't understand something, he stayed away from it – that had always been the peasant's way.

Once, on the train to Beiuș, a man told my father that the peasants of Căpâlna refused to thresh their wheat; and so did others from Ginta, Cheșa and Rohan. They were protesting against the increased quotas on cereals, imposed on them by the newly-installed Communist government. The local authorities asked the Prefect to come and solve the situation. The Prefect came but had to flee through the back window of the municipal building as his car burned. A prosecutor from Oradea was sent down with a police inspector and a company of gendarmes ready for combat. Men, women and children surrounded the gendarmes with pitchforks, axes, and sticks. The irate and frightened police inspector asked the prosecutor to authorize him to fire on the rebels. The peasants shouted at the prosecutor, telling him that they were not going to give their wheat to the state, to be sent to Russia, while their own children were starving.

The prosecutor's oily nose flared as he tried to convince the peasants that the quotas were to pay for war damages. The crowd shouted that Bessarabia and Bucovina, taken by Russia, were damages enough. And how about the men who had died in the war, leaving widows and children behind – wasn't that enough quota for the peasants to pay?

The prosecutor admitted that mistakes may have been made when quotas were set and that he would take their complaints to the authorities to be resolved. They never heard from him again.

A Pumpkin Trap and a Sledge

My first memory involves my paternal grandpa Teodorea, a frightened sparrow and a pumpkin bird trap – and my maternal grandma Saveta fighting furiously over me.

I was not yet three years old when I got interested in the sparrows, that populated the bare fruit trees in our garden as winter settled in.

"*Vabie, vabie,*" I said, pointing out the sparrows to Grandpa Toderea.

"Grandpa will make a pumpkin trap and catch one for you," he said to me. I did not know what a pumpkin trap was and kept saying to him, as soon I opened my eyes every morning, "c*usa, cusa,*" until he decided to make one. He brought a big pumpkin inside the small room, cut it in half, spooned the seeds out, made a hole in the side of each one of its halves and tied them on top of each other with a small cord. He cut a stick the length of the pumpkin's diameter and made a bridge to part the two halves enough for the sparrow to enter. He put sunflower seeds and grain inside. When the sparrow entered, the top half of the pumpkin fell and trapped her inside.

The next morning I was jumping up and down like a cat on hot bricks, not because of the snow sticking to my bare soles but in excitement at seeing the sparrow, crouched and motionless, in the yellow pumpkin trap. As soon as she saw the light of day, she helplessly fluttered her small wings in my Grandpa's huge and rough, yet gentle, hands.

"Oh, my God! You crazy old fool! What are you doing to my baby?" Grandma Saveta shrieked, her bony arms flapping about as she launched herself towards me with the agility of a racehorse and lifted me into the air. In her mind there was nothing more important than her instinct to save me, the apple of her eye, from the clutches of the brainless, dangerous old man.

An outburst of blasphemous insults stopped Grandma in her tracks, her usually smiling jaw hanging slack.

"Don't you dare touch him, you old bag! The boy needs to become a man!" Grandpa commanded. He snatched me from her arms and put me back on my feet.

Grandma Saveta shook her fists in the air. She couldn't bear the sight of me barefoot on the snow, my frail little body covered only by a long white hemp shirt. She realised she was no match for the old man and so began screeching at the top of her voice for my young parents to come and rescue me.

I have thought about this incident many times and, no matter which angle I look at it from, it warms me to know how much they loved me. According to the big town doctors, I was not supposed to be born; but here I was, a first grandson for both of them, with my feet in the snow, enjoying a trembling sparrow in a trap. I clutched Grandpa's arms, wanting to touch the little brown bird with its speckled belly.

Once in the house, Grandpa tied a string around one of the sparrow's legs and gave it to me. I was scared and excited when the bird started flying around the room, banging her head against the windows. Grandpa taught me how to hold the string so that the sparrow would not harm herself, and how to prevent her from resting her tiny feet on the hot stove. He explained that sparrow babies might be waiting for her in a nest out there in the cold, wanting to be fed.

When she eventually got tired, she rested motionless on my tiny palm, her heart beating a hundred times a second, and I went to bed a happy child. When I got up, the sparrow was gone. Grandpa must have decided that there were better ways to entertain a little boy than trapping birds.

In early December, Grandpa Teodorea told me he was going to build a sledge for me, because children had to have fun in the snow.

"*Sanie... sanie*," I said excited.

"And you are going to slide down Hurupa faster than the wind," Grandpa said, caressing my head.

"*Sanie... ulupa*."

"Yes, Grandpa's big boy is going to be faster than lightning."

I sat next to him by the stove. The embers were like a million red stars flickering. I tried not to fidget too much in my chair but it was difficult, because I was so excited. From a plum branch he cut two sticks no thicker than my forearm and planed them smoothly. He laid them a palm breadth apart, then nailed two shorter sticks to them, one near the front and the other near the back. There it was – the base of the sledge. It gave me such joy, that I wanted to take it out, unfinished as it was.

"We have to make a seat for you, don't we? My Teodor will have the best sledge in the village. That's how it's going to be." He pinched my cheek and I pulled his moustache, in our special routine.

"*Sanie... sanie*," I shook my body with pleasure.

The seat was made of three more sticks and, when it was attached onto the base, Grandpa tied a corded string to the front, wrapped me in my father's thick jacket, put on his own padded coat, took me by the hand and we went outside. The snow rose almost to my knees and I had to try extra hard to move forward in my *opinci*. My legs were heavy. My father's jacket so weighed down my shoulders that, but for Grandpa's hand, I would have tumbled. I looked over my shoulder and saw our footprints, side by side, in the snow. I wondered if my feet would ever be as large as Grandpa's and if I would ever grow enough to fill out my father's jacket.

When we were a few yards away from the house, he sat me carefully on the sledge and pulled me around the courtyard. Then he started running and I felt the cold air cutting into my cheeks, running up my nostrils, filling my forehead; and that made me squeal with excitement.

"*Ulupa… lepede … lepede*," I screamed.

I wanted my Grandpa to keep his promise and take me down the slope of Hurupa. But, all of a sudden, Grandpa stopped, gasping for air. He bent forward with his hands clasping his chest. I wanted him to keep pulling my sledge and for us to keep laughing together. Instead, bent over, he went inside and left me alone on the sledge.

I trudged back through the snow and walked to the house. I was sad to leave my sledge behind; but my father's jacket hindered me and I was not strong enough to pull it even a few inches. The mud floor in the corridor was wet with the snow from Grandpa's boots. I followed the wet prints into the small room where I found him on the bed; his wet *opinci*, hanging over the edge, dripped like a slow spigot. I climbed on top of the bed and pulled Grandpa's moustache, as I always did when I wanted him to play with me.

The next day my father left the *cazan* in the care of his half-brother, Mitru's. After Mama had prepared a comfortable bed in the cart, with sheets, pillows and doona, my father took Grandpa to the doctor in Ceica.

"You are going to be well again, Papa, you'll see," my father told him, grasping his shirt, as if he could transfer his own determination into the old man. Grandpa did not reply. Mama and I looked at him from the side of the cart and the urge to pull his moustache overcame me. Mama lifted me onto the back wheel of the cart, her tears falling on my cheek, and I did just that. Grandpa managed a smile; but a strange noise was coming from his heaving chest. Mama put me down and my father turned his red eyes away from me.

"Yah! Yah!" my father shouted. He whipped the oxen; his hand seemed to move in slow motion. Walking beside the cart, he looked back at us, standing at the open gate, then disappeared at the bend near Iosive. The road was uneven and the cart's wheels sank down to the axle in mud. The oxen strained their necks under the yoke, while Grandpa Teodorea was breathing heavily, his chest pounding hard. My father yelled at his oxen, cracked the whip with a sense of urgency. His father couldn't die before getting to the doctor. He moved his lips in a prayer and raised his desperate eyes to heaven, begging God to do something to alleviate his father's pain. He wished he could do something himself, instead of only praying and spurring on his oxen. His father had always been there for him, pushing him hard at times, encouraging him to do what was right. He remembered how Grandpa saved him from going to the Russian front.

Grandpa went all the way to Bucharest well prepared – that is with a demijohn of *pălinca*, lard, sausages, ham and exquisite sweets prepared by Grandma Maria. He found the Captain's house, and the Captain appreciated the offerings so much that, when Teodorea asked him directly how Pavelea could be spared the dangers of war, he immediately offered to make him his orderly. My father ended up fighting his war, either sheltered in the Captain's house or at home in Lupoaia, while the Captain and his regiment fought alongside the Germans on the Crimean front.

The doctor, a small man with a white coat, kind eyes and greyish hair, came to the cart, felt Grandpa's pulse and listened to his heart. He looked at my father askew while still bent over Grandpa. "For how long has he been like this?"

"Since yesterday."

"I'm afraid his heart…" He was interrupted by a terrible rattle in Grandpa's throat.

With shaking hands my father gently lifted Grandpa's head and pulled up the cushion. The doctor shook his head.

"Could you give him something?"

The doctor opened his arms, then made signs for my father to wait. He disappeared inside his modest house and came back with two white tablets on a napkin.

"He won't need more," he said.

My father tried to rearrange Grandpa's cushion again, then he gripped the side of the cart with his left hand, leaned his head on it and sobbed. The doctor patted him on the back and left him in the cold with his sorrow. My father covered his eyes with a

handkerchief and voiced a deep lament. It took him a while before
he turned around his oxen and took the road back to Lupoaia.

Grandpa's rattle increased with the cart's, the two moving
seemingly in time until they entered the forest, then his body
ceased to heave and start. His face, blanched and chapped with
the cold, grew peaceful and my father thought he had died. He
stopped the oxen, jumped off the cart and went to check. Grandpa,
though barely breathing, was still alive. Flakes of snow started
falling on his face and my father spread a sheet across the cart to
protect him. He thanked God for keeping his father alive, got in
the cart and continued the voyage, hoping they would reach home
before evening. But he couldn't sit there on that board while his
father was dying, without checking on him again and again. He
stopped the oxen just before leaving the forest to enter Dumbrava,
lifted the sheet covering Grandpa's face and looked at him. Too
peaceful, it seemed. He jumped off the cart, put his hand on his
father's forehead and it was cold as ice.

"Papa, what have you done to me?" He clenched both his fists,
raised them to his temples, squeezed tightly and cried, moaned,
wailed. He crouched, leaned forward and both his hands crushed
the little layer of snow that had gathered since morning. "Papa,
Papa…," he lamented.

It seemed so unfair and cruel for death to have walked with
them all the way through the dense forest, only to take Grandpa
just before entering the welcoming light of the village. When he
found the strength, he started the oxen again, resting his hand on
the side of the cart and moving along with his head uncovered. He
found comfort in walking so close to his father. He remembered
little things and big things about Grandpa, things he had forgotten:
like when he was a small boy and stole pieces of his fried polenta
in the mornings, and his father looked away pretending not to
see him. Or the excuses he had to invent for missing school
when they ploughed their parcels of land; and how his teacher
accepted them because Grandpa was the president of the parents'
association. And, after he left school, he wanted desperately to
learn carpentry, but his work-load on his father's property and on

his uncle Moanea's was such that he did not have any time to rest and do what young boys of his age did, let alone learn new things. One evening, coming home from his uncle's house, my father felt so tired and dejected that, when he turned his head towards Scurtu's house, he was struck down by the vision of a candle burning in a candlestick. His legs would not move anymore and his whole body was shivering. He must have stayed there for minutes on end, eyes glued to the image glowing in the dark on Scurtu's little veranda, until he slowly managed to move his feet and drag himself home exhausted. Seeing the devastated look on his face, Grandpa Teodorea understood how much he had pushed the young boy and never sent him back to work for Moanea again. And he not only allowed him to learn carpentry, but also did the best he could to encourage him. He knew how much young Pavelea liked that.

Mama, hearing the heavy noise of the iron-clad wheels, looked out of the window and saw my father walking alongside the cart, his head uncovered.

"Grandpa is dead!" she cried.

A hectic time followed. That night they laid Grandpa on a door frame in our big room and, for two nights in a row, people came in for the wake. The men drank a lot of *pălinca* and they stayed up the whole night playing cards and reminiscing about Grandpa's time on earth.

The *cazan* had to be stopped for the funeral and Inspector Bozga had to be brought in from Oradea, to seal it with red wax patches.

Apart from Father Milea, two other priests officiated at the funeral. My Grandpa did not have his wife Maria to grieve for him, but Grandma Saveta, a very convincing mourner, wailed her best for the old man. Auntie Puica did her part well; but what most impressed everybody was Grandpa's youngest daughter Raluca's chant. Her voice, as crystalline and uplifting as the thrills of a nightingale, left the villagers in wonderment.

On our way to the cemetery, I sat on top of the coffin and every time the women looked at me, they cried even more. I couldn't understand why. The *comandare* afterwards was a dinner to remember, with baskets full of *colaci* – little buns made of the whitest flour – pork sausages, *sarmale* – cabbage rolls filled with rice and minced pork – and plenty of *pălinca*, which not only filled the belly of the mourners but cheered their souls to the point that some of them started singing happy songs. This was considered disrespectful to the dead; but I think Grandpa Teodorea would have approved.

A week later the Inspector restarted the *cazan*. With Grandpa dead, Mitru informed my father that, as the eldest son from the first marriage, he was entitled to half of the *cazan*. A squat man with cruel, furtive eyes and a permanent sneer etched on his face, he barred my father from entering the *cazan* premises as the land, on which it was installed, belonged to him.

Grandpa had been married for only a few weeks when he had to leave and fight for Franz Joseph and his empire. While he was at the front, his son Mitru was born and soon after his wife died of cholera. On his return, for Mitru's sake, he married a young woman his in-laws had chosen for him. By doing so, he had alienated his father. When Grandpa's new wife fell pregnant with my father, things did not work out with his in-laws anymore and the young couple were thrown out of the house. They found shelter in the family stables outside the village. There, at the onset of spring, my father was born. He loved telling me the story of his birth over and over again, every Christmas during my childhood. Grandpa's family grew by four more children: Teodor, who died at birth, Puica, Gligorea and Raluca.

Now, all of them wanted a share in the *cazan*.

My father, who had contributed ideas and money, was shocked and angered at the greed displayed by his own flesh and blood. The only option he had was an expensive one: resorting to the law, which he did. Before the trial started, Puica, Gligorea and Raluca, in their spite and twisted, selfish stubbornness, unexpectedly sold their share to Mitru. This influenced the court, making the task for Mitru's lawyer easier. My father was left only an eighth of the *cazan*; and Mitru ordered him never even to come near it.

Eventually, my father sent word to Mitru, through Puica, that he was prepared to sell him his share in the *cazan* but Mitru was no longer interested. He had what he wanted, anyway.

And my father never ever saw a drop of *pălinca* from his share.

To hell with you, brother Mitru, my father thought angrily. Not one to take anything lying down, he decided, then and there, to have a *cazan* of his own. He went to Olok, the Hungarian *cazan* master-builder in Tinca, and ordered a three hundred and fifty litre *cazan*, bigger than Mitru's, to be made from the best Czechoslovakian copper available. After all, my father thought defiantly, it was his idea in the first place and he was able to run a *cazan* better than his dishonest half-brother. Mitru, whom the villagers were already calling greedy, could barely write his own name, let alone do sums properly. To keep the rudimentary books required of him, he had to resort to a Council employee. My father, on the other hand, may not have had the schooling but was sharp, intelligent and determined to best his brother.

A year later my father made a new tub for the cold water, a new barrel to collect the *pălinca* and installed his new *cazan* in Râturi in a newly built hut, bigger than the previous one, which now Mitru used. He was on his feet again, attracting more customers than Mitru. My father's sisters, especially Puica, sided with Mitru in the hope of scrounging something out of him and Mitru put pressure on Puica to ask my father for a share in his new *cazan*. When my father heard her claim, he treated her as every brother in Lupoaia treated a sister in such a case: he beat the hell out of her.

Those Who Are Not with Us Are Against Us

Times were changing fast. In 1947 the politicians, who opposed the elections of the Communists in parliament, were arrested. The old police cadres were purged and replaced by brutal, new men, with no real education, but selected for their cruelty. The royal army officers, who had fought on the Eastern and Western fronts, were sacked and imprisoned. One thousand five hundred politicians, from the National Peasant Party and some other minor groups, were incarcerated in a single night. Gradually, the Communists eliminated other parties from the political arena. Ordinary people, who expressed their dissent, were labelled enemies. All those, deemed to be enemies, had to be re-educated and the dissenters had to be destroyed. The year concluded with the exile of the king, the last obstacle in the Communists' subjugation of the country. "Those who are not with us are against us," the peasants heard too often. They had heard the priest telling them that Jesus said something like that too but, as far as the peasants knew, Jesus did not set out to destroy, eliminate and exterminate people. On the contrary, he was the one who ended up being crucified. They became more confused. Day-to-day life was difficult enough; but the future looked bleak, impenetrable.

By 1948 the Workers' Party was in charge of the country. No

opposition. The problem of leadership was still unresolved, however. There were two contenders jockeying for the position – Ana Pauker, of Jewish origin, and Gheorghe Gheorghiu-Dej, a Romanian electrician. Advice had to be sought from the father of all liberated countries, the great genius of mankind, Comrade Stalin. He had answers to everything.

Brief answers.

Infallible gems of wisdom.

Orders.

He said just one name – Gheorghiu-Dej – and that was heard loud and clear.

"We have a severe drought and we cannot feed our people," the Romanian leaders said. They did not mention the convoy of trains, filled to the brim with cereals, or the petroleum products, the machinery, the river and maritime ships leaving Romania for Russia. Nor did they mention the 19 carriages of Romanian gold reserves being taken by the friendliest country in the world.

"This will be solved later, after the construction of the Danube-Black Sea canal," Stalin declared.

The Romanians had a model in the Soviet Volga-Don Canal. The machinery from that Soviet project would be sold to them. At a friendly overvalued price, of course.

Nothing to worry about.

The Volga-Don canal, Stalin told the Romanian leaders, had been useful for the extermination of the enemies of the people. He could have shot them or deported them to Siberia; but he put them to good use, he said. In the process, most of them died anyway. That was one of the aims of the Revolution, after all.

On May 25th, 1949, the Romanian Workers' Party Politburo announced the decision to build the canal and, in 1950, a Great National Assembly decree designated it suitable for the re-education of hostile elements.

Who were the hostile elements?

Fertile minds went to work. Ideas, names and lists were produced. First on the lists were members of the old traditional political parties; second, factory owners; and third, landowners. While it was easy to deal with the members of the old parties and the factory owners, given their more limited number, it was more complicated to deal with the landowners. Almost every peasant, even in the remotest corner of the country, was the owner of at least a small parcel of land. So in the new classless society, three classes were created overnight: poor peasants, middle peasants and rich peasants. *Chiabur* was the name given to the rich peasants. That made them exploiters; and *chiabur* was invested with the same meaning *kulak* had in the vocabulary of our liberators.

The class of *chiaburs* was officially created at the Plenum of the Party, 3-5 March, 1949. They were peasants who owned over 50 hectares of land and employed a poor peasant for more than thirty days a year.

And they were guilty, even if the land had been in the family for countless generations. They had to be treated as the most dangerous criminals; they had to be exterminated. The new society had to be clean, disciplined; its members would work for it to the best of their ability and would take from it only as much as they needed.

That was the idea.

A wave of persecutions started in every corner of the country, including Lupoaia. The villagers would learn to behave, by example. The more suffering inflicted on the enemies of the people, the more the rest of the population would learn to accept the quota they had to give the state on cereals, which was as high as the production. The quota on milk was more than their cows could produce and the quota on wool was more than the sheep could yield; but they came to accept it. Compulsory voluntary work for building roads, mending bridges and digging ditches did not leave the peasants enough time to work the land to obtain enough cereals to pay the quota to the state, to look after their cows adequately to get the quantity of milk required to pay the quota and to feed their sheep appropriately to obtain enough wool. Those that managed somehow to comply with the requirements imposed by the state, had their quota increased the year after. The peasants were caught in a vicious circle, with no escape. That's how the workers' paradise was achieved in the Soviet Union.

It was easy to be labelled: just a tiny shade of the imagination, an anonymous letter, hatred for your neighbour's life, for life in general. It wasn't so difficult. After all, everybody must have hated somebody at some time. The Church had tried to teach love through fear, for centuries, and failed. Perhaps, because the fear it tried to instil in people was too intangible, too remote, too hidden for the dormant minds of the peasants. The God to be feared was nowhere to be seen. The new ideology was teaching hatred through fear too; and that was bound to succeed because the fear was here and now, physical and personal. The gods were real – you could stare them in the face. This fear was going to spread like wildfire. Then it would be easy to keep it constantly present in the mind of every citizen, to make him feel defenceless before the mighty force of the Party machine.

This had to last for a long, long, time, until the enemies were exhausted, eliminated, until everybody had forgotten what 'love thy neighbour' meant, until the new man emerged with a pure love for the idea forever and ever, because the new society was perfection itself.

Chiabur or the Enemy of the People

When my father was not working in the fields, he did carpentry and repair work in a room next to the stable, which was divided into two small sections: his work shed and a pigsty. When I complained about the dirt and general stink in the cramped but cosy space, he said he did not mind the stench of fresh pig manure or the pigs' squealing. If he got used to it, so would I. This was when, at the age of four, I was handed the copy book and pencil, given to me at my birth. My father sat me on the big rock in the middle of the room and taught me how to write, lighting up with pride at my progress.

At times I could hear my friends, Mircea and Dolea, Floarea and Domnica, playing outside, shouting and laughing and calling each other names. I wanted to go and play with them. Instead, my father set me goals: only a hundred slashes more, only fifty ovals more, only twenty hooks more, only ten circles more. I was learning to count, too, and the hundred slashes seemed an eternity to finish. I whined, as all children do, but in the end I did the hooks, the ovals, the slashes and the circles, until his curt nod told me he was satisfied. Then I was allowed to go and play.

By the time I was five, I was reading about a mother goose losing her goslings on a river and, after some apprehensive moments, finding them frightened and hiding under a bush by the riverside. From then on, every time I passed the Hodişel creek, I paused to see if any poor mother goose were looking for her lost goslings.

All the light was now coming from the East; and it looked breathtakingly new. In a very short time, everything was nationalized, from banks to factories, from pharmacies to little distilleries. The Party was on its way towards creating a new society; but how can you build anything new with old-type people? You can't teach an old dog new tricks – everybody knew that. The solution was to destroy the old dogs. The former members of traditional political parties, together with many intellectuals, endangered the new society. They were arrested, imprisoned, tortured. Many were sent to be re-educated on the Danube-Black Sea canal. The same treatment was reserved for the *chiaburs*.

Micula, our neighbour, was the village crier and jack of all trades at the People's Council. One evening, while my father and I were having dinner, he scurried to our house, his head down, his coat flapping open in the wind and carrying a brown envelope in his hand.

"I have come at the right moment, by the look of it," he said.

"Would you like some potato soup?" asked Mama, standing by the stove with a plate in her hand and a smile on her face, ever the perfect hostess.

"I've had dinner, Nuţa. Thank you, all the same," Micula answered and sat on the bench next to my father.

"I bet you won't say no to a glass of *pălinca*," my father laughed.

"If it's the one you make, how could I?" Micula joked, elbowing my father.

Having been my Grandpa Teodorea's war companion, he enjoyed a special status in my family. Later on, in spite of our age difference, he became my friend too. I was the only one allowed to cut his hair, or what was left of it; and, in exchange, he would delight me with stories about the old times and my family's past.

Mama took the bottle from the cupboard and filled two glasses, one for Micula and one for my father. After Micula emptied his glass, he wiped his mouth with his sleeve and handed my father the envelope

"I brought you this," he said. His gaze dropped to the floor.

"What is it?" my father asked, as he reached for the envelope.

"It's not good, Pavelea, it's not good."

My father opened the envelope and read the piece of paper. We were not used to receiving letters and expected him to say something. What he said didn't make much sense to me but it struck me for the novelty of one word.

"They declare me a *chiabur*," my father said. His voice was grave, unusually grave; and his face had the expression of someone who had lost something dear to him.

"What's *chiabur*, Dad?" I asked.

"Oh... I really don't know, son. I only know they are considered enemies of the people," he said. My question seemed to surprise him.

This time the word enemy bugged me. He explained that enemies were people who did not like each other and fought one another. As I'd never seen him fight with anybody, he gave me an analogy with some petty quarrels he used to have with Vantica over the boundary between our properties; but he said it was worse than that.

"Which people are you an enemy of?" I insisted.

"I don't know, son, I don't know," he said, scratching his head. "It's not true... it's a lie." He ran his hand through his hair.

"You tell them, Dad, tell them. They'll believe you."

"I'll do that, son, don't worry."

"My God, what will happen to us now, Micula?" Mama asked, holding her face with both hands, her eyes wide open as if popping out of her head, and her fear draining the warmth from the room.

"They'll make you pay very high taxes, Nuṭa. It's all I know," said Micula.

"Who knows what's in store for us? I'll have to do whatever they want," my father said. His voice, barely audible, sounded sad.

"And if you don't?" I interjected.

"They take him to prison," Micula said solemnly, shaking his head.

I asked, "What's a prison?"

Mama, who was standing close to me, put her hand on my head as if protecting me.

"Don't bother Dad, Teodor. He's got plenty on his mind right now."

"It's a small place, where they lock you up," my father replied.

"It's like the birds when you catch them? Are they in prison?"

"Yes, son, yes. Like the birds when they are no longer free."

In Lupoaia there were to be seven *chiaburs*: Traian, who had more land than everybody in the village but was still short of the fifty hectares prescribed by the Party; Mitru, my father's half-brother, who had inherited his mother's few hectares and now had the *cazan*; Iosive with some nine hectares, an old troublemaker with legionnaire leanings; Licu with roughly eight hectares and a past as a legionnaire leader; Ionelu, a former mayor of the National Peasant's Party; Zoltan, a Hungarian gypsy, who was barely scraping a living by running an old water mill on the Hodişel creek, and my father.

Traian paid a magistrate to falsify forms and documents; and suddenly, he was not a *chiabur* anymore. Mitru was saved by a famous public prosecutor in Oradea, who was related to his wife's family.

So now the *chiaburs* of Lupoaia numbered five. My father was the youngest, only twenty-nine years old. He had less than four hectares of land, which included Mama's share and the *cazan* he had just acquired. Unfortunately, he did not have anybody to save him, even though his would have been the easiest case of all. On his identity card his profession was registered, not as a peasant like the rest of the villagers, but as a *chiabur*. This pursued me throughout my life, because in the society of the luminous future, the sins of the fathers were made to fall on their children.

Licu was a special case. In the 1930s he was approached by Lobica from Oradea, with new ideas and booklets of new patriotic songs. It did not take long for Licu to get hooked. There was a new movement, the Legion of the Archangel Michael, which put God and the nation above everything else. This movement had its own voluntary army called the Iron Guard, made up of young peasants and students, Lobica explained. The Legion paid attention to the particular needs of the peasants, who would become a force to reckon with. Licu liked a movement where prayers were important; and he also liked songs that appealed directly to the simple soul of people without much schooling, like himself. The songs evoked the national heroes from the past like Horia, Cloşca and Crişan, and went as far back as Trajan, the Roman Emperor, who gave the Romanians their language. They sang of the dawn of a luminous future, which was there for the taking, but not without sacrifice and death. The creation of a new man justified the ultimate sacrifice of a few, they said. Licu believed that no one could remain indifferent to these glorious words full of promise, particularly as the Peasants' Party achieved little for the betterment of the peasants' condition.

The songs made Licu dream, and dreaming was so beautiful. He wanted so much to be part of it that he could barely wait for Lobica's second visit.

A week later Lobica came back, accompanied by Corbu, a lawyer from Ceica, and a teacher from Taşad. They lectured Licu on the Legion and its great Leader, the Captain, the one chosen by God to take the people's destiny in his hands. When they finished, they showed Licu the green shirt, which he found beautiful. It was the green colour of the fresh grass of the fields of Lupoaia, of all the fields of the motherland, they said. He was ready to swear allegiance to the Captain and die for the Legion. Corbu appointed him head of the Lupoaia garrison, with control over the neighbouring villages. After they left, Licu donned his green shirt and started organizing his friends in *cuiburi*, cells of twelve men – like the apostles – each with its own leader. They organized formal ceremonies to swear their allegiance to the Captain and declared themselves ready to die for the Legion. Above all, they were proud to exchange their soiled, coarse hemp shirts for the green shirts made of soft material, which they could never have afforded. They often met at night, had their collective prayer and sang patriotic songs. The more they sang, the more they broke the moral code of the Legion, by making *pălinca* part of their meetings. Soon most men of the village joined the movement; and so did the men from the neighbouring villages. They started learning hymns, marches and other rousing songs. They organized processions through the village, forcing the gypsies to accompany their songs with violins and drums. The women soon found their singing more appealing than that of the priest at mass.

When the famine was at its peak, they brought corn, beans and potatoes at cheap prices. Those who couldn't pay, did not pay at all.

In September 1940, the Legion joined General Antonescu in an alliance to create the National Legionnaire State, and force King Carol II to abdicate in favour of his young son. As part of their deal, the Legion became the only legal party. Their coalition was short-lived, as the Legion perceived Antonescu to be too tolerant of the old structures. The Legionnaires wanted a totalitarian fascist regime, the only one which could produce the new man able to bring about their luminous future with God. The Jews and all the other political rivals were to be eliminated.

When the Legion came to power, Licu thought it was time to assert its supremacy in Lupoaia. He decided to erect a flagpole in the centre of the Valley, just in front of Ionelu's house. Men were sent to the timberyard of Dobreşti for a 30m pole, which was speedily smoothed, painted green and lifted towards the sky with a pulley. The big inauguration day came and hordes of green shirts, from the neighbouring villages, joined their Legionnaire colleagues from Lupoaia, to attend the raising of the flag, and to renew their vows of allegiance in front of the high ranking officials, who had come from as far as Beiuş and Oradea.

A gendarme from Holod came to watch the ceremony and sat with the authorities, at the end of the front row. Overcome with the crowd's euphoria, he gave the Roman salute to the flag, like everybody else. That was too much for Corbu, who interrupted the ceremony and reminded him that he was not a member of the Legion and had no right to take part in the sacred flag-raising ceremony. Moreover, his Roman salute was a cowardly act, characteristic of those who wanted only the benefits, brought by the Legion, but were not prepared to put in the work. He went on with his tirade, shouting more loudly, expounding all the values the Legion stood for. The humiliated gendarme left quietly, amid the laughter and applause of the green shirts. No gendarme had ever been treated like that before.

On the night of the 21st January, 1941, Gavrila, Licu's son, heard a commotion in the relatively quiet street of Lupoaia. He was employed as a working hand by the public notary and slept in the stable at the back of the house. He put on his breeches and rushed past the house, catching sight of the silhouette of the notary through the dark window. The street was in turmoil. Peasants, armed with hoes, axes, shovels, scythes and pitchforks shouted slogans against Antonescu. They were led by Trincu, the mayor, who was himself red in the face, from the exertion of shouting in an effort to stir up the mob.

"What is happening?" Gavrila asked the Mayor.

Trincu scolded him. "Can't you see, boy, we are going to defeat that traitor dog of Antonescu and get back our sacred rights to rule this country. What are you waiting for? Go and get a pitchfork and let's go to Beiuș to teach the bastard a lesson. Make it quick, there is not much time left. Now or never!"

Gavrila said that the notary wouldn't allow him to go.

"There are no notaries any more, there is no authority beside us, the Legionnaires. Understand?" Trincu shouted.

Gavrila looked at the excited crowd, at the young *frățiori de cruce* – little brethren of the cross – much younger than he was, ready to fight for a better world. He couldn't sit on the fence; he was going to get dressed in a hurry and join them. Now or never!

The public notary, not a Legionnaire sympathizer, had followed Gavrila's every move. He opened the window softly and whistled at Gavrila, gesturing him to come in. Gavrila obeyed and found the notary pacing the lounge in his underpants.

"What were you doing out there?" the notary asked, wringing his hands, as the commotion seemed to increase right outside his door.

"I was trying to find out what this noise was all about. I am thinking of going to Beiuș," Gavrila answered.

The notary looked into his eyes, shock clearly written over his thin, angular face. "Are you completely mad?" After a brief pause he said, "Tell me where your father is right now!"

"In Beiuș," Gavrila admitted.

"Do you know what he's there for?"

"He's been conscripted by the army."

"So you will be going to Beiuș with your damn pitchfork, to fight against your father, who will be pointing a machine gun at you. Is that so?"

The notary gave him a long stare, but Gavrila couldn't raise his head to face him, keeping his eyes trained on the floor as realisation dawned on him.

"You will die and the old man will live. Is that what you want?"

The slogans and the chants of the Legionnaires were fading into the darkness of the night.

Time passed before the notary came closer to Gavrila, placed a hand on his shoulder and, in a soft voice, said, "Be a good boy, go to bed now."

Gavrila obeyed.

That night the Legionnaires of Lupoaia joined forces with other groups from neighbouring villages and, in the morning, converged onto the square in front of the army barracks in Beiuș. The conscripted soldiers were already lined up in war formation, with cannons and machine guns, instantly dampening the rebellious spirits of the tired Legionnaires. The two enemies measured each other; pitchforks, axes and scythes were raised.

Licu, who was now a soldier, recognized Trincu and other faces from his village; they were worn out by the journey, lack of sleep and bitter January temperatures. He felt his heart sink. How could he shoot at Mayor Trincu, his best mate, following a stranger's orders? His son Gavrila might be in the crowd. What sort of father could shoot at his own blood? He took out the bullet chamber of

his gun and slammed it onto the stone, cutting into his knee. He
thought he would later be able to make the excuse that his gun
was defective. After all, the equipment was fairly antiquated,
particularly that given to the conscripts. The sound of the chamber
being dashed against the stone broke the silence, and it was then
that Colonel Istrate advanced towards the undecided crowd. He
was no further than ten metres from the leaders' row.

"Good people," he said, "this is madness. There is no reason in
the world that sons should fight against fathers or brothers against
brothers or friends against friends."

Some Legionnaires, behind the front row, raised their farm
tools and shouted a slogan or two; but they were silenced by the
leaders.

Colonel Istrate saw that his words had made an impact but, at
the same time, he was aware that some elements in the crowd were
fairly radical. That's why he changed his initial idea of giving the
mob an ultimatum to retreat from the square and disperse. On the
contrary, he told them they had as much a right to be there as the
soldiers had. The only thing he asked them was not to invade the
soldiers' private space. If that were to happen, the soldiers would
have to defend themselves with their guns.

Murmurs rose in the rebels' camp.

The back rows of the Legionnaires, hungry, cold and tired,
moved away from the square, then the middle rows followed until
the leaders of the rebellion found themselves with no followers,
looking at each other in disbelief.

In one night, on their way to Beiuş, they had done great things;
they had replaced all the mayors belonging to the other parties with
their own loyalists, had chased away the suspected gendarmes and
replaced them with trustworthy Iron Guard members. They saw all
that work come unstuck, right there, in that very moment. Their
mighty rule, which everybody had had to follow unquestioningly,
surely couldn't end in that square, in front of the barracks of Beiuş.
But it did.

Their eventual downfall was caused by their natural ally, Hitler,
who wanted stability in this little country with such important oil

reserves, vital for his war efforts. He gave Antonescu the nod to do away with the Legion.

The Legion's reign ended that January but during its short time in government more than 60 political assassinations had been carried out and a series of pogroms instigated. Antonescu found out that a coup d'état was planned by the Legion and managed to suppress it, with support from the German army. After a three day civil war in Bucharest, more than a hundred Jews were brutally murdered by the Legion and hung up in the abattoir according to the kosher technique of butchering animals.

There was no place for people like Licu in the Communist new order. His luminous future was not the brilliant red of the new regime. While the new Legionnaire man eliminated his enemies in the name of God, with a cross in his hand, the new Communist man eliminated God altogether and stood on His pedestal. They were both equally thirsty for blood.

The Basement

The *duba* that took my father away, that cold night of February, stopped a few times in other villages – Dumbrăviţa, Sâmbăta, Ceica, Calea Mare – to pick up other *chiaburs*. It entered Oradea, with its prey of silent, traumatized human flesh, just before dawn.

The *chiaburs* were hurled inside the Militia headquarters and ordered to take off their clothes. Soon afterwards, they were pushed naked down the narrow, dark stairs of the building into the basement.

It was cold and, in the pitch darkness, they could hear heavy breathing and moaning. The stench of excreta was overpowering. The door shut behind them with a metallic screech and they bumped into bodies lying on the concrete floor.

"Pavelea, you are here too," my father heard.

"Yes. I can't see a thing. Who are you?" he asked, craning his neck and peering through the darkness, trying to make out the shapes of his fellow captives.

"Cornu from Sâmbăta."

"It's you, Cornu?"

"Yes, Pavelea. I can see you. I've been here for two days now. I can see in the dark." The old man's voice was weak and gravelly. He spoke with difficulty, pausing between words.

"Did they beat you up?" my father asked.

"They beat everybody here."

"What do they want?"

"I don't know, Pavelea. I don't understand anything. One thing they always repeat is that they want to exterminate us. They say that continuously. They also want us to give them a reason for doing so," he explained.

My father listened. He tried not to think about the filth or the stench.

"What harm did we do? Is it wrong to work more than other people? Is it wrong to have more land than the average?" Cornu asked. "It seems so. Why don't they kill us straight away, instead of treating us like animals? It's beyond comprehension, Pavelea. It's beyond anything I've seen in my life."

"Do you know anyone else here?" my father asked after a while, the eerie silence making him feel uncomfortable.

"Zaru from Inceşti. Yesterday they broke his jaw."

"How is he now?" my father asked.

"He is here on my left, lying like a corpse, he can't talk..."

"But he doesn't have much land," my father said. His shoulder hurt, where the men had twisted his arm behind his back. My father shifted his position to try to get more comfortable.

"They know it... they know everything," Cornu sighed.

"Why then?" My father tried to make sense of this.

"For the threshing machine... he is an exploiter, they say... as they will say of you, for owning the *cazan*. One should be poor... poor, everyone poor."

It was freezing in the basement. The exhausted men leaned against the cold walls or sat on the equally cold cement floor. Some had been there for ten days and had lost the sense of time. The stink of human excreta came from the overflowing latrine, an improvised leaking tub in a corner.

At dawn, a young militiaman opened the door with a bang. Many of the men got on their feet.

"Flonta Pavel!" he shouted.

"Yes."

"Come here."

My father quivered at the thought of what might be in store for him, but squared his shoulders, took a deep breath and held his head high as he was pushed upstairs and into a large room, with creaking boards and the Party leaders on the wall. A Securitate Captain was sitting at a desk, browsing through a file.

"Name?" said the Captain, a tall man in a spotless uniform, without looking at him.

"Flonta Pavel."

"How old are you?" asked the Captain, raising his gaze from the papers, his dour face offering no compassion.

"Thirty."

The Captain stood up and looked towards a window on his right.

"You know why you have been declared a *chiabur*, don't you?" he asked.

"No, sir."

"You don't know?" said the Captain, his mocking tone feigning surprise.

"No, sir. I have done nothing wrong."

The Captain came closer. My father could feel his hot breath on his face. "You have done nothing wrong. All you vermin do nothing wrong!" he shouted, somehow frustrated. He was now very close, his eyes piercing my father through and through. "Tell me, Flonta, how long were you a fascist?"

"I was never a fascist, Captain." My father swallowed hard.

Unexpectedly, the Captain slapped him so brutally around the face that my father's ears would be ringing for days after.

"Liar!" the Captain shouted with all his might and grabbed hold of my father's shirt. "Do you remember when the fascists erected the flagpole in the village square?" He shook my father. "Do you?"

"It was a long time ago."

"Do you remember, I say?"

"Yes, sir," admitted my father.

"And you helped them, didn't you?"

"No, sir."

"You helped them, confess!"

"If you say so, sir."

"Who else was there?"

"The whole village, sir."

"How come?"

My father wondered if it was prudent to tell the truth. He had to. "They were giving away corn flour, potatoes and food parcels. There was a famine going on, sir."

"How generous and friendly, these fascists!"

"I don't know, sir."

"You know damn well, you were there."

"I was never in politics, sir."

The Captain approached the desk, took a sheet of paper from the file, an anonymous letter, and dangled it in front of my father.

"It says here that you were a young fascist. You were seen in the village square, erecting the flagpole for the fascists."

My father remembered what a big event the flagpole ceremony was for the peasants, something out of the ordinary and a festive occasion for the young kids. A week before the erection of the flagpole, men dressed in green shirts came to the Valley with a lorry full of corn, potatoes and beans; but later the fascists behaved just the way the Communists were behaving now, beating up their opponents or people thought to be their opponents. He wasn't going to tell the Captain that. "I was very young at the time, Captain sir."

The Captain looked at him for a long minute. My father was expecting the worst, when the Captain called the young militiaman and had my father taken out of the room.

Instead of going back to the basement, he was put in a solitary cell, a tiny cell, one metre by one and a half metres. A light bulb hung from the ceiling at eye level, permanently on and blinding him. His only companion was a tub which served as a latrine. The walls dripped with water while the floor grate, which cut into his feet, covered a stream of cold water. The overflowing latrine reeked, and the drop of water, made to fall onto his head at regular intervals, drove him mad. It was cold, so cold; and he was naked. He leaned his head against the wet wall to try to ease his agony. Unexpectedly, the door would open and the guard would beat him severely, never allowing his bleeding to stop. Nights and days were identical.

Then a guard opened the peephole, "Prisoner Flonta Pavel, turn your back to the door."

My father started, thinking that he recognized that voice. He was almost sure of it.

"Yes, sir," he obeyed.

"Have you turned your back?" the guard asked.

"Yes, I have."

"Don't turn around! Cover your eyes!" The guard handed him a cloth.

My father couldn't resist. "I'll do whatever you say, Purdelea."

He knew the man. He had sold him *pălinca* now and then.

The guard hit him with his gun on the back of the neck.

"You don't know me, scum!" he said in a harsh voice.

"Oh, yes, I know you too well, Purdelea," my father insisted. Another blow almost made him lose consciousness.

"Keep your mouth shut!" the guard said, kicking him with his hard boots.

The guard then dragged him out of the cell and pushed him with the barrel of his gun through the dark corridor. He was taken to an office upstairs, where he found the same Captain strolling around an iron table. When my father entered, the Captain asked the guard to wait outside.

"What happened to you?" he said to my father, as if it mattered.

My father was surprised by the Captain's attention. He covered his private parts with the cloth the guard had given him. "I must have said the wrong words, sir."

"You see, Flonta Pavel," the Captain stressed my father's surname. "In this world you have to say the right words. You have to do the right thing, otherwise you make a nuisance of yourself. We don't want that, do we?"

"No, sir."

The Captain paced up and down in front of my father, looking calmer and calmer. "Tell me, do you have relatives outside your village?"

"Yes, sir."

"Tell me their names!"

My father thought of his mother who came from Duşeşti and he told the Captain.

Then the Captain really surprised him. "Anybody in the Securitate?" he asked.

Blood surged to my father's head. His heart began to race. Was this going to be good or bad? What was he going to tell the Captain? That Flonta in the Securitate was real, but he had never seen him, did not know what he looked like. Did not know his first name. He had only heard about him. Hard man. Typical Securitate carrier man. Son of peasants, from a little village not far from Ceica. That's what he had heard. They could have been distant relatives. Who could know? Flonta was a rare surname. You stayed away from Securitate men, relatives or not. You didn't go to them, they came to you.

"Yes, there is a Flonta, in Beiuş," my father said hesitantly.

"What is he doing in Beiuş?"

"He is a lieutenant."

"A lieutenant, ha?"

"Yes, sir."

"How closely related are you?"

"Cousins," he lied.

"Cousins? I see," said the Captain, raising his eyebrows in surprise. His attitude towards my father improved. "Now, listen to me, Flonta Pavel," and again he stressed the surname, "you are a *chiabur*, the youngest in the region, as a matter of fact." He glared at my father, as if determined to get his point across. "You do know what that means."

"I can only judge from what I have already been through, sir," my father said. "But I don't understand all this."

"Well, if you are intelligent enough, you'll understand that this could be only the beginning of what you could go through. You see this?" he asked, pointing to a thick file stuffed full of well-thumbed sheets of paper. "It's already sizable and will become even larger. It contains evidence that could destroy your life."

He sat behind the table.

My father didn't reply.

"I'll give you a piece of advice," continued the Captain. "Watch what you say, what you do and with whom you are seen, if you know what's good for you. You have many enemies in the village; and perhaps you'll be brought here again, and it may be very soon. You should be fine for a while, if you follow my advice."

Then he scribbled something on the file.

"I'll let you go home, now. But Flonta," he said, again stressing that surname, "not a word about this to anybody. Understood?"

"Yes, sir. God bless you, Mr. Captain," my father said.

"Guard," the Captain called.

"Yes, Comrade Captain."

"Release him," he said, waving his hand in dismissal and turning his back on my father.

My father was given his belongings and allowed to go home. He cleaned himself up a bit at the Oradea station and took the evening train to Holod. He did not recognize anyone on the train and slept until it stopped somewhere. He awoke to find himself alone in the compartment and worried that he had passed Holod. He jumped off the train, rolled into a ditch on the wrong side of the tracks, towards the forest. He couldn't see the station's name and, by the time he realised that the place wasn't Holod, the train had already started moving, so he lay there for a moment. When he got up, he read the sign – "Duşeşti". The relief! Holod was only four kilometres away. Only a few hours ago, he was confined in a small space with faeces and blood. He was thrown into a dark world he did not know existed and now here, in front of him, lay the forest he knew. He savoured his freedom. As he entered the usually dark, ominous and sinister forest, he looked at the leaves on the trees, so fresh and vibrant in the breeze, he looked at the leaves on the ground, moist and thick; and he felt alive again. With each step he took, he was getting closer and closer to his Nuţa and Teodor. He understood what happiness meant.

This part of the forest was as dense as it was when his grandpa Pavelea came to Lupoaia, perhaps following the same path, to start a new life – young, bold and looking towards the future. My father, although young, could neither be bold nor look towards a future at all. How could he expect the future to hold anything good for him? The present was harsh and, if the future was anything like the present, life was going to be unbearable.

All of a sudden, just as his thoughts grew darker and gloomier, my father heard violins playing and a drum chasing away the wolves and the spirits of the forest. He hurried to catch up with them. The gypsies stopped and one of them lit a cigarette. It was Ciotu, his old schoolfriend. My father coughed and dragged his feet through the foliage, to let the gypsies know somebody was approaching them.

"Who is there?" Zambil asked.

He didn't answer and, as he came closer, Ciotu lit a match and brought it close to his face.

"Pavelea! My friend!" Ciotu shouted. "Am I glad to see you!" He shifted his drum and embraced him. Neither Ciotu nor Pavelea had done well at school; and both had often been forced to sit together on the donkey's bench, at the back of the classroom. Now his smiling and familiar face, spooky in the light of the cigarette, was the most welcoming sight Pavelea had seen for days.

"You're back, Pavelea," said the tall Zambil. "That's good, man, that's good."

"None of the others have come back yet, Pavelea," Corcodel said, pursing his thin lips.

My father understood that the other *chiaburs* had been arrested too. A lump in his throat prevented him from saying anything. He was happy to have met the gypsies; and he was happy to cry.

"Cry, friend, cry," Ciotu said, placing a gentle hand on his shoulder in consolation. "It helps soothe the sorrow.'

"Let's drink to your freedom," said Zambil, handing him a bottle of *pălinca.*

"It's good to see you," Pavelea said, and drank with gusto.

"Tonight we'll play the night away, just for you, Pavelea. But first give me that bottle," Ciotu said.

"Don't give up, man, don't give up." Corcodel patted him on the back. Then, with a swift movement of his bow, his violin made a harsh defiant sound

"How is my family? Do you know anything?" Pavelea asked.

"Nothing new. They've been waiting for you every day," Ciotu said.

Pavelea nodded, "If you only knew…" Tears ran down his cheeks.

"We know, we know," Zambil pushed the bottle into Pavelea's hand again.

"Where have you been?" said Pavelea, after he took a long swig from the bottle.

"To a wedding, in Dobreşti," Zambil answered.

"Where did they keep you, Pavelea?" Corcodel asked.

"In Oradea… somewhere…" he replied. "If you only knew…"

"Man, it's good to have you back," said Ciotu, borrowing the violin from Corcodel. "Let's sing one of those old tunes, you know, when we were young…"

The gypsies sang and drank, until the bottle was empty. My father sang and cried with them. The gypsies did not go home that night. They played with gusto, causing the villagers to curse them for disturbing their sleep. They didn't mind, as they were used to being cursed for no reason at all.

When my father finally arrived home, Mama crossed herself, thanking God for his freedom. She woke me up and took me to the porch, carrying me in her gentle arms as I continued to doze. At the sight of my father, my sleepiness disappeared completely and I ran towards him. He picked me up and I was so happy that I couldn't stop talking.

"Did they put you in prison, Dad?" I asked. His face was unshaven, his clothes stank like our outdoor toilet. The long stubble on his face made him look older and tired.

"Sort of," my father replied, unwilling to ignore my questions, but reluctant to answer them honestly.

"Was it a cage?"

"A big cage with many people, many…" he said.

"Did they tie your leg to a string?" I insisted.

"No, but they were not nice, for sure."

Mama lifted me from my father's arms. I wanted to tell him about my plan to become the bad, old wolf Grandma told me about, if the Securitate came to take him away again. Trapped by the villagers in a barrel of nails, which lacerated his flesh, the wolf farted so loud that the barrel exploded, and he ran away. I wanted to blow up these Securitate men's faces into many pieces, just as I imagined the wolf have made the barrel's staves fly all over the fields of Dumbrava. But I couldn't tell him that, because some neighbours wanted to know details of his plight in Oradea. I noticed that my father, otherwise a man who had plenty of words for every occasion, did not want to talk about what had happened to him. His replies were vague and short. Mama was staring at him and I could see that look of eagerness to help him on her face, like the one she adopted when he had drunk too much; but this time it was not a scolding woman's look, reproaching him for his behaviour, but that of a bewildered and deeply compassionate wife, who was trying to fathom the depths of hell her man had been through. She had never seen him so broken before. My father asked Mama to bring *pălinca* for everybody. That made the men happy and diverted their attention from him. Then he quietly slipped out into the night. Thirty years later, he told me that a man, who can bear the humiliation of being stripped of his clothes in public, can go through many unpleasant things in life. That was the first lesson he learnt from his arrest, he said.

The other *chiaburs* had been taken away some days after my father. A few weeks later, Iosive, Licu and Ionelu returned, or rather, their ghosts came back, so thin and wretched they were. Iosive, especially, wouldn't talk to anybody and would not leave his house, except for his bodily needs. He stayed in the big room for days and nights on end, alone and in the dark. Licu would do some work around the house but he wouldn't talk either, not even to my father, who wanted to know what had happened to them. Ionelu seemed to be the one least harmed by the experience. People said it was because his uncle, the archbishop, prayed for him; and the higher the cleric who prayed for you, the better your luck.

Zoltan was released last and he walked on crutches for months.

On the second Sunday after his release, my father went to Sâmbăta to see what had happened to Cornu. As he entered the village, he heard mourners crying and chanting, and he crossed himself. As he approached Cornu's house, the chanting and crying became louder and louder and suddenly he realised that it was coming from Cornu's house. He took his hat off, gripping the brim in despair and helplessness, and stood at the back of the crowd, looking at Cornu's name on the coffin. The man's wife, petite and haggard, looked a tragic apparition in her black clothes, as she sat down beside the coffin and leant her head on it. Everybody was crying. My father cried too.

He joined the crowd and walked behind the cart carrying Cornu's earthly remains to the cemetery. Devastated by the death of the old man, he introduced himself to Cornu's wife. She insisted that he go back home with her and tell her about the time in the Securitate basement. People were gathering at her home for the *comandare* and the woman asked my father to accompany her to the end of the orchard, so they could speak in peace. She couldn't stand still, sighing and flinging her arms out in despair.

"What happened to Cornu?" my father asked.

"He hanged himself, Pavelea, he hanged himself," she said, beating her cheeks with her hands. "He couldn't take it anymore. They just would not let him be. He was beaten, trampled on, spat at – he had to lick one Securitate officer's boots. But he didn't like talking about it. They told him we were going to be sent somewhere, to Bărăgan. He couldn't take that. We are too old for that kind of thing."

There were many stories about enemies of the people being deported to Bărăgan, the vast plain in the south of Romania, more than 600km away. Many of these people never reached their destination, destroyed by diseases, hunger, desperation and homesickness. The most difficult thing, the fatal thing for a peasant, was to be uprooted, separated from the land that he had tended year after year, season after season, day after day. It was unthinkable for an old peasant to leave the land of his fathers, for which he struggled all his life, not only against the whimsical forces of nature, but against his neighbour, who tried to shift the boundary each year, and against his relatives, who never stopped claiming part of it, bitterly cursing the soil covering their parents' remains, over the lack of a bequest.

My father knew the likelihood of deportation and he knew that, in spite of his youth, he would never be able to cope with exile. He did his own research and decided that if ever he was sent to Bărăgan, he would escape and hide somewhere in Banat. The land was good, far better than the uneven fields in Lupoaia that had a tendency to be just as stubborn as the local people; and he had the will to begin again.

"They did the same to me."

"He told me you were together for one night, then you were released."

"Yes, we met in that dark basement. Cornu sounded as depressed as anyone could be in those circumstances. They didn't release me that night. I was put in a solitary cell."

"He was in a cell too, until last week. Then he went to see Zaru in Incești on Monday and came back a destroyed man. Zaru was already in his grave. He had killed himself by drinking a bottle of poison. I think Cornu decided to put an end to it all, after that."

"I am sorry to hear about Zaru too. They beat him very hard. The night I was in the basement, he was lying unconscious on the floor," my father said.

"What am I going to do, Pavelea? What am I going to do?" She broke into sobs, wringing her hands as cries racked her fragile old body.

My father wanted to console her, but what could he say to a woman whose husband had taken his life, because he was persecuted for reasons he couldn't understand? For centuries, life had continued in that part of the world, with some people having more land than others. Some people drank their land away and remained poor, while others took advantage of them. But that was of their own doing, which everybody could understand and come to terms with, in one way or another. There was nothing to be understood now. A man got up one morning, worked hard all day long and, when he came home, found a piece of paper that changed his life. In Cornu and Zaru's cases, that piece of paper took the lives of two men. For what? They were just peasants, all sweat and ignorance, nothing else, except for common sense. Yes, it was their common sense that helped them through life, helped them understand what was good and what was bad, what was right and what was wrong. When that common sense around them was destroyed, they didn't have anything to follow; not even their survival instinct was enough anymore.

Illiteracy Eradication and a Musical Bucket

After my father arrived home from jail, the local militiaman, Mititescu, paid him a visit. He told my father to report to the police station every Monday morning. The *chiaburs* had to be kept in check, he said.

One such morning, while he was at the police station, Comrade Avramescu, the Party activist, knocked on our door. Mama was surprised to see him and immediately thought something might have happened to my father.

"Don't worry," he said to Mama, "I've come to see you."

"What for?"

"I need your help," he said.

"My help?" she almost screamed in absolute disbelief, her eyes wide and jaw hanging slack.

He straightened his posture as if shrugging off her surprise, and explained that all the illiterate peasants had to learn to read and write. In the shortest time possible. The Party was grappling with the question of how to replace the enemy with the new men, remade from peasants. As the majority of them were illiterate, the Party's latest directive ordered the immediate eradication of illiteracy. To cut the story short, he said, he wanted to put Mama in charge of the literacy program on the Hill.

Mama smugly pointed out to him that we were *chiaburs*,

thinking that it was as good an excuse as any

"The Party orders you, Nuṭa."

"Your Party cannot order me anything. I am not a member of the Party and never will be."

Mama folded her arms across her chest, squared her shoulders and stared ahead, never blinking. She cut quite a formidable figure when she got angry.

"Come on Nuṭa," the activist said in a conciliatory tone, "we don't have anybody else in the Hill as good as you are."

Perhaps flattered, or thinking that she shouldn't irritate the Comrade too much, Mama accepted. She had to teach all the illiterate women and men to read and write – in other words, the majority of the villagers. After all, they had to learn to write their names in preparation for signing the collectivization application. This had not yet started in Lupoaia, because the big villages on the plains of Banat and Bărăgan kept the cadres occupied.

So Mama tried. She cleaned the small room thoroughly. Grandma Saveta helped, because she was going to be one of the students. The class was supposed to start at 7pm. Micula, the Council Messenger, had announced it for the second time that week, telling everybody to bring pencil and paper. His wife, Vioara, who lived just across the road from us and had the worst breath imaginable, arrived on time. I remember that I was always repulsed by her lips, which were pasty and white like boiled chicken meat. She was also known in the village for her tasty piss. Micula revealed that his cigarettes, which he kept under the pillow at night, fell in her urine bucket. He said she dried them on the stove and he smoked them. This made Micula the talk of the village, and the men did not miss the opportunity of asking him frequently how the cigarettes tasted. Micula, who had a good sense of humour, invariably answered, "Nothing tastes better than the piss of a woman, you should try it."

Ten minutes later, the troubled Veta Bodorili from Dumbrava arrived. Now in her 50s, she carried a weight of guilt on her shoulders. When her only son was 8, she whipped him and the tip of the cane blinded him in one eye. She couldn't forgive herself and her smile disappeared forever – her damaged son couldn't find a wife in the village.

The third arrival was Norca Mitri, a middle aged woman, who was short and chubby, with a reputation for smiling at the men, particularly when out in the fields.

Nobody else arrived. Mama did not know what to do, especially since those who did attend had no pencil or paper with them. She eventually used brown paper bags; but the first hurdle for the women was to learn how to hold the pencil.

"May the devil fuck me," Norca Mitri said, "this is harder than holding a sickle and cutting hay all day long."

"I will never be able to do this," Micula's wife complained.

Veta Bodorili did not say much but her sighing and grimaces said it all.

The week after that, a few more women came; but the more the group grew, the more the giggling did. The women soon concluded they were dummies and may the devil fuck them if they would ever learn anything. They had lived so far without writing their names and they had better things to do. After that, some brought their needlework and treated the lesson as a girls' get-together.

Although I was not going to school yet, I could write and Mama assigned Grandma to me. She was good with money but, after we tried hard a few times to write her name, she gave up.

"Let me be, darling," she said, touching my head with her thin, chapped fingers. "This is for young people. Teach somebody else, be a good boy."

Seeing her refusal to learn, I teased her with a poem I had written for the occasion, which made me an instant hit with all the women of the Hill.

> *Bunica mea cu cârpă neagră* (My granny with a black scarf)
> *În loc să-nveţe alfabetul* (Instead of learning the alphabet)
> *Ar înghiţi o ceapă întreagă* (She'd rather swallow a whole onion)
> *Literele-i curg şuvoaie* (So the letters run aplenty)
> *Din ochi încetul cu încetul* (Slowly, slowly from her eyes)
> *Ca mici picături de ploaie* (Like little drops of rain)

She loved my poem, as she herself always wailed mourning verses, at the village funerals. From then on, when she saw me sad or worried about something, she would come and cheer me up by asking how that poem of mine was going. She died more than 35 years later, without ever learning how to read or write her name.

I did have other students but they were all the same. Nobody learned a thing. Paper and pencils were not their tools and learning words and letters was a waste of time for them. Mama had to keep an attendance register, which was checked monthly by the Party activist. When he checked it the first time, he was furious. He went to every house and threatened to impose heavy fines if they did not attend the literacy classes. They did, after that, because for a peasant with no regular income, fines were the worst thing that could happen. Non-attendance was further punished with the prohibition of selling their produce on the open market, thus taking away their means of survival, particularly during those times when the quotas were very high.

A few months later, the literacy program was considered a success and a few months after that, the Party declared the successful eradication of illiteracy.

In the spring of 1951, my parents loaded the hay into the attic of our stable. I climbed the outside ladder and ended up in the attic. Mama wanted me to get down; my father said I could stay in the corner near the trapdoor. So I stayed. When Uncle Ionica pushed a pitchfork full of hay through the trapdoor, I panicked, stepped backwards, where there was a broken plank in the ceiling, and fell 4 metres into the shed below. I landed with my head just 10 centimetres from the rock I used to sit on, when my father taught me how to write.

"Nooo!" Mama screamed, her hands flying to her face and the colour draining from her completely.

My father fled down the ladder as fast as his legs could carry him, his face as white as his hemp shirt.

Grandma Saveta heard Mama's scream. "What's happened?" she shrieked, running out of the house, her black scarf flying through the air behind her. She arrived at the shed, just as my father was bending over me. "My God, what have you done?" she shouted, her hands pulling at the grey plaits that were gathered in a spiral at the back of her head. As soon as she saw Mama, she scolded her, "How could you allow him to go up there?" She scolded Uncle Ionica, my aunties, my father, who was picking me up... everybody. "How could you be so careless with the little boy and let him go up into the attic?"

I was the apple of my Grandma Saveta's eye.

My left arm lay at a strange angle to my body and was clearly broken. I was in pain. Grandma cut a wide strip from a hemp sheet and they put my arm in a sling. My father took me to the Duşeşti train station, on foot, and we caught the train to Oradea where I had my left arm put in plaster for five weeks. When they took the plaster off, my arm was brown from the dirt that had accumulated underneath and I had the sensation that it was longer than the right one.

We stayed with my father's cousin in Oradea. Next to his flat there was a grocer's shop, where next to the apples, in a wooden box, I saw what looked like coloured balls, but their porous skin and flowery, sweet scent told me they were not made of rubber.

"What are these, Dad?" I asked.

"Oranges."

"What do you do with them?"

"You eat them."

"They smell nice," I said, looking pleadingly at my father.

"You can have one," he said. He gave me money to buy one and showed me how to peel it. It was delicious, better than anything I had ever tasted. I kept the peel and I sniffed it during our trip on the tram to the town center to see the Moon Church. The church was important, my father said, because its clock showed the phases of the moon. On our way back home, we passed the grocery again. He gave me money to buy another orange and I was very happy.

In the town centre, I was amazed by the electric poles with buckets near the top, from which popular music was playing. When the music stopped, somebody talked about the Soviet Union, the

Party, the workers, the dictatorship of the proletariat, the new man with a luminous future, and about our strangely-named leaders. I wondered how a man could squeeze into that bucket, let alone an entire band? My father laughed. He said that those people were somewhere else, not in the bucket. They could be as far away as Bucharest – hundreds of kilometres away – and their voices travelled through the air. It did not make sense to me. I would have loved to see inside that bucket.

Quotas and Tears

The harvest started and the wheat was piled up in ricks of different sizes on the fields of Dumbrava. The arrival of the threshing machine was always an event and here it was, dragged at a snail's pace by a puffing old locomotive along the Valley road. The deafening sound of the engine, the acid smoke billowing out of its large pipe, the huge back wheels that were taller than the men walking beside it, and the grinding sound, as it moved over the protruding stones of the dry road, enthralled me. It was the best spectacle of the year.

A procession of children followed the thresher, running and chasing each other. I ran down the slope to join in the fun, while men from the Hill were waiting, with three pairs of oxen and thick ropes, at the bottom of the Colnic. The oxen replaced the old locomotive, which did not have the power to drag the machine up the steep slope. When it reached the top, at the edge of our property, ropes were tied on its right side and secured around our huge ash trees, to keep it upright on the narrowing track and stop it rolling down the Hurupa slope. For us boys, it was a great show. The noisy chaos of the scene was thrilling. When the danger of overturning had passed, we were allowed to follow the machine to its destination in Dumbrava and see how it was fixed into place and checked, before it started the roaring sound that would be heard in the Valley until late every evening.

The thrill reached its climax for me, when our own wheat was due for threshing. My friends and I were allowed to stay and roll freely in the straw, playing hide and seek among the remaining ricks with all the other children.

When our turn came, I was there with Mircea, Dolea, Domnica, Floarea, and a horde of others from the Valley and the neighbouring gypsy encampment. There was frantic activity on the threshing ground. Two huge men, on top of our rick, threw sheaves down to two other men, on the machine; one of them cut the sheaves loose and the other fed them into the machine's belly. A short distance away, a few men were transporting and stacking the straw in a row, while women hauled away heaps of husks.

I was playing with Mircea and other children through the maze of the wheat ricks, when Mama called me. We had to pick up our sacks of wheat and go home, because the threshing machine was to be moved onto the next lot of four ricks. The fun was over. A man weighed our twenty sacks of wheat. With the operation concluded, the sacks were loaded onto a truck that was so rickety it seemed barely able to take the weight of the heavy bundles. Our cart and oxen were just a few metres away and it seemed strange to me that a truck would be transporting our wheat. A truck, with a motor and everything. It had never happened before. Nobody in the village would do such a thing. I looked at my father and I saw him watch the scene in dismay. Mama also seemed dumbfounded. I couldn't understand why.

At the end of the loading, the man in charge handed my father a receipt.

"This is yours," he said.

"Do you have to take all my wheat?" my father asked, his eyes darting between the sacks and the man who, I had already decided, was a thief.

"It's not even enough to cover your quota. You are a *chiabur*, aren't you?"

"It can't be that much!" my father said, his voice raised and his arms thrown out in despair.

"As I said, it doesn't cover your quota," the man repeated. "Sorry, I have to do my job."

Mama started crying. She buried her face in her hands.

The man in charge took my father to one side and spoke softly. "If you want to buy back some wheat, let me know later. But... mum's the word. Understood?"

My father nodded. The veins in his neck seemed to darken and pop as despair morphed into sheer rage.

We walked to the cart, Mama crying and my father pensive and speechless. Normally I always had to keep pace with them but now they were walking so slowly I had to wait for them. Mama was covering her mouth with the tip of her scarf and was crying in her hand, her shoulders heaving silently and the tracks of tears tracing lines down her dusty cheeks. My father seemed bent with age and walked like Micula, his head ahead of his body. Before getting into the cart, he stopped, his foot on a spoke, as if not able to decide whether to get in or to go back to that truck, which was taking away his year's work.

Seated on the board sobbing, Mama kept asking, "What are we going to do?"

"We'll think of something," my father said.

I knew that something was terribly wrong. "Where is that man taking our wheat, Dad?"

"To the collection station in Rogoz," he said.

"All of it? Everybody takes some wheat home."

"They say it's our quota, son."

"What is a quota?"

"The part that the State takes."

"Why does the State take it all from us?" I asked, confused and scared.

"You'll find out, son... one day," he said raising his eyes towards the spotless sky. I looked at his sweaty neck and I saw the coarse chaff had formed a dark brown crust on it. The deep creases on his forehead, his nostrils and his ears were all full of dusty particles of chaff and husks too. I felt sad.

Some days later, the *chiaburs* were standing in the Council's courtyard in front of Popescu, the new Secretary. Popescu was shouting like one possessed, red in the face, with arms flailing as if independent from his body. He called them names of all kinds but he labelled my father a monster.

"You did not fulfil your obligation to the State. You did not produce enough to pay your quota. Why?" he asked rhetorically. "Because you are saboteurs!" His voice was like thunder. "You are monsters!"

I knew the word monster. But saboteur? Never heard of it. It must be bad, because Popescu said it first.

"If you don't pay your quota immediately, your household goods will be confiscated. Before we do that, you will undergo some corrective lessons."

My father had heard about these re-education lessons, where people were humiliated and beaten to a pulp, and he expected the worst.

"I'll leave you to it," Popescu said.

The *chiaburs* were now under Mititescu's orders and he had a reputation for being heavy-handed.

"Le-e-e-ft! March! ... Out! One, two, one, two..." he shouted.

The *chiaburs* could do nothing but obey. They marched towards the communal bull stable, keeping in line in front of Mititescu.

"When I give the order to run, you run... hear me? And you run fast! Up to the fence and back! I count to three: one, two, three..."

And they started running. They wanted to please Mititescu to avoid more punishment. They were accustomed to the sufferings of the flesh, but four of them were old and tired quickly. Zoltan had slowed down and was looking pleadingly at Mititescu.

"What's wrong with you, Mr. Zoltan ? You don't want to run anymore?"

"I am old, Mititescu sir, I can't ... I can't keep up," he panted.

"Yes you can, you dirty scum!" shouted Mititescu. "Run!" He kicked the old man hard with his military boot. Zoltan fell to the ground and looked up at the shiny revolver, pointed at his head.

"If you can't run, then you can do something else! Isn't that so?"

"Anything, Mr. Mititescu... anything, may God bless you..."

"Then eat the grass, you animal! Eat!" he yelled, his boot pushing Zoltan's head towards the ground.

The other men ran more feverishly, with the strength of desperation and fear. At the same time, they watched the scene from the corner of their eyes.

Zoltan, exhausted and hopeless, freed his head from under Mititescu's boot for a moment, then bent over, his teeth against the ground, and started grazing.

After Mititescu locked the *chiaburs* in the Council annexe, two militiamen came to our house to seize goods in lieu of the unpaid quota. They carried out the two long benches alongside the beds, the table and the cupboard from the small room. They also wanted to take some of the embroidered cushions from the beds in the big room.

Mama cried out, moving forwards and grasping anything the militiamen picked up in their disgustingly grubby hands, trying to prevent them from taking it all. She pulled the other end of the cushions. The brute pushed her against the corridor wall and slapped her a few times, enjoyment etched over his ugly, pock-marked face. He won. Once he had loaded the cushions, his narrow eyes fixed on the sledge Grandpa Teodorea built for me. He stepped forward and reached for it. No! This militiaman was not going to take my sledge away. I grabbed his legs, determined to keep my last physical tie to my late grandpa. He tried to shake me off and I bit hard. He dropped the sledge, grabbed my hair and dragged me up like a puppet dangling in the air.

Then he dropped me. I hit my head against the wall.

Mama charged like a bull and pushed him aside with all her might and the man fell over my sledge. He got up, kicked Mama in the face with his boot, cursed God and all our ancestors and got out of the house, carrying my sledge with him. In my rage I wanted to be a *zmeu* to steal back my sledge, our cushions, our table, our cupboard and our benches from the militiaman; but I was just a little boy, with a father locked up in the Council annexe.

By now, we were left without wheat, without furniture, apart from the beds, and with no means of avoiding a famine. My father had a barrel of *pălinca* in the garden, covered by some layers of old timber with hay on top. It had to be hidden better. It was our only hope. Released after two days of re-education in the Council annexe, he dug a hole under the bed in our big room. The barrel had to be buried there, until better times, or until a buyer could be found. I was allowed to help, despite the late hour but only after I promised I would not tell a soul about the barrel, no matter what. I held up the lamp, which was covered by a cloth, while my parents carried the barrel inside.

After my father placed the barrel inside the hole, he felt satisfied.

"The bastards won't find it now. Let them think they can starve us." He patted the barrel with satisfaction and said, "This will bring back our wheat."

"May God help us." Mama crossed herself. "Cover it well and wet the floor, so when it dries up there won't be any tell-tale sign."

My father checked the cork, placed a rug on top, and covered the barrel with earth.

It was too late, when Mititescu came to look for the barrel a week later. Not that he knew about it, but they often checked on the *chiaburs,* just in case they were plotting something. Once a week, the *chiaburs* were summoned to the Council for re-education lessons, which consisted of forcing them to run from one end of the courtyard to the other, slap each other and spit into each other's faces. When Mititescu thought his instructions were not properly obeyed, he took it upon himself to humiliate them, by making them lick his boots and lap muddy water from the courtyard puddles like dogs, before locking them in the Council annexe for the night. The nights my father was at home after the re-education lessons, Mititescu and Popescu hid behind bushes in Hurupa, spying on his movements.

Micula had an agreement with my father: he would play his fife any time we were in danger from the authorities. His song was always a *doina*, a slow, wailing tune, which would make my father run as fast as he could. When we heard the fife the week after we had buried the barrel, my father ran through the garden towards Râturi and hid in Norea's oak plantation. Mama and I ran the opposite way, towards Dumbrava, then crossed the road at Doanea's and slowly walked back to Micula's house.

"Come quickly," Micula said, grabbing Mama's hand and dragging her inside.

"What's happening?" Mama asked.

"Look," he pointed towards our house, "they are jumping the fence into your garden now. They were behind that bush over there." He pointed to a spot in Hurupa, just opposite our house.

We stayed at Micula's until late that night. It must have been well after midnight when we got back home. Father was already there, looking at the damage made by the two uninvited guests. The front door had been kicked off its hinges and the wreckage left by their search was devastating. Our beautiful icon of the Virgin Mary and Child was smashed to pieces. My father said that our mounds of potatoes and carrots in the garden were no more, everything flattened out. The two men must have been looking for *pălinca*. Angry for not having found any, they scattered all our few provisions around and trod on them.

We went to the garden and could pick up only what we felt under our fingers in the dark. I went to bed, just as a new dawn was breaking the darkness, bringing with it more suffering for my weeping parents.

Comrade Teacher

Mrs Elena Petroi, the short, chubby teacher with round lenses, thick as the bottom of jars, came to visit us. She did not have enough students for grade one and wanted to persuade the parents of younger children, like Mircea and me, to enrol a year earlier. Chioara, the cleaner – a taller, thinner woman with no hint of humour on her face – followed her with a wicker basket on her arm.

Mama sat me at the table with the teacher and wanted to offer her something, but did not find anything that she felt was good enough. I got frightened by the thick glasses Mrs Petroi displayed on her nose. Nobody else wore glasses in Lupoaia, even if they were as blind as bats.

Mama signed a register and Mrs Petroi promised me a piece of candy when I started school in September, while Chioara eyed our sour cabbage on the stove.

"From now on, you call me Comrade Teacher, right?" Mrs Petroi said to me imperiously, on her way out.

A few days later, Mama heard rumours that Comrade Petroi was disappointed about the lack of attention to her comfort, when she had visited our home. Mama went straight to Chioara and asked her what those rumours were about. At first Chioara said it was nothing but, when Mama had turned her back, she mumbled, "You could have given the teacher something, like everybody else. You had cabbage all over the place."

A week later Mama bought a sour cabbage from the Ceica

market and handed it to Comrade Petroi herself. She was all smiles.

My father had to repeat the fifth grade, and stopped going to school altogether. He realised what he had missed because, in later years when I was doing well at school, he always told me that he didn't want me to work in the fields as he did, when he was a child and that, if I did well in school, he wasn't going to ask me to.

He kept his word.

When the first day of school came, Mama tried to get me out of bed.

"Come on, big boy, it's your first day of school," she said kissing my forehead.

"I don't want to go. I want to sleep," I said. An only child, I was a bit of a whiner.

She pulled the blanket off me and gave me a gentle smack on the backside, as she often did, her laughter at my laziness tinkling around the room like a beautiful melody.

"Come on now, you'll be late and Comrade Petroi doesn't like that. Didn't you hear that she'll give you candy?"

"I don't want her candy," I mumbled.

Rays of light streamed through the window onto our stove. A nice perfume of fried lard and eggs titillated my nostrils. I loved how Mama always crested the lard slices and, while frying, they would curl back. I imagined them as combs with big teeth. I used to eat them tooth by tooth and then crush the rind, pretending to be a hungry wolf. When Mama fried eggs on top of the lard, I would enjoy stripping the combs bare and lick my lips because they were tastier.

Mama took me in her arms, kissed me on the chest and tickled me. That woke me up.

"You like candy. I know that," she said, laughing and pushing her face into my chest.

"You like candy, don't you?" she insisted and, just to make her stop doing that, I said: "Yes, yes."

"I've prepared clean clothes for you and a tasty snack; and you'll play with lots of children. I bet Mircea is ready to go."

Mircea, my neighbour, and I were the youngest in the class. We were six years old and everybody else in grade one was seven. That early morning Mircea and I ran down Hurupa with our new school bags made of wood, like little suitcases, proudly resting on our backs. I wore a pair of trousers made by Mama from harsh hemp cloth and dyed dark blue. They were uncomfortable, after the long, white shirt I had worn until then, and they made me fidget.

The school courtyard was filled with the screams of boys, running around chasing girls or tussling with each other.

Dorel, a boy from the Valley, took us to the classroom. When we entered, there was silence. The beginners, seven in all, were on one side of the room, the older children of grade three, on the other. Comrade Petroi was our teacher. Her husband, the principal, taught grades two and four. Mircea and I sat down at the same desk, eyeing the other boys and girls.

On the wall behind the teacher's desk, hung four large portraits, some with hairy faces and long beards. Soon we had to learn how to spell their foreign names: Marx, Engels, Lenin, Stalin. We were told that only the last one was alive and he was the greatest genius on earth, the father of us all.

Father of us all?

I knew who my father was and I was itching to tell Comrade Petroi that but I was too intimidated. I knew who the father of my father was, my Grandpa Teodorea. And I knew the fathers of the majority of the kids in the class. What was this woman, with glasses thicker than dry cow dung, talking about?

On the right hand wall stood an old cast-iron stove and above it, a series of nine portraits, this time of Romanians – the leaders of our dear Workers' Party, who were watching over us, sometimes grudgingly, especially when we mixed up their names or simply forgot them. There were some strange names amongst them, which did not sound Romanian – Pauker, Chişinevski, Moghioroş, Bodnăraş. Pauker was a woman, who disappeared from the wall after a few weeks. My father told me she was a Jew and, as I had never seen a Jew before, I had some questions about that. Mircea said he heard from his father that the Jews had salami shops in

Oradea and they had a trapdoor in the floor of the shop, just in front of the counter. When a Romanian went into the shop, the owner pressed a button and the person fell into the basement, to be chopped into pieces and made into salami. The Jews did not sell that salami to their own kind, only to Romanians, and he said that the Hungarians did the same. The Jews and the Hungarians did not like Romanians at all.

I told my father not to buy salami anymore. We had our sausages and they were made with our own pig's meat. He laughed before adding that he had heard that Stalin had a trapdoor in his office too and, if he did not like some of our leaders, he could just push the button and away they went. That's why Tito did not want to go to Stalin's office anymore – he would have been killed for sure. I asked him if Stalin was a Jew and he said he did not think so, but he was the biggest criminal on earth. I asked him why, then, did Comrade Petroi say that Stalin was the father of us all? He looked at me, as if he did not understand my question. After a while, he asked me if she really said that to us in class. When I nodded, he shook his head in dismay.

"She says those things because she is paid to say them," he said.

He told me not to believe her when she talked like that, but to ask him and he was going to tell me the truth. Always.

"Stalin is not even a Romanian," he continued. "How can he be your father or my father or grandpa's father? Can you understand that?"

I shook my head, but this story of fatherhood was a bit tricky, if somebody like Comrade Petroi could play with it like that, saying things that were not true. I was happy with the father I had. Who wanted Stalin for a father anyway? Apart from her and the red banners in our class and on the Council building, I hadn't heard anybody say good things about him.

It seemed to me that the first three of the Romanian leaders on the wall, were looking askew, with one eye on the four giants and with the other on us, the new men of tomorrow, as Comrade Petroi called us. I didn't have the courage to ask her why she didn't put Jesus Christ or the Virgin Mary on the wall, like everybody else.

Were these people more important than them?

I asked my father. He said that these people were criminals and that Jesus Christ and the Virgin Mary were angels, just the opposite, and that I would be able to understand the difference later. His suffering, he said fervently and with much bitterness in his voice, came from the minds and deeds of those four foreign people on the wall behind Comrade Petroi's desk. The other nine people were the portraits of men of straw. This made me think. I had seen a lot of straw – we were living in it, our mattresses were made of it – but I had never seen men of straw before. I explained to him that they looked neat, well dressed.

He laughed at my naivety and explained his meaning: they were puppets of Stalin, because he made them do what he wanted. They were incapable of saying no to him. That was why everybody was suffering. It was too hard for me to understand how everybody suffered because of these people on the wall of our school, until he said that he was declared a *chiabur*, because those four people on the wall behind the teacher's desk had taught the nine Romanians, the men of straw, how to become criminals too. The fourth man with the big moustache was the biggest criminal on earth and his power extended over many countries. It was not for this that Horia, Cloşca and Crişan died. They fought to free us from Hungarian domination. They fought for a free country, governed by its own citizens.

"And where are we now?" His eyes focused on mine as he spoke.

He answered himself, saying that we had passed from one form of domination to another. Now it was the Russians' turn to dominate us, through people who did not bear the Romanian seed inside them, such as Pauker, Chişinevski, Moghioroş, Bodnăraş and the like. All of them were taught, in Russia, how to ruin our country. If Avram Iancu had seen this, he would have gone mad again, he explained.

Comrade Petroi was not quite the candy-lady Mama had talked about. Her thick glasses and the cane in her hand scared the hell out of us. She talked and talked about things that we couldn't understand. Then she talked about the *chiaburs*, and that I understood better.

I was the son of one.

She wanted us to take part in the struggle against the *chiaburs* and other hostile elements, who were our enemies. All the enemies of the dictatorship – the alliance of the workers and the peasants – had to be exterminated. That was the Party's directive. She told us that she had arranged, with the Party and the Securitate authorities, to give us a demonstration of such a struggle, here in our very village, against the *chiaburs*. And for those who did naughty things, like skipping homework or failing to prove themselves worthy members of the Communist society, "There is this!" She lashed the cane against the desk. The cracking sound made us all jump in our seats.

She looked at us through her thick glasses for a moment, before adding in a gentler tone: "Now it's time for a break. If you are good and don't shout in the courtyard, I'll give you candy." Her promise did not diminish my fear or my dislike of her. She shouldn't have talked about the *chiaburs*. I did not like that at all. Neither did I like her huge eyes; magnified by the jam-jar glasses, they scared me.

When we were out in the courtyard, I told Mircea, "I don't like it here. She is bad. I don't like her."

He didn't like her either.

"Let's go home," I proposed, and moved furtively towards the end of the courtyard, where the main entrance was, looking behind me with every other step.

"She will see us and beat us up," Mircea said solemnly, beginning to shake with fear.

He followed me, though, as I backed toward the entrance.

"She won't catch us. We can run fast," I spurred him on, a confidence in my voice that I definitely didn't feel.

"My mum will kill me," he worried aloud.

I was already at the door, looking around to see if anybody was paying attention to us.

"We'll say we don't feel well," I said. "Are you coming or not?"

I asked, pointing to the door. I did not wait for a reply, just opened it and ran for my life, my large blue trousers slowing me down.

I heard Mircea behind me. "Wait for me!"

I didn't.

I ran past a peasant.

"Have you finished school already?" He laughed. "Look behind you. They are coming after you!"

Mircea was only a few metres behind me, and we both turned and saw a group of three boys from grade three, pursuing us at great speed. They almost caught Mircea as he was doing the fastest poo ever on Hurupa.

When the boys entered my house panting, I was already in bed.

"Teodor and Mircea ran away from school," said Nelu, the tallest and son of the school cleaner. "Comrade Petroi sent us to take them back," he announced to Mama, sounding like a grown up.

"I don't want to go. I am sick." I pulled the cover over my head.

"Get up, Teodor, you'll see that it'll pass," Mama said. There was not a hint of playfulness in her voice.

"She didn't even give us candy. She said she'll beat us with the cane," I protested. "I don't want to go."

"Comrade Petroi sent my mother to buy candy," Nelu announced.

That moment Mircea ran into the room, head bowed and sweat dripping down his fearful face, followed by his angry mother, brandishing a rolling pin.

"Naughty devil, I'll kill you if you do this again." She raised the pin to hit him, but Mama defended Mircea.

"If he comes with us, he'll get candy," said one of the boys.

"I'll give him candy!" Mircea's mother managed to hit him from behind Mama's back. "Just tell Comrade Petroi to straighten him out, whatever it takes," she said to the boy, while glaring at Mircea.

Comrade Petroi kept her promise. Everybody received a frog shaped candy. The boys who chased us received two and they were very proud of themselves.

Fusu's Death and Another Arrest

Mircea and I were playing at the top of Hurupa, throwing stones into the bushes to scare the lizards out. We egged on Fusu, Mircea's little black and white dog, to get them. We heard a cart coming up the Colnic towards my house. It was a rare sight, a horse-drawn cart with a driver we did not know and the two local militiamen, Mititescu and Ciorescu, sitting on top like two important visitors.

Fusu ran after the cart and made such a fracas, barking and jumping up and down circling the cart, that we were afraid a kick from one of the horses would land on his little body and kill him. Mititescu shouted that he would shoot the dog, if we didn't take it away, his dirty black teeth bared in a menacing smile. Mircea managed to get hold of the little creature, but he was too eager to show us his skills at nipping the wheels of the cart or the hooves of the horses. Suddenly, he escaped from Mircea's grip. He jumped at the horse's tail, barking with all his might, but the bullet from Mititescu's gun made him fall backward; he whimpered, then fell and lay still. I bent down to caress Fusu. Blood was trickling from under one eye onto his white cheek. Mircea looked at me, with such grief in his heart, that I thought he was going to die too. Big tears dripped from his eyes onto the dog's fur, and he wiped them with the back of his hand. Fusu was very dear to us both. We'd played with him in Dumbrava, training him to herd the piglets and keep them together in one place. Every time he did that, we rewarded him with pieces of lard or sausages and he ate everything, looking up at us for more. He even ate the sweet *pancove* and tomatoes.

We couldn't believe he was dead. Only minutes before, he had been having such fun with the lizards and the cart and the horses. I hated adults, when they killed animals out of anger, revenge, fun or for no good reason other than they did not want them, as they did with kittens, when there were too many in a litter – they put them in a sack and drowned them in the waterholes.

Alerted by the gunshot, women came over shrieking, their hands flying to their horrified faces, and calling the men to stand up to Mititescu. The men didn't move a finger, just stood there like gutless statues in grotesque poses.

The cart was in front of Iosive's house, two doors up from ours. My father, working in his workshop, heard the gunshot but was unaware of what was happening on the road. Mititescu took him by surprise and led him to the cart as he was, half undressed, in only his worn, greying trousers. Seeing Mircea and me crying over Fusu's dead body, my father furiously asked Mititescu why he was so cruel. Mititescu responded by shoving the gun barrel into his ribs and ordering him to climb into the cart.

We heard Iosive's wife crying and Iosive's desperate pleading, before we saw Ciorescu dragging him out of the house. The men and the women, who had seen Mititescu shoot Fusu, stood on their porches, watching in dismay.

"They are taking me away! Villagers, help! What did I do? Let me go!" Iosive screamed.

Ciorescu wasn't impressed by his screams and ordered him to get into the cart. Iosive didn't budge and both militiamen pushed him up, while he continued screaming.

"Shut up, fool, or I'll shoot you on the spot!" Mititescu yelled.

The old man kept quiet but, when they rolled him into the cart, he got up and struggled to get off. He untied his pants and dropped them to his knees, taking the militiamen by surprise. The women covered their faces and some men wolf-whistled at the view offered by the old man.

Mircea and I caressed the lifeless body of Fusu and nobody cared about our grief.

Mititescu took the gun from his shoulder, aimed at Iosive's large white hemp trousers and pulled the trigger. The bullet made a hole in the trousers. Iosive started shaking. The women ran into their courtyards and the men were stunned.

"Your turn next," warned Mititescu, redirecting the gun towards Iosive's face.

"Yes, sir, yes. I'll shut up... I am finished, I know it..."

"*Mucles*!" shouted Mititescu, scorning the old man with the gypsy shut up.

Iosive sank down, his face in his hands, crying pitifully, as though his heart were breaking. He didn't say another word. Only when my father patted him on the back did he mumble between sobs. "What did we do to deserve this? What did we do, Pavelea?"

My father was slack jawed and speechless. He watched me and Mircea, with Fusu in his arms, following the cart until Ciorescu pointed his gun at us. I was a bit confused at seeing my father quiet, unlike the time the Securitate took him away in the middle of the night. Mama did not say anything either. Was this a good thing? I did not think it was, when a man was taken from his house by militiamen with guns in their hands, making him scream the way Iosive screamed. On one hand, old Iosive made you laugh with those screams of his, because he behaved like a child being punished by his parents. On the other, he made you almost cry, because he was an old man being treated like a little child, with no respect. What distressed me most was that our neighbours, grown-up men and women, were standing there on their porches, with their mouths hanging open and their eyes wide, not doing anything. They just watched the militiamen take my father away, as they did when the wretched Mititescu shot Fusu. That silly look on their faces made me really angry. When one of our gang of children from the Hill was mocked by the Valley boys, we all threw stones at them, all of us with no exceptions. It was hard to understand why these grown-ups, particularly the men, who often came and drank my father's *pălinca*, did not help him. The cranes I watched in the evening skies of Dumbrava all stuck together, flying in a V formation. When the crane in front was tired, another one took her place. Micula had told me that if a crane were sick, all the cranes would stop and wait for her to get well and, only then, would they continue their flight. Why couldn't our neighbours behave like the cranes? Why should cranes be better than men? If I were my father, I would give my *pălinca* to the cranes, not to these hopeless men.

The cart was now on its way down the Colnic. Mircea and I took Fusu to his garden and placed him under a big plum tree. Then Mircea went into the house and grabbed a tablecloth to cover the little dog's body, already cold and stiff. He said we were going to dig a hole under the plum tree and bury him there.

Mama called me and told me to see where the cart was going. I didn't feel like leaving Mircea alone but Mama said my father was more important than Fusu. That made me panic, thinking that my father could be shot, just like the little dog.

I quickly went to Hurupa, where we had played with Fusu, chasing the lizards and climbing into the old orchards. The tall grass scratched my ankles. I ran through the church's land, crossed the cemetery and reached the Council's garden. I hid behind the communal bull stables, knowing that the cart had to come that way. I heard the cart wheels grinding over the stones on the mud road and then saw it entering the Council's premises. Iosive and my father – still without a shirt – were taken in. After a few minutes, another militiaman, unknown to me, pushed Zoltan into the courtyard with the barrel of his gun. Zoltan looked sad and bewildered, his head hung low and uncovered, as if he were going to a funeral.

I stayed in my hiding-place until I saw the men being locked up in the Council annexe, where the rags collected from the villagers were kept. I ran home and told Mama. She thanked God that my father was not taken to town. I didn't understand the difference and Mama told me that in town, he would be in prison and that was not a good place at all.

I ran to Mircea's house. He was not home. His mother had chased him away, scolding him for having taken her tablecloth to cover Fusu. I went to Hurupa and found him there cursing his mother and calling her a bitch for hitting him with the rolling pin because of her stupid tablecloth. I persuaded him to come back with me and bury Fusu.

He followed me into the garden and we started digging a little hole; but his mother came out with her rolling pin and this time, Mircea raised the shovel and invited her to come closer, with a rather manic expression on his innocent, unlined face. She stopped, continuing to curse him and threatening to tell his father about the tablecloth and his raising the shovel at her. We buried Fusu and sat there for a long time, until Mama called me again. Mircea came to our house, intending to spend the night with us, because he knew he was going to be beaten by his parents. Late in the evening, his father came and dragged him home by his hair, crying.

And I cried for him, for Fusu and for my father, thanking God that Mama never cursed me and never beat me with the rolling pin.

Class Struggle, New Men or Dead Men

Comrade Petroi told the students to form two rows in the courtyard. We were taken to the Council, where a Securitate captain was waiting for us. Mititescu and Ciorescu escorted five men into the muddy backyard. Horrified and equally embarrassed, I saw my father among them. I recognised them all: Iosive, Zoltan, Ionelu and Licu. Apart from my father, they were all old men, unshaven, tired, disheartened. Comrade Petroi made us stand in a line in front of the men's row, a sly smile on her grotesque face, as if relishing their humiliation. My father looked straight into my eyes, while I avoided his gaze. I was embarrassed, because the other students were casting furtive glances at me. Just in front of us stood Comrade Petroi and the Captain; the two militiamen flanked the *chiaburs*.

Comrade Petroi couldn't resist explaining the meaning of the word *chiabur*, how the Party would exterminate all its enemies, how the dictatorship of the proletariat would triumph all over the world and bury imperialism in its own ashes, how we would be the new men of tomorrow, in a society where there would be no exploitation of man, and what a luminous future awaited us thanks to the care and wisdom of the Party. The Soviet Union, led by the wisest man on earth, Comrade Stalin, who was watching over us, would make sure our generation benefited from the great successes of Socialism and Communism.

The bewildered men, in front of us, hung their heads low.

Comrade Petroi's ramblings, in front of the kids, humiliated them more than any blows and kicks they might have had to endure from the militiamen.

"Lazăr Iosif, one step forward!" the Captain ordered.

Old Iosive stepped forward, his graying eyebrows drawn together in confusion.

"Your father has lived in America," the Captain stated. He stood with his feet apart and his square chin jutting forward.

"Yes, sir."

"Where?"

"In Detroit."

"In your house, we found shares in an American company. Would you like to explain?"

"My father brought them, when he returned home," Iosive said.

"Why didn't you hand them to the Militia organs? It is against our policy to keep imperialist documents at home!" The Captain's voice sounded like thunder.

"I didn't even know I had them. When my father died, they just stayed there," he explained.

I pricked my ears, when I heard the word 'American', thinking that the Captain would understand that Iosive had good friends. The Americans were good and the Russians were bad. That's what I always heard the peasants around me saying. Surely the Captain would see that the old man was a good man, because he liked the Americans; and the Americans liked his father, if they gave him presents to bring home. However, the word 'imperialist' didn't sound too good the way the Captain said it, although I did not know what it meant.

The Captain approached him, as if wanting to hit him, but stopped and screamed at him, like a man possessed.

"You scum! You are all the same! You can't face reality! You always lie!" He spat at him and grabbed Iosive's trembling skeleton by the chest. "Listen to me, you bastard. You are our enemy, our children's enemy. You don't deserve to live!"

He released him, spitting out one final question. "What do you have to say for yourself?"

The confused and helpless old man didn't seem to know what to say and wrung his hands, searching for the right answer. He repeated the only thing he always told them, the only thing any of the *chiaburs* could say: "I didn't do anything wrong."

I knew he didn't do anything wrong. He had tried to tell the militiamen the same thing, when they picked him and my father up; but they wouldn't listen. Why didn't people, like the militiamen and the Captain, listen to people like Iosive and my father? They didn't do anything wrong. I knew that, because nobody in the village talked about them and, if the villagers didn't talk about you, it meant that you didn't do anything wrong. Somebody could have told this Captain and the militiamen how things worked in Lupoaia.

"How dare you? Viper!" the Captain shouted, spraying spittle all over the cowering old man, before kicking him in the groin. "Get him out of my sight!" he ordered.

I felt sorry for Iosive as I watched him bending over with pain and then being dragged away by Ciorescu. Nobody should treat an old man like that. Well, some did. Vancea beat up his father and gave him only crusts to eat, even though the old man did not have teeth, and all this because Manca had given most of his land to his daughter, who later refused to look after him. However, it was funny hearing the Captain calling Iosive viper, because the viper I killed with Mircea, near the Valea Ştefani a few weeks before, was tiny and did not scare us at all. How could a big man like Iosive be a viper? I just did not understand this Captain and the silly names he gave to people.

Pacing in front of the men, the Captain called my father. "Flonta Pavel!"

"Yes, Comrade Captain," my father said, squaring his shoulders and raising his head high.

"I am not your comrade, Mr. Flonta!" he shouted, stressing both the words comrade and Mr. His eyes glared at my father and he stopped for a moment, as if waiting for his words to sink into our minds.

I knew that all the other children were looking at me and, as I tried to avoid their gaze, I wondered for a moment why my father called the Captain 'comrade.' He hated that word, just as he hated being called a *chiabur* or an enemy of the people.

"You are an enemy of the people! You are exploiting persons from the village," he said.

"They are working for a wage, Captain sir," my father said.

"That is called exploitation in our society, Mister," he said, half turning towards us. "When a man owns land or a business or a factory and has other persons working for him to make him richer and richer, that is exploitation. Got that?" he asked, raising his voice. As my father's answer didn't come, he got louder. "Answer, swine! Answer!"

"If you say so, Captain sir," my father said, shrugging a little, as if dismissing the shorter, but much louder, man in the shabby uniform in front of him.

"Anyone who does that, has no place in our society. The exploitation of man by his fellow men is to be eliminated forever. This is a priority for our Party. To achieve this, exploiters have to be re-educated or... eliminated. You have two choices, when we finish with you: to be a new man or a dead man, Flonta Pavel," he warned.

I started to panic, my eyes opening wider and wider with every word. First the Captain called my father a swine and now he was telling him that he was a dead man. Was this man going to kill my father, as the villagers killed the pigs at Christmas? I had never heard such a thing before; but that thought terrified me and stayed with me for a long time. These people in uniform were really nasty. They just call you a pig and then kill you, I thought. What would happen to me? What would happen to Mama?

"I bought the *cazan* with my father's help, sir. The State did not help me. I am not harming anybody... on the contrary, I am employing two people who never before, in their entire lives, received a wage," my father dared.

Tell him, dad, tell him. If he doesn't listen, become a *zmeu* and hang him by his tongue on the Council's gate, so everybody can see what happens to a Captain, who calls people silly names and humiliates them in front of children, who will laugh at me for weeks to come.

"You want to argue with me? Scum! We'll show you the way. Wait and see," he threatened. "Take the disgusting swine out of my sight!" he told the militiaman.

Oh, no! Not swine again. Is this man really going to kill my father? What about the other men? He did not call Iosive a swine.

Zoltan, Licu and Ionelu went through the same routine, with the difference that Zoltan was made to kneel and pray to see if God, whom he had mentioned, would help him out of his troubles.

The Captain approached Comrade Petroi, his face glowing with pride.

"We thank you, Comrade Captain," she said, her head inclined towards him and her voice taking on a breathless schoolgirl quality. "I am sure the students will never forget this lesson."

"It was good of you to wish to familiarize them with what we have to contend with, day by day. After all, they are the Communists of tomorrow. They will have to advance our ideas and make them work for the benefit of our society. We have a difficult task, as long as the class struggle goes on. We are only at the beginning. But they," he said pointing at us, "will have less to do in that respect, because we initiated this revolutionary process and we might even be able to do away with the old class and its prejudices, in our own lifetime."

"Thank you again, Comrade Captain. The children want to express their appreciation. Don't you?" she said looking at us. She made a sign to Mitrea, a small boy in third grade, who stepped forward and recited: "Comrade Captain, we, the students of first and third grade from the Lupoaia Elementary School, solemnly promise to become good Communists and to fight against the old class of exploiters."

"Wonderful, comrade, wonderful," the Captain said. "You'll make very fine Communists, I can see that." He shook the proud boy's hand.

Pacing in front of the classroom, Comrade Petroi wanted to see what we had learned. "What is a *chiabur*?" she asked.

A few children put their hands up.

"Marişca," she said and smiled, adjusting her grey blouse on her shoulder.

"A *chiabur* is an enemy of the people."

"Good, very good. What does a *chiabur* do?" She pointed at Anton in the middle rows.

"A *chiabur* exploits working people and enriches himself."

"Excellent answer, Anton." Comrade Petroi put a hand on his shoulder and looked complacently at him.

"What is the attitude of the Party towards the *chiaburs*?" she asked, moving away towards Gusti at the bottom of the classroom.

"The *chiaburs* class will be eliminated. We will build a class-free society and will fight against any influence of imperialism," Gusti said, reciting as if from a script that he barely understood.

"Who can give me an example of *chiaburs* in our village?" she asked everybody.

All the students except me raised their hands. My gaze sank to the floor.

"Teodor, don't you want to participate in the discussion?" she asked. Her voice was tight and laced with sarcasm.

I didn't say anything. I wanted to smash her ugly glasses.

"Try!" she insisted, staring at me.

"I don't know," I said, with my head bent down.

"Your father is one," Ion said from behind Comrade Petroi's back and laughed.

"My father is not! He is my father!" I replied. My face and neck felt hot.

"Yes, he is a *chiabur* too!" Anton mocked me.

I couldn't restrain myself. I got up and tried to hit Anton.

Comrade Petroi intervened. "Stop that! Immediately! Teodor, come here!" she ordered me. As I did not obey, she shouted, "Come here, I say!"

I did not move. Then she came running to my desk, grabbed me by the ear and dragged me in front of the class. When she released my ear, I ran out of the room, heedless of her shouting my name.

I hid in the bushes of Hurupa. When I didn't come home after school, Mama went to Mircea's house. He told her I had run out of school, because Comrade Petroi called my father a *chiabur*. She came down to Hurupa calling my name, but I did not answer. I could hear her desperate cry. "Teodor, my boy! Where are you?"

She sat crying on the roadside. I could see her shoulders slumped forward, like those of a much older woman.

"Teodor, come home my boy. Come out of there. I know you've had a bad day. We have to get some food to your father. Would you do it? Come darling, come. We already have so many troubles, don't make me feel worse. You understand me, don't you?"

I didn't show myself, but I said, "Do you promise to let me go with food to Dad?"

"I promise but you have to be careful. Nobody must see you." She dried her eyes with the backs of her hands.

"Nobody will see me, Mama," I said, finally coming out of the bushes.

I remember her hug, so strong I almost couldn't breathe.

"My boy, my boy," she cried aloud. "What would I do without you?"

I took her hand and went home. Clouds drifted overhead, leaving us in shadow.

In the evening, we approached the Council courtyard from the cemetery side. It was nearly dark and we stopped behind the fence, to spy on movements or sounds coming from that direction. Mama nodded and gave me the cloth bag containing food for my father. On tiptoe, bent low, I crept towards the annexe, where the men had been detained for two days. They were not allowed food or drink; but they were lucky because, in the centre of the room, was a mountain of rags, collected from the village, on which they could sleep, protected against the cold.

As I got closer to the annexe, I waited, listening for any suspicious noises. When I did not hear anything move, I ran to the annexe, stretched up and peered through its small, barred window. The men were silent.

"Dad! It's me!" I whispered.

"Teodor!" my father said, and came to the window grating.

I managed to squeeze the bag with food through the bars. "Take this. Have you eaten anything?"

"No, they don't give us food. Where is Mama?"

"Hiding behind the fence," I said and took fright as I heard the sound of a door opening.

"Run!" my father said.

And I ran as fast as I could.

A militiaman was coming out of the Council's building.

"Who is there?" he shouted. "Stop or I'll shoot!"

He fired a shot in the dark.

By now I was already beyond the fence, running with Mama for our lives.

The School Play

My father was now arrested every second week and imprisoned in the Council annexe, for three or four days at a time. He got used to it and always told us not to worry. We had to get used to it too. Every second week, Mama prepared the little bag with basic food items for me to sneak in through the bars of the Council annexe's door. Sometimes I did not succeed on my first attempt; but I was always lucky on my second. I missed my father and worried about him.

At school, Comrade Petroi decided we had to put on a play for the parents.

I hated being in that play, but I couldn't do anything about it. I complained to Mama and she convinced me that it was better to do what Comrade Petroi wanted, otherwise we could all suffer. I didn't see why that should happen but I didn't insist. Mama was so distressed by my father's arrests that she looked twice her age and always seemed to be hunched over, as if the weight of the world were on her shoulders. I didn't want to give her any more to worry about, so I dragged my feet but went along with the stupid play.

On the Sunday of the play, Mama came with Grandma Saveta to see me. The hall of the People's House was filled with women and children and the occasional drunk man. They were all wearing their Sunday best. I hated my part, which wasn't much of a talking part anyway. I walked on stage with a fur cap on my head, a moustache, leather boots on my feet, a heavy jacket and a pipe in my mouth, while a boy and a girl, in shabby clothes, performed as peasants, bending down and working hard on what was supposed to be my land. When I tried to light my pipe with proper matches, the match died. I tried again and I failed. I gave up lighting my pipe and pretended the vapours coming out of my mouth were smoke. That made me feel bad but the people laughed. All of a sudden, a group of boys and girls came on stage to the rhythm of the Internationale, carrying a red flag with hammer and sickle on it and singing at the top of their voices. When they stopped singing, they freed the two peasants working for me, handcuffed me and took me away. I was the centre of attention in the last scene, where I was crawling from a boy, dressed as a militiaman, to another in the uniform of a Securitate Captain. The latter was shouting insults at me that echoed those hurled at the *chiaburs* in the Council courtyard.

"Listen to me, you bastard!" he was yelling with his strident boyish voice. "You are our enemy, our children's enemy! You don't deserve to live! You are exploiting your fellow villagers. They work for you, don't they? That is called exploitation of your fellow man in our society. When an individual employs other people to make him richer and richer, that is exploitation. Got that?" said the boy and suddenly he seemed lost for words.

Comrade Petroi did her best to prompt him, while I was waiting on all fours for him to finish, so that I could make the turn to the militiaman.

"Answer, swine! Answer!" he yelled, watching Comrade Petroi's lips. "Anyone who does that has no place in our society. The exploitation of man by his fellow men is to be eliminated. To achieve that, the exploiters have to be eliminated. This is a priority for our Party," he said.

The young people in the audience were laughing, more for the boy's difficulty in remembering his lines than for the content of the play, while their mothers were elbowing them to shut up. I saw Mama's grave face with tears running down on her cheeks. I wanted to run to her and tell her that it was alright with me. I could finish Comrade's Petroi silly little play. I would have given anything in the world to see her smile; but I knew that was not possible. How could she smile when I was treated, in the play, the way my father was treated, in the Council's courtyard? Why had Comrade Petroi wanted me to play the part of the *chiabur*? Why me and not somebody else? Was it because my father was considered to be one? Did that make me different from the other children too?

Hailstones, the Bible, Coloured Eggs and Cane Strokes

Micula used to come to our house in the evenings. He kept my father informed about the bits of phone conversations or verbal exchanges, between the Party and Council authorities, that he had overheard during the day. My father would then make up his mind to stay at home and possibly be arrested, or hide in relatives' houses somewhere in the neighbouring villages, and face the consequences on his return.

One day, when my father was hiding in Duşeşti, Mama was out in the fields, close to the forest, harvesting the wheat. I looked after our cows and oxen on the green pastures of Dumbrava, which seemed to stretch in multiple superimposed vistas, as far as the eye could see. Big, black clouds gathered over the forest, but it was noon and hot, so Mama and Grandma Saveta went on harvesting. I noticed the sky becoming darker. The black clouds moved faster overhead and suddenly the day became night, the warm air turned chilly and big hailstones started hurting my head. I was only wearing an ankle-length white hemp shirt and I couldn't breathe properly. The cows had disappeared into the forest, looking for shelter, but I was on top of the hill overlooking Valea Gavri, buffeted by the strong wind, covering my head with my hands and gasping for air. I crouched down crying. Then I heard a voice close to me calling my name. My sixteen-year-old cousin, Floarea, had seen me alone and come to rescue me. She sat over me and covered me with her skirts, like a mother hen protecting her little chicks. I passed out.

I woke up in Florica's house on the edge of the fields. When I opened my eyes, I saw Mama.

"Where am I?" I asked, looking around the room. My mouth felt dry.

"You are in Auntie Florica's house, Teodor. You slept for two days, do you know that?" Mama smiled. "You fainted out there."

"Where is Dad?" I asked.

Auntie Florica and Mama looked at each other.

"He is not home, Teodor, you know that... he would be here if he could," Mama said, fighting off tears.

"I want to go home."

Father Iordan came to see me. He was my father's age, although a little shorter, and they shared many a joke together. I liked Father Iordan, because he was kind and he came to bless our land and house, at the end of winter every year. Before his arrival, my father would light three big straw fires, one in the courtyard and two in the garden, and would spread the ashes around the house, stable and garden. My father would jump over the fires when the flames were at their highest, and then move some burning straw to the side for me to jump too. He said that the smoke in our clothes purified us and made us resistant to sickness and sin. Mama never jumped over the fire and scolded my father for making me do it, wagging her finger in his face, when he ignored her and encouraged me just the same. When Father Iordan came, he made me shake his golden censer all around our house, wafting clouds of incense, while he sprinkled the house walls and the plants nearby with the basil bunch, dipped in holy water. We were doing this to chase the serpents and the insects away, he said. They gave too much trouble to people and crops in summer. When he finished the blessing inside the house, Mama made him sit at the table in front of a plate full of *pancove* and buns of different shapes. Of course, my father made him drink four glasses of *pălinca*. Father

Iordan said that he only drank the four glasses with my father and that every glass of *pălinca* counted for ten of wine, because that's what priests drank in church.

"How is our sick boy?" he asked Mama. She got up from the bench next to the bed, each line on her face looking deeper in the low light of the house, and not even her shawl could hide just how bony she had become, as a result of constant stress and worry.

"He is much better, Father... tell Father, Teodor... he slept for hours..." Mama said. "Please, take a seat, Father," she indicated the bench. Father Iordan sat down there and touched my arm.

"I feel better, Father," I confirmed.

"Good boy... good boy," he passed his fingers through my hair. "Your father would be proud of you," He turned to Mama. "Any news of Pavelea?"

"No, Father. I pray to God to keep him well."

"You have to keep your faith in God, Nuţa. These are hard times, hard times indeed."

"I don't know what to do anymore. I don't have time to come to church every Sunday, now that Pavelea is away. I have to look after the house and the cattle..." She sat next to Father and touched the doona covering my feet.

"I know, my dear, I know. I just heard about Teodor and I came to see how you are coping."

"Not very well, not very well at all. It seems like a punishment from God, Father."

"These are the times of the Antichrist. Nobody can trust anybody. A man is driven away from his own home for no reason at all. I heard that some people are writing anonymous letters to the Securitate... brother against brother... it is terrible!" said the priest in a resigned tone.

Mama crossed herself.

"May God help us, Father," she said.

"He will, He will, eventually. But we have to help ourselves first, Nuţa. I thought of having all the children in church, every Thursday night until Easter, for catechism lessons; and at Easter, we will have them take Holy Communion."

"I would like that, Father. When will you start?"

"The sooner the better. Next week, perhaps."

"That's wonderful, Father. You are not afraid of them?"

"I am old enough now and, besides, we have God on our side. These are hard times and we need courage to get through them. Let it be His will."

I had not gone to church since I started school. Comrade Picu Petroi, the Principal, forbade us to go and warned that we would be punished, if we did. He said that religion did not have a place in the new society. The Party replaced God, who was not real.

"Have you ever seen God?" he asked us.

God was an invention of the rich, to oppress the poor and make them even poorer. God was a distraction for the masses and took away the focus from the important task of building the new society. Marx and Comrade Lenin, two faces on the wall behind the teacher's desk, taught us that religion was the opium of the people. We were all atheists, he proclaimed, without a shadow of doubt.

When I asked Mama what atheists were, she said that it was something to do with the church but she did not know exactly. As for opium, she had not heard that word before. It must be something bad, she said, because anything people like Comrade Petroi say, is bad. I agreed and slowly built the two words into my defence system. I started ignoring the two Comrades, when they talked like that. I pretended to understand, so they let me be.

Mama borrowed an old Bible from Pițurca, the only one in the whole village, and started reading to me in the evening. On Thursday night, we would creep into the church, terrified that we would be seen and reported to Comrade Petroi. The church was dimly lit. We would sit on the cold and hard floor in front of the altar, jumping at any slight flicker of the shadows. Father Iordan said that we were like the early Christians, who had to practice their religion in secret. At the end, we would leave only after checking that nobody was on the road. This went on until Easter Thursday, when we were allowed to hammer on the *toaca* until sunset, to announce the death of Christ. The *toaca* was a 20cm wide board on a 2m pole in the church courtyard. After sunset, neither hammering on the *toaca* nor the ringing of bells was allowed until Sunday, the day of the Resurrection.

On Easter Sunday women placed little baskets full of coloured hard-boiled eggs and cross-shaped loaves of white bread in front of the altar for the blessing. The children, dressed in white shirts, took the first Communion in front of the congregation. However, the spectacle we were waiting for was to come later in the church courtyard during the frenzied egg-cracking competition. We wrapped one hand across our egg, exposing only the pointy end, and hit each other's eggs hard. If your egg cracked, you lost your egg.

"Mircea, I bet I can take away your eggs," I challenged him outside the church.

He gave me a push and responded, "Try this, smarty."

I tried and lost.

"You want to try another one?" he asked.

I suspected he was so confident because there was something fishy about his egg. So I accepted the challenge, pulling out from my pocket my special egg. I hit hard and a funny, thick sound, not at all like the sound of an egg cracking, was the result.

"What did you do, stupid? You have a wooden egg," said Mircea.

I ran away laughing.

"And yours is filled with pitch. I could hear it," I said.

My father had come out of hiding on Easter Friday and had worked late at night to make the egg for me. Mama had dyed it in onion peels and it looked like a real boiled egg. Mircea, in his eagerness to steal my eggs, couldn't spot the difference.

Our good time was suddenly interrupted by the appearance of Comrade Picu Petroi passing by the church on his bike. Seeing us, he stopped and approached the fence with a fixed smile on his twisted face that did not quite make it to his eyes. Some of the children hid behind others' backs, but he caught sight of me and beckoned me to come over to the fence.

"What are you doing here?" he asked, a crooked smile on his

face.

"I came to church," I answered, feeling somehow guilty, unable to quite meet his eye and kicking my feet against the mud.

"You came to church, ha? And the other students?"

"They came too."

"This is how you obey the rules? We'll see about that tomorrow, at school," he said and rode away on his bike without looking back.

The next day Comrade Picu Petroi came to our class and the first thing he did was to reach for the cane behind the blackboard. He called me out in front of the class.

"Tell me who else has been to church with you?" he asked.

"Mama," I said.

The children started to laugh.

"I mean the students, idiot!" he shouted, leaning as close as possible to my face, with a look of sheer madness in his eyes.

"You saw them, Comrade Principal," I said.

"I want you to tell me," he said.

I did not answer.

"Why don't you answer?" he yelled and hit me on the head with the cane. "You are no better than your father, are you?" He bent down and poked his nose right into my face. His breath smelled sour. "I want to hear their names from your mouth! You hear me?"

I started sobbing. "I hear you," I said.

"The names!"

I didn't see myself having much choice. Nonetheless, after a while I said, "Ask them, they can tell you." I shouldn't have said anything, because he flew off the handle and hit me repeatedly. His sentences followed the rhythm of his strokes.

"No wonder your father is an enemy of the people. You are as stubborn and uncooperative as he is. There is no place in our society for people like you, unless you change. The alliance between the workers' class and the peasants' class will make sure of that! You will change, my word, you'll become like everybody else in our society, a new man! I assure you of that!"

I did my best to protect my head with my hands, but the blows on my body hurt worse than the hailstones. Some of the boys were hiding their faces, laughing at my struggle to defend myself. Comrade Picu Petroi did not get the names from me. He then summoned all the students to the front of the class and administered two blows of the cane on each hand. I could have laughed at the way they were trying to withdraw their hand before the blow landed, and at how they rubbed their hands between their legs after each blow. I did not laugh but I enjoyed seeing this mountain of a man, foaming at the mouth and showing all the veins in his red neck.

When he finished with our punishment, Comrade Picu Petroi started rambling again about our non-existent God, atheists and religious opium, not that anyone in the village knew what opium was. He said that priests were enemies of the people, just like the *chiaburs*, because they did exactly the same thing to people. That made me prick up my ears. He said that the *chiaburs* exploited poor people's work, while priests exploited poor people's minds, bullying them into giving money at Mass, baptisms, weddings, even funerals. People who exploited others were parasites of society and had to be eliminated. He said he was going to teach the priest a lesson. I thought he would go to Father Iordan's house with some books and try to teach him something, just as he taught us.

I told my father about that. My father's look made me understand that Comrade Picu Petroi was up to mischief but I still felt I had to ask him what lesson he could teach the priest.

"I think he is going to denounce him to the Securitate. He is not a good man," my father said.

I knew he was not a good man. You couldn't say that a man was good when he was always there with his stupid cane to cut your hands and head for nothing. His wife with her thick glasses was no better than him.

My father said he feared Father Iordan might be arrested when I told him Comrade Picu Petroi called him an enemy of the people. He scratched his head, went outside and disappeared into the garden.

I went to bed, thinking about Father Iordan and Comrade Picu Petroi. After a while I heard our entrance gate squeak, then I heard whispering voices in the courtyard and I recognized Modru and Ghiona, Mircea's father. I stretched up from the bed and looked through the window but it was already dark. The men had their backs turned and had lowered their voices. I couldn't work out who the others were. My father had brought out a bottle and passed it around. The butts of the men's cigarettes were like fireflies in the night.

The day after, when I went to school, Mircea and I saw Chioara brushing away glass from under Comrade Picu Petroi's windows. She was complaining aloud about our not having found anything better to do on Sunday than going to church. If we had stayed home, this would not have happened. Comrade Picu Petroi knew who broke his windows and why. He was going to denounce those people and the priest to the Militia.

It turned out that Comrade Picu Petroi did not know who broke his windows and never talked about priests, as enemies of the people, again.

Sovrom and Uranium

Micula, our neighbour, was often on the road, tin drum around his neck, to inform the villagers on matters like impending storms or hail, deadlines for paying quotas, the arrival of a new bull, availability of seeds for better crops and general assemblies about Party activists' new instructions on anything. The latter was the kind of news he would announce more often. In his over-patched military jacket, which was caught in at the waist, he would stop in the middle of the road, bang the two sticks on his tin drum for a couple of minutes and then yell the message at the top of his voice. One morning, when my father was detained in the Council annexe, he was about to go out to make an announcement to the villagers, when he overheard Mititescu's telephone call. Mititescu was saying, "Yes, comrade Colonel... tomorrow morning, before dawn. They'll be ready."

Micula understood that they were talking about the detained men and hurried up the Hill.

"It is brought to everybody's attention that a general assembly will be held at the People's House today at 2pm. One person from each household is required to attend," he yelled, cupping his chapped hands around his mouth. Then he beat the drum again to signal the end of the message.

Vioara, his wife, saw him on the road in front of our house. She draped herself in a black shawl and hurried towards him, with a sandwich wrapped in a towel. When she placed the sandwich in the little leather bag around his neck, he beat the drum softly to cover his words. At the same time he kept an eye out for possible onlookers. Then Vioara walked slowly and deliberately down the road, facing straight ahead so as not to attract attention, but her eyes darted everywhere to see if anyone was watching. She came to our fence and continued walking, until she found a small opening. She looked around again, before running into our garden calling Mama.

"Come here," Vioara waved her hand.

"What's happening?" Mama said, her voice sounding uneasy.

"It's about Pavelea."

"Oh, my God!" Mama gasped and placed her hand to her heart. "What did they do to him?"

"They are coming to take him tomorrow morning. This time it is the canal... you have to get him out tonight... listen for Micula's fife... he'll play... you go then!" she whispered. Then she hurried again out of our courtyard the same way she came in.

That night, when we heard Micula's fife breaking into the dark, Mama and I hurried through the fields to the Council building. As we passed the back of houses, the dogs barked furiously and, by the time the people came out to see what was happening, we were already well ahead, holding onto each other to avoid tripping over weeds, furrows and tree trunks. In the distance, we could hear owl-calls and drunk people singing obscene songs, outside the general store. We had to stop suddenly and lie low in the high grass because we heard a man spitting phlegm, talking to another who was urinating near him, only a few paces away from us.

I carried a small bag containing a pair of pliers, some iron wire and a hammer, to help Father open the annexe door. When we reached the back of the Council, we stopped and Mama gave me her instructions.

"You can go now," she said, holding my hand. "There is no light in the Militia room. Be careful, darling... run if you hear any noise. Alright?"

I nodded. "Don't worry, Mama... don't worry." I left her there and I got down on my hands and knees to inch towards the annexe.

Because the tools were clattering in my bag, I stopped from time to time, to make sure I wasn't seen or heard. The militiaman on guard must have already been asleep in the main building. The annexe was a mud brick, square room with a flat roof, just opposite the stairs leading into the main Council building. It was often used to store sacks of cereals or furniture, confiscated from peasants who did not pay their quotas, and was half full of rags, freshly collected from the villagers, waiting to be sent to the Oradea textile factory to be recycled. Moon beams poured into the room through the barred window. I could see the men. Two of them, Zoltan and Ionelu, were lying supine on a pile of rags facing the door. Iosive was snoring next to Licu, who was all curled up. When I called out, they didn't wake up. My father had his back against the door. He lay on the side, his head in his hands. He was surprised to see me there at that hour and made sure it was me.

"Yes, it's me," I said, keeping my voice low. "You have to get out of here tonight... they plan to take you to the canal tomorrow."

"Who told you?"

"Micula's wife," I said. "I've brought you some tools... make a picklock... don't make any noise... I will remove the outside bar..."

I asked him if he understood and he said he did, a curiously blank look on his face.

"Tell Mama to bring me some money and clothes... I'll be waiting for her in Râturi by the creek," he said.

My father picked the lock under the older men's gaze. They were now awake, sitting on top of the rag heap. When he finished, he urged them to follow. None of the men moved. My father stared at them for a moment as if paralysed, then serious doubts about what to do overcame him. "Let's go. What are you waiting for?"

"Go on, Pavelea. Don't bother about us... we are too old for this…" Zoltan said.

"We've lived our lives... what will be will be," Iosive said.

"Be very careful... they'll look for you everywhere. Go, Pavelea, don't waste your time with us... go as far as you can," Licu said. "We'll pray for you... if we don't meet again, we'll know you are safe," he added.

"We'll meet again, you'll see," my father said.

"Pray not to, my boy, pray not to," said Licu.

Ionelu did not say a word. He only nodded when the others talked.

My father stared at them for a moment again, then his eager face dropped as he knew they were right. He bent down and crawled out into the courtyard, while Licu closed the door behind him. He crept across the road. Keeping close to Pilu's fence, he walked towards the river. He followed the river bed to Râturi, where he waited in a bush, close to the path leading to the Holod railway station.

At home Mama fetched clothes and put bread, lard and onions into a bag.

"Can I come with you, Mama?" I asked.

"You go to bed, darling, it's late... you have school tomorrow..."

"Please, Mama, please," I begged.

She looked at me, drew me closer to her and kissed me on the forehead.

"Let's go then," she said, taking my hand.

We closed the door but left the petrol lamp burning, the light turned down to the minimum. The sky was full of stars and the full moon was shining, which didn't please Mama, because it forced us to go through the cornfields. The corn husks cut our hands and faces and we were afraid that our rustling would attract some wandering villager's attention. We left the cornfields, crossed the beaten track and reached a hay field on the river bank. Mama, still keeping us off the track, coughed loudly and called my name as if I were somewhere else. She explained to me that it wasn't prudent to call my father's, in case somebody should hear. A shadow came out of a bush on the river bank and scared me. I pointed it out to Mama. It was Dad. He embraced us for long moments.

"I'll try to catch the train to Ştei," he explained to Mama. "Don't let anybody know where I am. Alright, my boy?" He caressed my head. I nodded.

"Look after yourselves. I'll come back when I can," he said in a tone of voice I had never heard before, like that of a man who did not believe what he was saying. In the moonlight his wide forehead was wrinkled like old Micula's. When he turned his back on us, Mama lifted her apron to her face and I saw her bite it hard, to quell her sorrow and resist the urge to yell. As it was the first time I saw my father go into hiding, somehow, I felt that the separation was going to be definitive. Only for a moment though. I changed my mind, telling myself that he would come back, as he had always done before. I was swinging between extremes and now Mama sobbed so hard her shoulders shook. Seeing her cry this way brought tears into my own eyes. I didn't want my father to go anywhere either. I couldn't understand why a man, who loved his family and his home, had to run into the night like that, chased by other men whom he had never bothered in his life. When the darkness had enveloped my father, I felt Mama's hand, still wet with tears, reaching for mine. I squeezed it, to reassure her that everything would be alright. But it wouldn't, and we both knew that. Mama's sobs became louder for a while, then she stopped. I stopped too and, in silence, we went up towards the Colnic. At home I could see inconsolable sorrow in her eyes in the petrol lamp light and, for a brief moment, the urge to cry again almost overcame me. I hid my face in the pillow, turning my thoughts to my father, to the night that had swallowed him as if he'd never existed, to the men pursuing him, to Mama, to our family and the questions I would be asked by the militiaman and the children at school.

Sorrowfully, my father walked to Holod station, thinking of what was going to happen to the older men left in the Council annexe, at the mercy of the heartless militiamen and Securitate officers. He waited in a bush, close to the railway station, until he heard the train in Rogoz and then, as the train passed, he emerged from the bush and ran behind it. The train stopped only for a minute and, running up to it from the side opposite the station, he grabbed hold of the doorhandle of the last carriage. From there he managed to climb onto the top of the carriage to avoid the ticket controller.

For the *chiaburs* in the Council annexe dawn erupted. It was a miracle that Mititescu, in his fits of rage, did not kill any of the men. As soon as he realised my father was gone, he started driving his bayonet repeatedly into the pile of rags, like a madman, then hit the men with the butt of his rifle, uncontrollably. With blood on their faces, he forced them out into the muddy courtyard and made them run to exhaustion. The *duba* came at noon and took them to Oradea. A search dog was brought in from Beiuş to look for my father. The dog followed his footsteps up to Râturi, where he had met Mama and me but, when the dog was taken over the creek, he lost track of my father. Mititescu made fruitless enquiries at the train station. Then he had only Mama left to torment.

In the meantime, my father walked from Ştei to Băiţa, where he slept in an abandoned mine gallery for a few days. As the lard and onions Mama had given him were soon gone, he cautiously entered the village early one morning. As soon as the shopkeeper opened the store, he went in and bought a full salami, a kilo of feta cheese and two loaves and disappeared quickly, walking in the opposite direction to the gallery, as the local militiaman was making his way towards the shop.

There was a mine in Băiţa run by a *sovrom*, a Soviet-Romanian joint enterprise. It was called *Sovromquarţit* and was supposed to exploit quartz. Instead, it extracted uranium for the first Russian atomic bomb. Initially, the workers were political prisoners and most of them died of radiation poisoning; so peasants, who knew nothing about uranium mining, were brought in. This was the price the Party was paying to our great friends from the East, for having liberated us. In exchange for the promise of a new society and a luminous future, they took our wheat, meat and other goods, as war damages. All in the name of our great and indestructible friendship.

My father had heard rumours that the Russians were looking for carpenters to build houses for their soldiers and administrative personnel. One day he visited Dricu's wife in the nearby Forosig. Dricu was a *chiabur* and, fearing arrest, had disappeared from home a couple of weeks before. His wife had just returned from the Securitate Headquarters in Beiuș, where they had interrogated and abused her for days. They wanted to find out Dricu's hiding place, but she did not tell them anything. She told my father she did not know where he was but mentioned the mines of Băița. For my father, that remark confirmed the rumours about the Russians.

He didn't go straight to the mine, because he was terrified they would discover his identity; so he spent more than a week in a ravine on the outskirts of the city. He felt he had no choice. He either had to risk being caught and sent to the canal or going home and, then, being sent to the canal.

He spent days worried about going to the mine, not knowing how to introduce himself without giving himself away. He circled the mining site every day, watching, from afar, the men coming out of the shaft at dusk and later, sitting in front of the barracks smoking and talking. Life seemed normal, apart from the locked gates that kept the men inside. Observation turrets, placed around the camp and the presence of numerous armed guards made it look like a prison camp. He could hear orders given in Russian and see the lights in the barracks being switched off at the same hour, early in the night. After many days of observation, he decided to go inside. A few hundred metres from the barracks, there was a tunnel, from which a series of small carriages brought out the uranium ore, which was then deposited on either side of the railway. When he showed himself near the tunnel, he was picked up by a soldier and taken to the personnel office. He said that he was a carpenter and was instantly given a job, much to his relief. He felt an enormous weight being lifted off his stooped shoulders, for the first time in months. They didn't ask too many questions. A man took him to one of the barracks, still under construction, and delivered him to a foreman. He was ordered to go onto the roof and start work. When he did, he was startled to see Dricu. He refrained from showing recognition and Dricu made a sign to pretend not to know each other.

"Give me a hand with this beam," he said. "How come you are here?" Dricu whispered, when the foreman had walked away.

"I had to hide somewhere. They are after me."

"Have you seen my wife lately? Has she been mistreated by the Securitate?" Dricu asked, worry creasing his forehead, as he struggled to keep his voice low.

"She is fine. She's been roughed up a bit, but she didn't tell them where you are."

The Soviet administration of the mine was like a state within a state, totally autonomous. The Soviet managers answered only to themselves; the Securitate was not allowed to come and inspect the place. After a few days my father began to feel relatively safe. He knew that he had to be alert and often pinched himself for not feeling persecuted by the Securitate. He felt as if he were in a foreign country, because he could purchase many things which were not available to Romanians outside, in the exclusive shops set up for the Russian personnel. The food at the canteen was excellent – meat, white bread, biscuits and jam, in abundance. They slept in barracks but there were stoves with a good supply of coke, which we often ran out of at school. The linen was made of cotton and changed weekly, which was better than at home. Soap was available on request and they even had toilet paper, which was in short supply elsewhere in the country. The latrines were outside, but cleaned daily; and even they were better than those at home, for most of the workers. In every barrack, they also had a Russian-built radio. The only bad thing, for my father and his co-workers, was that they didn't have their families with them and that was torture because they knew the Securitate was persecuting wives, parents and children.

The only things that mattered to the Russians were business and productivity. The uranium ore was loaded into huge train convoys and transported to Estonia, where the uranium concentrate was produced and, then, delivered exclusively to the Soviet Union. The Russians seemed to be in a hurry. They paid bonuses to the most productive miners and gave unsolicited promotions to the other workers. Within a few months my father had had two promotions and felt luck had come his way at last. He fondly remembered how eagerly Grandpa Teodorea had encouraged him to learn carpentry. Would the Russians have employed him if he did not have those skills? The thought, that perhaps this trade saved his life, crossed his mind. What better gift could a father give his son? Here, he was paid regularly every month, had hot food and a roof over his head every day and, what's more, was not tormented by the Securitate people. He kept his money in a handkerchief, tied to a cord around his neck, day and night. He could do a lot with that money – buy better food for his family, buy a new dress for his Nuța and something special for his boy. Teodor had asked him once for a ball, a big rubber ball, instead of the one he had made for him out of oxen hair. That was the first thing he was going to buy, he thought. The separation was a pain in his heart – the worst ever, much more so than the previous occasions when he hid from the Securitate. Who knew when he'd be able to walk out of this precinct, like a free man and not like a hunted one? He couldn't make sense of all this madness; but he knew he had to do everything to get out alive, for his son and for his Nuța. But he had to be careful. This was not a place for slackers: they worked on a daily quota and those who didn't fulfil it, were given the boot the same day. He had a lot at stake. He had to work harder to stay afloat, no matter what the cost.

Grandma's *Bocet*, Pioneers

The night after my father's escape I lay in bed thinking about his whereabouts. In the darkness Micula's *doina* was drowned out by the sound of the engine of the *duba*. The closer that vehicle drew to us, the farther away Micula's melody seemed to be. The *duba* stopped in front of our house with its lights off. Mama looked out of the window and I could hear Micula's melody again. Four huge and ominous shadows emerged from the *duba*. Two of them quietly entered our muddy courtyard, while the other two remained in the street. Mama was terrified but wouldn't escape without me. The men knocked on the door, making it sound as if they were about to break it down. Mama winced at the sound and then opened it. Mititescu and a young Securitate officer wanted to know where my father was. She wouldn't tell them. The young man lost his patience and slapped her, but she still wouldn't tell. He grabbed her by the throat, strangling her.

"You'd better talk, bitch, you'd better!" he was yelling.

I started crying and that annoyed them.

"Shut up, son of a bitch!" he shouted.

They searched the house – under the beds, in the attic, in the garden, everywhere.

It wasn't going to stop there. Mititescu grabbed my right arm and dragged me out of bed.

"Where is your Dad?" he asked me.

"I don't know," I said, swallowing hard as my limbs began

to shake in fear.

"You don't know, ha? You don't know," he measured me.

"I don't."

He yelled and made me start.

"Son of a bitch! You don't know!" He took me by the ear and pulled hard upwards. I stood on my tiptoes to lessen the pain.

"You still don't know, do you?"

I couldn't move my head and I only cried. Then he let my ear go.

"I don't know, Comrade Mititescu, I don't," I pleaded with him.

He grabbed my hand and dragged me towards the door, opened it, pushed my fingers in the door hinges and held them there in spite of my attempts to resist him.

Mama shouted at the top of her voice. "They are killing us! He-e-e-lp!"

The Securitate man gave her a mighty slap, that made her fall onto the bed and turned her cheek a crimson red.

"Where is your Dad?! Speak up, son of a bitch! Speak up!"

"I don't know, I told you." My eyes stung with tears. My heart felt like a rabbit kicking inside my chest.

He started to close the door on my fingers. The pain was terrible and sharp and I tried to free my hand.

"How about your Mama. Does she know?"

"No, she doesn't." I tried to speak quickly, so that he would stop, but he closed the door further on my fingers. I screamed so loud, it was more of a howling, tears rolling down my face. He let me go.

As Mititescu left, he said to Mama, "Let him know that we'll be waiting for him until tomorrow. If he doesn't report by then, he is a walking corpse. Is that clear?"

In the morning Vioara, Micula's wife, came.

"You shouldn't be home tonight. Micula heard them talking. They have orders to catch Pavelea dead or alive. They'll take it out on you."

"What shall I do, Vioara?" Mama asked.

"Hide somewhere and ask your mother to look after Teodor."

So Mama's wandering started that night too.

"You be a good boy and obey Grandma," she said to me. "If the militiamen ask you questions, you say you don't know. Okay?" She caressed my face, trying to reassure me and gave me a kiss.

"Where will you be?" Grandma Saveta asked. "To let you know when they've gone."

"I won't be far, Mama," she said, wiping her tears.

"It's a curse. My God, what a curse," Grandma said.

The singing of drunken men woke up the village. Old Druga, who had been to America for some years in his youth, and Petuc were surprised to see the *duba* passing by with no lights on. Druga asked, "What is this apparition in the night? Is it a miracle?"

"It's a car. Look," answered Petuc.

"It can't be... this is no place for cars... I haven't ever seen a car without lights in the middle of the night. Not even in America are there cars without lights at night," Druga said, lurching after the *duba*.

"It's a car, I tell you..." Petuc explained, and dragged him back.

The old man fell to the ground.

"Shit. Let me go," he complained.

Soon they started singing again and lost the car from sight. When they came by our house, there it was, a black lump blocking the way. They saw lights on in our house.

"Ssst. This is something. It's a *duba*!" Druga said.

"Pavelea is having guests. Listen," said Petuc.

They listened to the thundering voice coming from the house.

"Old bitch!" the voice was shouting. "Where is he? Where is he? Better talk!"

Grandma's crying was not real crying. She was trying to block their words, to not listen to them at all, and was intoning a *bocet* from the time of the oppression, a chant for the dying. She was very good at this chant, usually making up most of the words as she went. But this time she chanted as her mother and her grandmother had chanted before her, the heart-rending tale of the disappearance of a nation.

Maică mare, Maică mare (Great mother, great mother)
Ce-ai adus pe lume moare (Everything you gave birth to dies)
Pleacă toți să se înșire (Everybody is lining up)
Pe sub cruci de cimitire (Under cemetery crosses)
Maică mare, Maică bună (Great mother, good mother)

"Let's do something," Druga proposed. The chant made them think and plan. "Let's go in and ask for some *pălinca*... Ha? To see what's going on... come on... you have the courage? Ha?" He gave Petuc a pat on the back. "What do you say? Ha?"

"You go and see. I'll watch the car," Petuc said.

"Alright, chicken," Druga teased him.

"Don't let them take it away. It's State property, my boy," Druga laughed. "State property... my foot..." he laughed again, "State property... listen to that."

Minutes later Druga was thrown out of the courtyard into a pool of muddy water.

"This is against the law," he shouted. "I wasn't treated like this in America and I was there for twenty-five years. You take it out on our women and children. These are good people..."

A gunshot broke his words causing the neighbours to come out in the dark.

Petuc left his hiding place in Hurupa and ran towards the house.

"They shot at you, old man. Where are you? Answer me."

"I am here... in the mud... the bastards work at night... when normal people have done their work... Shit, I am all wet... I need a drink..."

"Let's go before they come out... let's go man... it's no use... get up," said Petuc, helping him. "Like this... okay."

They stopped on Micula's porch until they saw the Securitate men leave our house, then the old man started his singing again and Petuc joined him, staggering and leaning on each other all the way home.

As I arrived at school in the morning, I saw the Principal, Comrade Picu Petroi, with a visitor in the courtyard. I ran into the corridor, pretending not to see them. Soon after that we were all standing in a square formation in the courtyard with three flags flying – the national flag, the Party flag and the Pioneer Organisation flag – and singing the anthem. After the man's speech, the ceremony for the awarding of the title of pioneer took place, for the first time in our school. Almost all the students got the red scarf and the badge. I didn't get them and I was upset.

"Comrade Representative," I said raising my hand and genuinely confused, "why don't I get a red scarf and badge?"

Everybody started to laugh, but it wasn't a laughing matter for me.

"Probably because you have to improve your marks and become a model student like the others," he replied. "Then you will surely be worthy of becoming a pioneer."

"We'll talk about it later, Flonta," Comrade Petroi dismissed me.

But I wasn't going to give in.

"I have the best marks in my class," I insisted.

"Flonta!" shouted the Principal, Comrade Picu Petroi. His face turned red and his eyes narrowed.

The Representative looked at my teacher, Comrade Petroi. She whispered something to him and he nodded.

"Go and play," she ordered, piercing me with her stare.

I was disappointed. I knew why they didn't give me the red scarf; but then they shouldn't say that they gave it for merit. The other kids also knew why I hadn't received it and started teasing me. Mircea annoyed me more than any other boy, because he was an arsehole and passed the year, only because he copied my homework.

"You don't have the red scarf! You don't have the badge! Look at them, they are beautiful!" he taunted me, waving the scarf an inch from my nose.

I pushed him as hard as I could, and he fell to the ground.

"Idiot!" I shouted.

He sulked and ran straight to Comrade Petroi.

"Comrade Teacher, Flonta pushed me!"

I was called by Comrade Petroi. The other children gathered around, to enjoy my punishment. We always enjoyed the spectacle of someone being in trouble.

"Why did you do that?" she asked me.

I did not answer and kept my head down.

"He is jealous because he was not made a pioneer," Mircea said, sticking out his tongue.

"You must know, Flonta, that sons of *chiaburs* cannot be pioneers," she said rubbing salt into my open wound.

"My father is not that!" I rebelled and turned, walking away.

"Come here!" she shouted. Her voice sounded like an out-of-tune trumpet.

I wouldn't have gone back, but the boys from the higher grades took hold of me and kept me still, like a prisoner.

Comrade Petroi walked towards me and I thought she was going to crush me.

"How dare you talk to me like that! You are just like your father, aren't you?" she shouted. "We'll talk about this, just you wait." She jabbed her finger at my eyes.

Later, after the visitor's departure, Comrade Petroi summoned me to the front of the class. She took a cane from behind the blackboard and saw it was short. "Here is the knife, go and get a long and strong one. Be quick!" she told me.

The class was giggling.

I went outside to choose the instrument of my punishment. I hated the Comrade so much. I chose a thin lilac branch, hoping it would do less damage to my hands. I cleaned it well, all the while panicking before returning to the classroom. I thought of running away but then I gathered my courage and said to myself that I wasn't going to give Comrade Petroi that satisfaction. I was in the right, after all. She had lied many times about this pioneer business. All good students would get the red scarf, she said, and in the end, all the arseholes of the school got it and I didn't. I took my time, though, to spite her. When I entered the classroom, the idiots started giggling again; some of them covered their faces, others mimicked me getting the caning.

Comrade Petroi was transformed into an infuriated beast when I handed her the cane.

"You cretin, I told you to bring a strong cane! Didn't I?" she roared. And she broke the cane on my head. "How dare you disobey my orders." The cane strokes hurt and, although I covered my head with my hands, some of them fell on my ears and on my face. "Go back and bring a good one, as I told you! March!"

The situation was getting serious. Now I was crying. I kept on crying until I came back with a thicker cane.

"Hand!"

I obeyed, but she missed as I had jerked my hand back.

"If you do that again, I'll expel you from school!" she yelled. Perspiration filled the creases of her neck.

I gritted my teeth, closed my eyes and was dealt two mighty strokes on my right hand and one on my left. They left their marks for a few days, in spite of my rubbing them together between my knees and Mama's cool compresses.

I could hardly wait to get out of the classroom and out of that dreadful woman's sight.

The Danube-Black Sea Canal

The Securitate searched everywhere for my father. The *duba* was like a thief who hated the light. It was often stationed in front of our house at night, to the point where it became a habit for the villagers to ignore its presence. Mama hid when she had a warning from Micula, or simply just put up with the Securitate men's insults and violence as best she could. Grandma Saveta stayed with us most of the time now, especially with me, and tried to console Mama, who broke down under the pressure and harassment. They sent Grandma and me out of the house and remained there with Mama on her own. We often found her crying in a corner, her bony knees drawn up to her chest – and refusing to talk.

Every time this happened, I went and sat on her lap. She did not cuddle me as usual, squeeze my cheek to see the pink coming out or pass her hand through my hair; she just sat there, without looking at me and without looking at Grandma. If I had been able to, I would have killed those cruel bastards with one shot in the head, just as Mititescu killed Fusu. I thought that was the only way to keep them away from Mama.

One night the *duba* took Trincu away. He had been mayor of Lupoaia under the fascists. On 19 July 1952, he was sent to a forced labor unit at the Danube-Black Sea Canal, without a trial or the possibility of contesting the decision.

Unconstitutional.

Illegal.

Immoral.

Inhuman.

He was told to take a suitcase with clothes. Norca, his wife, a softly spoken woman, asked a militiaman where they were taking him. They refused to tell her. Instead, one of the militiamen sequestered her bed cover. Norca pleaded with him, begging him not to take it, because it was made by her mother; but that made no difference. Six months later the family found out that Trincu was at the canal, when they were informed that the prisoners could receive parcels from home.

After two days in a cattle carriage with other men, Trincu had arrived at the canal and been put in a work-gang of eighty people. His gang had a leader, Voiculescu, a gendarme from the previous regime, with a reputation for cruelty. Trincu was given a bed, in one of the barracks with cardboard walls and no doors. They cropped his hair, but did not give him a prisoner uniform. He had to wear his own clothes.

Trincu's gang's task was to build a railway and maintain the existing one. He worked twelve hours a day at the beginning, but when winter came, there were three shifts of eight hours each. The food was mainly boiled cabbage or boiled onions. He lost several pounds and his strength was not up to the task. This attracted the foreman's attention and Trincu was beaten up, as punishment for being weak. His bread ration was cut.

And still he was lucky. Luckier than most.

One day, a gang working on the opposite side of the canal was ordered to dig under a 7m high wall. The foreman hurried them and they did not realise the danger. All of a sudden the upper wall came down, crushing all of them. No survivors. It seemed that the order had come from above.

Exterminate.

Eliminate.

Liquidate.

Bury alive.

The soldiers, standing guard over the prisoners, had the order to shoot if a prisoner misbehaved. As a reward, the soldier received fifteen days leave and a sum of money.

Life was hard. One old man said he couldn't go on. He started walking towards the wire fence that separated the camp from the outside world. The sentry shouted at him to stop. The old man continued walking. The soldier shot him dead and received his reward.

Winter came, the first for Trincu at the canal. He was still in summer clothes. His hands froze, transporting frosty iron rails. He told the brigadier and showed the brigadier his hands; but the foreman made him work on regardless. In the barrack at night, Trincu's fingers throbbed and oozed pus. The next day he showed the foreman; the foreman made him work more. Trincu's pain grew unbearable. He uncovered his left hand from under the rags he had wrapped around it, and his middle finger dropped off. He showed the foreman, just before he fainted. At the infirmary, the doctor said he was lucky that he had lost only three and a half fingers. The only finger saved was the little finger. The half finger was his thumb.

He made friends with a Brătianu, from the famous family that has produced several prime ministers. The mining enterprise was on land confiscated from the Brătianu family. This Brătianu had to shine the shoes of the Securitate officers – they wanted to humiliate him.

One day Trincu heard the sirens wailing and the bells tolling. Someone whispered that Stalin had died. Never more joy for the death of a man. Hope; more food; less torture.

Autumn came and Trincu was summoned to the Camp Commandant. He was terrified. Lots of thoughts, all associated with fear, passed through his head. What had he done? Somebody must have dobbed on him. He approached the barrack and told the soldier on guard he was summoned. The soldier let him pass. Racked with worry, he pushed the door with his good hand and found himself in a little room no bigger than a turret, where another soldier stood guard. He had to wait standing. Then the door opened and the Commandant himself appeared.

"Come in," he said and returned to his seat.

Trincu entered, his cap in his hand, thinking of how best to behave. The office was bare except for two portraits on the wall – one of Stalin and the other of Gheorghiu-Dej. On the desk a pistol and a whip sat next to each other; and in the darker corner of the room, stood a small table with a chair. It was dark inside and that made Trincu shiver.

"Take a seat, Comrade."

Had he heard right? Normally prisoners would stand at attention, but what puzzled him, was the use of the word 'comrade'. How come? Was it a mistake? He sat on the wooden chair opposite the Commandant.

"How is your hand coming on, Comrade?"

"Much better, Commandant Sir." Trincu rubbed the purplish stumps on his hand.

"That's good, very good."

Then suddenly the Commandant changed the subject.

"Do you know Burca Nistor, Comrade?"

"Burca Nistor from Lupoaia?" Trincu asked.

"Yes, Burca Nistor from Lupoaia."

"Yes, I know him very well. It's a small village, Commandant Sir."

"Do you know what his function in the village is?"

"Oh, yes. He is the secretary of the local Workers' Party branch."

The Commandant cleared his throat. "What is that, in your opinion?"

"Well, Commandant sir, he is the local authority. He knows what happens to everybody in the village."

"Good. In two days shake his hand, Comrade."

Trincu understood the Commandant's words. He heard them loud and clear, but for a brief moment he sat there, stunned, as if his brain had frozen.

The Commandant woke him from his trance.

"You heard me right, Comrade. You are free. Go and organize your trip home."

"Thank you, thank you, Comrade Commandant. Thank you so much."

Words of thanks came easily to him now.

Burca Nistor or Nistorea, the Party Secretary in Lupoaia, was one of those people who always fell on their feet, in spite of themselves. He was a soldier in Bucharest with my father. On one of the first days in the army, Nistorea stole money from another recruit. A full body search revealed he had hidden the money between his buttocks. He received twenty-five lashes and fainted. My father looked after him. When Nistorea came to, the only thing in his mind was how to escape. He borrowed money from my father, money he would never give back, and disappeared. He walked 700km home and remained in hiding for two years, until the end of the war, lucky that, in the meantime, the Romanian army had changed sides.

Gherea, who looked after the communal bulls, talked to Nistorea about Trincu. He asked Nistorea if he, the most important authority in Lupoaia, couldn't do something to bring him home. It was not flattering for Lupoaia that one of its citizens, who had done only good for the villagers, was in a place like the canal. After all, when Trincu was mayor in the late 1930s, he had brought food for everybody, helped build the church and, most importantly, he had helped Nistorea and his sister, when their mother abandoned them to follow her lover, Şurub.

Nistorea was a bit erratic but, this time, he listened. He immediately wrote a letter to the regional Workers' Party secretary. And now Trincu was shaking his hand.

When Nistorea was small, his father worked in Bucharest as a labourer for a few years, while his mother became infatuated with Şurub, who lived near the forest, alongside the gypsies and was renowned for initiating many a young gypsy girl into womanhood. Rumour had it that he made Brânduşa, the young gypsy widow, bathe with him in the Valea Droani creek and then made her bend forward and place her head into the fork formed by two oak branches, which became known as Surub's tree. He whipped her buttocks with a bundle of nettles, making her dance like a mare in heat; and then he charged from a few feet behind her, like a stallion eager to satisfy his lust.

The rumours gave him temporary fame; but he eventually became notorious as the winner of an unusual competition – he carried a bucket full of water on his aroused member. It was then that Milica, Nistorea's mother, fell in love with him and abandoned her children and husband. When Sivea, her husband, returned home for good, he took her back. By then Şurub was dying of syphilis.

This was the story Nistorea grew up with. He was the butt of jokes all his life, on his mother's account. That drove him to do things that other people did not do. Stealing, drinking, fighting and womanizing. People soon said that he was not the son of his father, but the result of an early affair of his mother with Şurub. Trincu looked after him and his sister, as if they were his own children. He gave them food and clothes and had men drop firewood at their place during winter.

Domnica's Poo and the Christmas Tree

A foul smell came from under the desks at school.

"Somebody shat himself," Mircea said in a loud voice that made us laugh.

Everybody was preparing their bags to go home. Mircea pointed at a round cone of shit under Domnica's desk. Splitting his sides laughing, he next pointed at the girl. "Look, Domnica did it under the desk!"

The girl was sitting down and turned around with an intense blush on her face. "Shut up. I didn't do it. I didn't."

Comrade Petroi, who had not intervened so far, came down between the rows of desks, took a look at the cone and, curling her thin, cruel lips and covering her nose, asked who did it. Mircea again blamed Domnica, who again denied it.

"I'll give you time to reach your homes. The mother of the person who did it must come and clean it up," Comrade Petroi decreed.

Nobody turned up. Chioara complained to Comrade Petroi, folding her arms across her chest and refusing to clean it up herself. Then Comrade Petroi had an idea. She told Chioara to call Mama to do it.

"Perhaps if you could write a note," suggested Chioara, not at all taken with the idea of telling Mama.

So, that afternoon, when our dog was barking its head off at Chioara, Mama walked to the front door to see what she wanted.

"I brought this from Comrade Petroi," she said and gave Mama the note. I had already told Mama about the incident.

"Teodor did not do it. One of the girls did," Mama said.

"I don't know, Nuţa, I am only the messenger."

"You should clean it, it's your job," Mama said.

Chioara straightened her shoulders and spoke in a high pitched voice. "I am not paid to clean your children's shit. You'd better come, otherwise Comrade Petroi might not like it."

Mama knew that.

"Just this time, tell her," Mama said. The muscles in her jaw clenched.

"Good. It's better not to go against your child's teacher," Chioara said, softening her tone.

At school, she did not want to lend Mama her broom and dustpan, until Mama threatened to leave the shit there. When Mama finished cleaning the mess and swept the classroom floor, Chioara insisted Mama wash the floor.

Mama looked at her with narrow eyes, squaring her shoulders and drawing herself up to her full height, in her indignation. "You can go to hell and tell your Comrade Petroi to do likewise."

It snowed heavily that winter. We didn't have wood for the fire, since Dad had fled for his safety; and Mama had to rely on the planks and posts pulled from the fence for the cooking. As Christmas neared, we felt increasingly desolate. The women neighbours came and stayed with us at night, spinning the threads out of that year's hemp or working on old embroideries. I couldn't hope for Christmas presents but I was pleased that Santa was coming around on his white horse.

On Christmas Eve it snowed, the flakes settling on the white branches of the trees that were already bent under the weight of ice, covering our small but cosy home with a pure and even blanket. I stared out the window for a while and thought about past Christmases. I wondered where my father was and if he would have any Christmas at all. I went to sleep, with the covers pulled up against my chin and tried hard to find a good dream.

That night, a man made his way along the side of the road from Holod to Lupoaia, his feet sinking deep into the snow. He carried a wooden box under his arm and a sack on his back. A small pine tree protruded from his sack. From time to time he stopped and put the box and sack onto the snow, blowing warm breath onto his hands, then rubbed them together to avoid freezing. At the same time he strained to listen, trying to detect any noise from any direction and ready to hide, at the shortest notice.

When he reached the intersection leading to the Hill, he left the main road and took the path, hoping that the bridge over Hodişel was still there or at least that the level of the water wasn't too high for him to cross. It would shorten his trip by half an hour.

The bridge wasn't there, but he managed to throw his burden over the river and jump to the other side without getting wet.

It must have been well past midnight when Mama heard soft knocks on the door, too soft to be the Securitate men. That's what she thought at first, but then she panicked at the thought of the Securitate and began to shake with fear. They were capable of anything. The windows were frosty and she couldn't see outside.

Then my father called her name.

I was sleeping soundly and did not hear anything.

She was so excited that she couldn't open the door immediately. Dad had to calm her down from outside, the mutual relief thawing the air around them and adding a little colour to their cheeks. Then they got down to work. Dad placed the Christmas tree on a wooden stand from his sack, and Mama prepared some basic decorations. She collected walnuts and apples from the attic and inserted a matchstick in the back of each walnut, before wrapping them in old silver paper. She chose apples with their stalk still on and tied them to the tree. Dad had also brought biscuits from the Russian canteen, and they found their way onto the Christmas tree as well. After the candles were lit, Mama came to wake me.

"Father Christmas came on his white horse. Come and see what he brought you!"

Still groggy, I didn't react until she took me in her arms and the light of the candles shone directly into my eyes. I half opened them bewildered and then opened them wide. It was the first time I had seen a Christmas tree in my house.

"Where did it come from?" I asked.

"Father Christmas. I told you he was going to come," she said.

"Why didn't you wake me up?" I had wanted to see him for myself.

"He comes only when kids are asleep."

"Let me go!" I kicked my feet against her and, as soon as I touched the ground, ran towards the table on which the tree was standing. I circled the tree, gazing at it from all sides. I couldn't stop staring at it. Suddenly, through the flickering of the candles, I saw a shadow by the bedside in the corner of the room. I was frightened and pulled away. Images of Securitate agents and Father Christmas chased each other in my mind. When the shadow moved out of the dark corner, I froze.

"It's me, my son," said my father. "I met Father Christmas outside the house. He couldn't get in because we don't have a chimney, so he gave me the Christmas tree to bring it to you. Come here!" He opened his arms and lifted me up. "Father Christmas said you were a good boy. That's why he brought you the tree." He smiled and rubbed his beard against my face.

"How does he know that?" I asked.

"He knows everything. Look what else he gave me for you," he said, pointing to the wooden box under the tree. "Do you want me to open it?"

"I'll open it!" I said, and freed myself from his arms. I took a knife from the table.

"Careful with the knife," my father warned.

I slid the knife between the boards of the box, but it wouldn't open.

"You are going to hurt yourself, Teodor. Let Dad do it," Mama said.

I continued to play with the knife.

"Please," she insisted gently, touching me on the shoulder. I handed her the knife and she passed it to my father.

"Watch!" said my father, "it's easy."

He inserted the knife under the lid, lifted it up and the top of the box was gone. Then he pulled away the paper cover. A beautiful slab of shiny red jam stared at us. It looked like a magnificent jewel. I couldn't resist poking it with my finger, my eyes shining with glee and my belly rumbling with hunger. My father cut slices with the knife and gave us both a piece.

"Tell me if it's good," he said.

It was so good that I filled my mouth and I couldn't answer. It tasted sweet and tart... like somewhere far away.

It was nearly dawn when I went to bed. I woke up late in the morning and I saw the tree without lights. I was disappointed. Nobody was in the room.

"Mama! Dad! Where are you?" I called.

I called again, since no response came the first time.

"I am coming," Mama replied. Her voice was broken, her face raw and her eyes almost swollen shut with crying.

"Where is Dad?" I asked.

"He had to go away again," she sobbed, and stroked my hair. "I don't know what will happen to us."

"When will he come back?" I insisted, feeling that same familiar despair.

"Only God knows, only God knows. Don't tell anyone Daddy has been home. Alright?" she begged me, wringing her hands and sniffing loudly.

I wanted to cry, but at the same time I wanted to show her that I wasn't the little boy she thought I was, so I played the grown up, "I know that, Mama."

Stalin Is Dead

That winter seemed endless and Comrade Petroi grew uglier, as the sneer she permanently wore on her face twisted her features still further. Although I had the best marks in my class, she picked on me more than on others. It got worse after the news spread that my father was in hiding. I complained to Mama. She said not to take any notice and not to talk back to her and she would let me be. I took Mama's suggestion and it seemed to work. Sometimes.

The spring brought floods, as the snow started to melt at the end of February and the water from the Hodişel filled part of the Valley, including the school courtyard. Men came out of flooded houses, with water up to their waist. For us children this was a festive occasion, as we did not have to go to school. We got in our mothers' bread tubs, which floated like little boats, and rowed with big wooden spoons as improvised oars. Then the sun came out again, the water receded to the river bed, leaving behind enough mud to swallow our boots; and we had to go back to school.

When Mircea and I arrived at school one morning in March, we found all the children lined up in pairs in front of the main door. Comrade Petroi stood on the steps; with a graver and uglier face than usual. It wasn't yet eight o'clock, so we waited until everybody came. Then Comrade Petroi, whose tears ran from under those thick glasses, started talking to us in a peculiar way.

"Children, this is a day of mourning. A great tragedy has struck us. The father of us all, our beloved Comrade Stalin, has died. We will mourn his memory forever. You go home and ask your parents to fly the national flag at half-mast on the porch. It is your duty, as members of the pioneer corps, to see that your neighbours do the same. Tomorrow, you will come to school wearing a black band on your left arm."

Her shoulders bowed and shook. She seemed barely able to refrain from sobbing.

"Go now in silence and be disciplined, as our beloved Comrade Stalin would want you to be," she said. Her voice trailed off, like the voice of someone exhausted.

We left the courtyard in silence, holding hands as customary, until we were in the street. There hell broke loose. Comrade Stalin's death was a gift to us all. We broke our ranks and ran around with grins plastered on our faces, giving the happy news to passersby and women in the courtyards of their houses.

"Stalin is dead! Stalin is dead! No school today!" we yelled. "Stalin is dead! No school today..." was a chant to linger in my ears for years to come.

Mama looked surprised to see me home early.

"We don't have school today, Stalin is dead," I told her.

"What are you talking about?"

"Stalin is dead, Mama," I repeated.

She crossed herself first, to allow the thought to sink in, and then a slow smile spread across her face.

"Let's tell Grandma... this is good news... thanks be to God," she said and ran into the house. I followed her.

Grandma looked at Mama, as if she were mad. "I don't believe it... the devil never dies," she said.

"It's true, Mama. The teacher sent the children home. Tell her, darling, tell her," she prodded me.

"Comrade Petroi told us, Grandma," I said.

Then Grandma crossed herself and reflected, "Pavelea might come home soon then."

"This is really good news, good news," Mama said, embracing me.

I told Mama that Comrade Petroi had asked me to raise the flag.

"What?"

I repeated that Comrade Petroi wanted her to raise the flag and to tell the neighbours to do so, as well.

"That will be the day," she said, raising her eyebrows. "May he burn in hell."

Rodna Rodoet

Soon after Stalin's death, tragedy came closer to home.

Grandpa Toderea had been sick for a while. His belly was getting bigger and bigger and he was telling me to listen to the waves in his tummy, when turning in his bed. Every time I went to visit, I pressed my ear against his belly and he played the gloo-gloo music for me. His breath smelled like sour cabbages and the lines around his mouth seemed deeper than ever before. Sometimes he moaned in his sleep.

As my father was still in hiding, one Sunday morning Mama prepared the cart and the oxen, a grim expression etched on her face, and took me to Grandpa's house. There she filled the cart to the brim with straw. Grandma Saveta put a heavy sheet on top and they loaded Grandpa onto it. Grandma Saveta brought another sheet and a heavy doona and placed them on top of Grandpa. Two cushions raised him slightly, so that he could see over the edge of the cart.

Grandpa joked that he had never been so comfortable and wanted me to sit next to him. I did, but I didn't go under the doona. It felt so nice in spite of the bumps in the road. Grandma Saveta, the worry showing in the lines on her old face, dressed in black from head to toe, with freshly combed hair, sat on the driver's seat next to Mama. It was spring. The sun was rising, the plum trees were in flower and there was not a cloud in the sky. It seemed wrong to waste such a glorious day going to the doctor.

We went to the dispensary at Ginta, some 10km away. The oxen were slow and the iron-clad wheels of the cart made a loud grinding noise as it kicked up dust on the road.

"Why are we going to Ginta, Grandpa?" I asked.

"I know a nice doctor there, who will take away the gloo-gloo from my belly," he said.

I wondered how the doctor could do that but did not have the courage to ask.

"But don't worry, we will be able to play again in a few weeks," he assured me.

The doctor, a tall man with grey hair and a pot belly, offered Grandpa a chair. Grandma took Grandpa's shirt off and the doctor played the gloo-gloo sound. Grandpa was looking at me, laughing, and I was amused by the doctor's friendliness. I thought of becoming a doctor myself, when I grew up. Everything looked so clean and tidy in the room. There was a medicinal smell that reminded me of my tonsil operation in Oradea, but apart from that, I liked the place.

A large woman brought a wide enamel wash-basin from the room next door and placed it at Grandpa's feet. When I saw the doctor with a long needle, I got scared and wanted to leave the room. Grandpa asked me to stand near him instead.

"Don't worry, it's nothing. Just a flea bite," he said, grabbing my arm.

I shook my head, trying to banish the image of the needle, and shivered.

"When this is finished, we'll have so much water that it will quench the thirst of both our oxen, you'll see," he smiled. The doctor nodded. Still, I covered my face when the doctor pushed the big needle into Grandpa's belly but, curious as I was, I saw everything. The yellowish foul smelling water gushed out and poured straight into the basin. It went on and on until the gush became a trickle, the basin was full and Grandpa had no big belly anymore.

He did not last long after that. For a few days following the extraction of the yellow liquid from his tummy, Grandpa got up from his bed and moved slowly from the house to the stables, hunched over as if in constant pain. Once, he even ventured to the orchard, to see his two rows of beloved old walnut trees in full bloom. Soon after, he restricted his movements to the house and its two rooms, often going into the big room to sit on the bench under the window and look at the people passing on the road. A few weeks after that, he did not get out of bed at all and I was not allowed to ask him to play the gloo-gloo music for me. At his funeral I cried a lot, remembering how he used to pick me up from Dumbrava when I took the family cattle to pasture, and how he used to go with me into the forest, to gather wild strawberries and teach me how to thread them onto a straw and make necklaces for Mama and Grandma. During the mushroom season, he would take me to the yellow German mushroom patches in the forest; and we would come home and fry them with an egg on top.

He often came home from the pub drunk, stinking of alcohol and staggering, his cap askew and barely able to stand, and would pull out a lolly from his pocket. Only once did he disappoint me, when he was so drunk that it took two men to bring him home. They couldn't straighten him up at all and came the whole way from the Valley, with Grandpa bent in half. After Grandma put him to bed, I checked his pockets and there was no lolly for me.

After his burial, Grandma Saveta wanted me to sleep with her because she was afraid of being alone. Many people feared the dead in Lupoaia. Grandma got very distressed, saying that Grandpa visited her, but she did not know if it was in her dream or if it was for real. He was telling her to go and feed the cow and that she forgot to close the pigsty overnight. She was too afraid to go and check during the night; but in the morning, she saw that the pigsty door was indeed wide open. This happened for a few weeks. He often came during the night to make noises and give her orders. Eventually, Auntie Catiţa, Grandpa's sister, found out, from a woman in the Ceica market, how to make Grandpa stop coming back from the grave. Grandma had to offer a Mass at midnight and write Grandpa's name in reverse on the entrance gate at dawn, the same day. This way he would not recognize the house anymore and would wander around until he gave up trying to come back.

Grandma had difficulty with the Mass arrangements but Mama fixed the problem with a litre of *pălinca* for the priest. As Grandma was illiterate, she asked me to write Grandpa's name on the gate. I asked her if she wanted me to write Toderea or Teodor. She settled for the name on Grandpa's identity card.

RODNA RODOET.

That's how I wrote Grandpa's name in reverse, with white chalk at the top of the entrance gate. I wrote it twice more, in pencil, on both sides of the gate.

Although Grandma couldn't read the letters, she was pleased with the result.

The night after, Grandma said, Grandpa made a fleeting appearance. He asked her, "What did you do to me, Saveta, what did you do?" He never came back again.

No Prize for the *Chiabur*'s Son

At the beginning of the summer of 1953, following Stalin's death, my father returned home. Minutes after his arrival, Mititescu entered our courtyard and asked him to go for a walk in the garden. Mama paced the floor and chewed the end of her thumb. However, Mititescu only wanted to know where my father had spent the last few months. My father did not tell him the truth. He told him that he had been in Bucharest instead. When Mititescu asked him for proof, my father told him he had walked all the way and back. That was all Mititescu was able to obtain from him. He was living on borrowed time, though, until the next less friendly visit from Mititescu.

The end of my first year at school came at last. We were all excitedly awaiting the summer vacation, with its chores, but also with its fun and games. We wouldn't miss Comrade Petroi, with her thick glasses and ugly, menacing mug.

First, though, we had to have our end-of-year celebration in the People's House, where the Principal, Comrade Picu Petroi, handed out the first three prizes for each grade and the mentions, minor prizes for those who did well, but were not among the top three in the class. This came at the end of a program of songs about the Party and its conquests, the national anthem, and poems about workers who worked overtime and were leaders in productivity, and mothers who had many children but managed to work with a higher motivation than other mothers with fewer babies. Other poems sang the praises of pioneers who helped elderly workers cross the street or showed them where the dispensary was, or the brave militiamen who worked day and night for our protection from the bourgeoisie, enemies of the people and imperialists.

There were two good students in our class apart from me – Gusti and Aurora, both from the Valley. There was also Dorel, who was good at the beginning of the year, as his elder sisters had taught him how to make hooks, slashes, circles and ovals in the notebook; but by mid-year he did not make much progress and was out of contention for any prize.

The prize-giving ceremony began with grade one. I had noted the marks Mrs Petroi had written on the cover of her book all year. Most of the time I was given 5, which was the top mark. Gusti and Aurora were given 4. The fact that Comrade Petroi gave me 5 made me forgive her bullying, and I was sure I would get first prize.

We were on the podium in front of the parents. I looked at Mama and Grandma Saveta, and at Dad who had told me how happy he was to be home to see me getting first prize. They all beamed at me with pride.

"First prize goes to … Augustin Zigrea," the Comrade Principal announced.

How could that be? I had seen the marks with my very own eyes. There had to be a mistake. Comrade Principal was not my teacher and he must have read Gusti's name by mistake. Gusti was supposed to get the second prize. What could I do?

"Second prize goes to … Aurora Burca," Comrade Picu Petroi continued.

That was not possible. I had told my parents I was going to get the first prize. It seemed they were looking at me now as if I had lied. My father's face – was he smiling or what?

"Third prize goes to … Teodor..."

I stepped forward.

"… Galea."

Dorel came forward and everybody laughed at me. I had to step back with my head bowed, more ashamed of having made a fool of myself than of not getting the prize.

"Your turn has come, Teodor," Comrade Picu Petroi said, and his words made the class burst again with laughter. "You were a good student and you get a mention," he said with a sly smile on his face.

I stepped forward, but I really didn't want to. I would have rather run away from all this business of prizes, where the teacher can play with your marks and give your prize to whomever she wanted.

After the ceremony, my parents tried to comfort me, saying that prizes come and go and that it was good enough for them that I got a mention; but it wasn't good enough for me. My father went to Comrade Principal and asked him why I had not been given a prize. He was told to go to Comrade Teacher and ask her. She told him that I was as good as the other three; but choices had to be made as to whom each prize was given. My father asked her if the other three students had as many 5s as I had during the year. He was very pleased with my marks and this was going to disappoint me. I might end up not wanting to go to school again. She told him to wait and called the Principal. After she had explained what my father said, Comrade Principal was more forthcoming.

"Have you forgotten that you are a *chiabur*, Pavelea?" he asked.

Comrade Teacher nodded.

My father was dumbfounded. He looked at them for a while, his mouth hanging open in disbelief, and could barely stop his jaws from clattering.

"In the Bible it's written, that the sins of the fathers shouldn't fall on their children," he managed to say.

Nothing he said could have changed the situation. We walked away and he told me there was no justice whatsoever in this world of Communists and, as I'd seen, they twisted the truth by not respecting their own words: what they said and what they did were two different things. Comrade Petroi gave me all those 5s and yet didn't give me the prize.

"She can't be trusted," my father said, looking past me. He stopped in front of me, put his hands on my shoulders, stooped to my level and said, "Prizes are good but are not the most important thing in life."

I told him that I didn't like it, when the children who got the prizes, acted as if they deserved them. "Gusti got my prize, that's not fair," I said resentfully and freed myself from his hands. I walked towards the main road.

"I understand that. I know and I'm sorry I couldn't do anything to correct that," he said remorsefully as he caught up with me.

"It's not your fault," I said.

We walked side by side and, after a few moments, he said that what the Comrades had done to me should make me stronger, should make me study harder. That was going to be my best answer to petty people like that.

"What's the point of studying harder, if they give the prizes to other people anyway?"

"Don't feel humiliated for what they've done to you. They should be humiliated and ashamed of themselves, because they cheated you. You've done your duty. You've got excellent results. You should always get good results, to beat them. Sooner or later you'll beat them. They are just patches of snow in your way. They'll melt away, as if they never existed," he said.

So many words and my head was so full of anger, that I couldn't understand it all. As I did not answer and was kicking the pebbles in my way, he placed a hand on my shoulder and stopped me again. He put his other hand on my other shoulder, stooped to my level, shook me gently and said, "I want you to remember one thing, my son. A very important thing this ignorant father is going to tell you."

"What?" I asked reluctantly.

"Never give up on learning because what you put up there in your brain," he indicated my head with his index finger, "the Communists won't ever be able to take away from you."

Then he released my shoulders and we walked again, side by side.

"Nobody. Ever."

Mischief on the Pasture Fields

Boys of twelve or thirteen worked in the fields alongside their fathers and mothers, whole families in grubby clothes, sweat dripping down their dust streaked faces, bent over crops that provided supplies all year round. We, the younger cattle herders, were slowly becoming aware of the difference between us and the girls. We started spying on the older girls and talking about what boys did with girls, when they grew up, and how they did it –things we heard from older boys who often embraced girls, threw them to the ground, and fought with them.

Any time an older girl went for her business behind a bush, she had to be on guard as one or more of us followed her and watched her. When she had finished, we shouted to everybody what she did.

The big girls had a plan. One day they lined four of us up and told us to lie down on our backs. They wanted to play with us. The younger girls were giggling, but we were not going to be fazed by that.

Once we were on our backs, the girls undid our flies, pulled their skirts up and started bouncing up and down on us and making strange noises.

Just as I was beginning to enjoy the moist warmth of Florița's pussy, a gunshot exploded in the air. Shrieking and cursing, the girls ran for cover behind the blackberry bushes. The forester, watching from the edge of the forest, was laughing madly.

We boys were left watching both the girls and the forester,

not knowing which way to go. We took our sticks and each went towards his herd, pretending nothing had happened. Mircea and Dolea said that once the forester was gone, we should ask the girls to play with us again.

During break the next day at school, we teased the girls and, when they ran away, we hopped around shouting a phrase we had heard many times from older men:

> *Tot mă mir şi mă ţuţur* (I always wonder and ask myself)
> *Cum stă puţa lângă cur* (How pussy and arse sit near)

Our fun did not last long. Comrade Petroi heard our voices and came out of her kitchen. When she understood what it was all about, she summoned us to the classroom, together with other boys who had joined our choir, lined us up, and caned our backsides.

As well as the two cows, I was looking after our two oxen – Iambor and Mojar – for the day. Free from slaving under the yoke, they grazed on the pasture just north of Dumbrava. We boys were playing the dog's game with sticks of different woods. The cornelian tree was the most prized, as it was more flexible than others. We also used the hornbeam, beech, ash, oak and willow, the latter only as a last resort. You beat the thin end of the stick on the hard ground until it was at its springiest. Then you released it, making it spring away. The boy, whose stick landed closest to the starting line, was the dog and his stick was used as the target for the others. Every time a player missed the target, he was out, while the last remaining player was the winner.

This was the game we were playing the morning Mutu made his way past us towards Dumbrăviţa. As soon as Mircea saw him, he began shouting, 'Mu-tu! Mu-tu!'

Mutu was a mute middle-aged man from Ceica, tall, with a receding hair line. He was well dressed in a brown jacket and white shirt, just like men in the city. We knew that he was living with his old mother and had never married; but from time to time, he wandered through the forest, going for long walks. He didn't harm anybody. But what can you say about children in a pack? Like hungry wolves, they are cruel and insensitive.

Mircea began shouting at the top of his voice and most of the others joined in.

Mutu, Mutu, gură mare (Mutu, Mutu, big mouth)
Unde te duci la plimbare (Where do you go strolling about)
Să-ţi pun la spate clopoţei (I'll tie some bells on your back)
Să-ţi deschizi calea cu ei (To help you on your way)

Lica, a younger boy, and I did not join in the chorus.

Nothing happened because Mutu was also deaf. He didn't even look in our direction.

The pack moved closer to him, advancing like wolves would on their prey. Mircea took a stone and threw it. The stone fell in front of Mutu and only then did he whip round. He continued on his way, watching us; but other boys started throwing stones too. One of them hit him on the head. He stopped, raised his elbows above his head to defend himself, as more stones came his way, some hitting the target.

Suddenly he crouched down, covering his head with both hands and getting his good trousers dirty in the process. The boys began to cheer like little warriors.

Mutu produced long, inarticulate wails, like a wounded beast. He became a crying baby, then a whining little boy who grew into a grunting old man who, in turn, became an enraged wolf scuffling with competitors for its prey.

The cowardly little army backed off. Some scattered in different directions like chickens.

Mutu got to his feet and headed straight for Mircea, who was so petrified at the sudden change, that he couldn't move. Mutu grabbed Mircea with his left hand and raised him above his head, holding him there for interminable seconds before he started circling on the spot countless times. Mircea was caught at his own game, crying his lungs out and shitting himself, but his remorse was ignored.

Lica and I stood our ground but wet ourselves, when Mutu advanced towards us, Mircea still held up high like a scarecrow, making snuffling noises.

Mutu stretched his arm towards us and we backed off. We had not wronged him.

Mutu smiled, his big high eyes crinkling in a friendly way, whilst he brushed the dirt off his clothes with his free hand. We smiled back with uncertainty, and he shook hands with us, big gentle hands swallowing our small shaky ones. The blood from his wound was now a long crusty stain on his cheek. Then he looked up at the miserable Mircea who was shaking like a leaf. He put him down and stared into his eyes.

Mircea bolted. Forgetting about his cow, he headed home in record time, crying that Mutu had beaten him up on his way to Dumbrăviţa. Lica and I put things right and teased Mircea for being a silly pissy pants.

The single tail whip was one of our toys as cowboys, although cowboy was not a word known to us, as everything American was forbidden. Yet I wanted to go to America – the land of the free, according to my father – to buy a tractor to free our oxen from the hard work of ploughing, harrowing and drawing the cart up the hills of Lupoaia, come rain or shine.

Making a whip was easy and we all learned how. First, it had to be longer than two metres and made of hemp. It started thick at the top and narrowed down to a thin tip. When it was ready, a piece of lard was used to grease it and protect it from rain. Some vicious children tied a little metal ball to its end, drawing blood from the cattle they whipped, their wounds making a feast for the flies.

The whip, apart from cracking to make a single pop or a double deafening pop, was used as a sling. Our game was dangerous. We tied a well shaped little stone or pebble, preferably round, to the thin end of the whip and cracked it violently. The pebble was released at a great speed and spun through the air with a long, whistling sound that we loved. There was an orchard stretching from Curătura to Blidu's house, a few hundred metres long, with apple, plum, pear, apricot, and cherry trees, and many sparrows and crows gathering on their branches. The unfortunate birds were our targets. We got wickedly excited until one of us, Vanu, the oldest and strongest, decided to try his sling in the direction of Valea Gavri. His stone shot through the beech trees and hit the forehead of Zoriţa, a young girl guarding her family cow. She started vomiting blood. She was put on a cart and taken home. As the vomiting did not stop overnight, they took her to the hospital in Beiuş. She did eventually recover, but none of us heroes, with lethal toys, were allowed to go near a whip for a whole year.

A Young Party Secretary Makes My Father Sing Sad Songs

Stalin's death did not bring the change for which my father yearned – a quieter life with less harassment from the Militia and less danger from the Securitate. He was still a *chiabur* and still on the list of the enemies to be eliminated. Now he was taken by Mititescu into the Council room to stand before Vidu, a young man from a mountainous village 40km away and newly appointed Council Secretary. Ciorescu guarded Iosive and Zoltan.

Vidu, thin and rather small, with sunken cheeks and a long nose, was the son of a poor peasant family and, in 1948, had to leave a vocational school, because his father couldn't pay the fees. That was the year the Communists established complete control over the country after the King's abdication. They needed young cadres in the Securitate, young – so as to be easily brainwashed, inexperienced – so as to be easily trainable, needy – so as to be easily controlled. They would be won over by the new ideology and become intoxicated by the power with which they were invested; power supported by a shiny, new revolver.

Once home, Vidu did not know what to do with his life. One day his cousin, a secretary of the Rural Youth Union, offered him a job. He sent Vidu to Comrade Vereş, the Party secretary in Vaşcău. Vereş was recruiting young people for the Securitate through the youth organizations. He offered Vidu a good salary and a new pistol.

Vidu went on missions for two or three days at a time and, when he came home, hid his pistol and wallet in the stable under the cattle manger.

Vidu's mission was to spy on people who spoke against the Workers' Party in bars, the streets, buses and trains. He was perfect for this because his unremarkable features allowed him to blend into the background. Whenever he heard something suspect, he had to demand the person's identification papers, note down his or her personal details and report to the Securitate headquarters in Vaşcău. If the person refused to show him the papers, Vidu was to do one of two things: pull out his shiny pistol, if there were no onlookers, or follow the person home to find out his or her address. He did a good job and there were cases when he had to draw his pistol and force the person to do what he wanted. The particular aspect of the job, that involved threats with the pistol, was very much appreciated at the top. The authorities believed any man, prepared to go as far as that, was a fighter for the cause and could be trusted.

In 1952 Vidu was sent to the Securitate Training Centre No. 17, in Turnu Măgurele, and then to the Securitate School in Găeşti, where he graduated as a Securitate officer, at an age when many of his contemporaries were just being recruited into the army. He was sent as a Securitate lieutenant to Caransebeş. There he fought the partisans, those who opposed the Communist regime and took refuge in the mountains.

But Comrade Vereş had other plans for him. As a Securitate officer, Vereş said he was perfect for the position of Council Secretary. This was not an administrative position, as the name suggested, but a political position. He was going to fight the *chiaburs*, the former Legionnaires and whoever he perceived to be an enemy of the Party and of the people.

"We have three positions available and you could choose any of them," Vereş told Vidu.

They were in Ginta, Holod and Lupoaia, all close together. Ginta was some 10km from Lupoaia and the majority of the inhabitants were of Hungarian descent. Holod was only a couple of kilometres away and had the railway station.

Vidu needed time to think. He knew he couldn't reject this proposition because he would risk being considered the opposite of what Vereş had described him as being. The fall from grace would be speedy and come with terrible consequences.

"Yes, think about it," Vereş said. "I have to remind you that this is a task the Party is assigning you. In other words you should do your best and take it without delay."

Vidu went back to the village and, when he arrived home, his father told him that all his hay had been taken from him as a state-imposed quota. The wheat, the maize and the rye had suffered a similar fate. They had worked hard for a whole year, had a good crop and were left with nothing.

Vereş' words started ringing in Vidu's ears. The Party needed people it could trust. They were engaged in a class struggle, had to create a new man and build a luminous future for the people – the peasant class and the working class were united in this aim… He looked at his father and couldn't see any of that. His father was engaged in a struggle for his family's survival; he was not interested at all in fighting anybody, or alongside any workers in the city. Vidu couldn't see how his father could become a new man with a luminous future, after having been deprived of the fruits of his work… Famine and despair don't create friends. They create enemies. The situation, he knew, was the same everywhere. It would be the same in Ginta, with the added complication that the inhabitants were Hungarians. It would be the same in Holod and Lupoaia.

He would have to enforce the Party policy, which directed him to take peasants' livelihoods. He would thus create enemies out of poor people living on a few acres of land; and then he would have to fight them and make them submit. The worst part was that he felt he had to explain this to them. Well, he thought again, he didn't have to explain. That's the law, he would say, and that would be explanation enough.

And they would have to endure it.

On the 17th of November 1953, Vidu arrived in Lupoaia and was installed as the new secretary of the People's Council. He had opted for Lupoaia because, of the three villages, it had fewer people, less access, less control from the higher authorities and he anticipated fewer problems.

Here he was at the age of 23, shiny revolver at his waist and head full of imperfectly acquired ideological terminology, feared and respected by the community of peasants. He knew they feared him and he knew that they respected his position, out of fear alone, but he could live with that. Being new to this post, he had to make a good first impression on his masters.

When he heard the name, Flonta, he was startled. Was there any connection with the Beiuş Securitate lieutenant he had met a few times? Perhaps this coincidence was going to be his test. Everybody will have the treatment prescribed by the law, no matter who they are, he thought. Exceptions were to be regarded as heresies. A sort of personal curiosity was creeping up on him but he rightly decided to leave that for later. For much later, when the case would be closed and curiosities of this kind were not going to be regarded as harmful as they might be now.

"Mr. Flonta," he said upon meeting my father for the first time, "I trust you received the notification that you've been declared a *chiabur*."

"More than two years ago, sir," my father replied.

"That's fine," Vidu answered with a curt nod, measuring my father from head to toe. "I would like you to understand that we, the Party and the State authorities, have a job to do. We need to make sure you realise that we cannot build a new society with recalcitrant elements, who think only about their own good and thereby damage the whole community. We have to convince you of that, to make you accept that. In other words, we must re-educate you. Therefore you have to demonstrate at all times that you are prepared to co-operate with us. If you fail to co-operate," he stopped his monologue, which had grown in fervour, and stared at my father, "there is no future for you or for your family. Is that clear?"

My father did not know what to say. He just looked at Vidu – so young, so vicious, so adept at using meaningless words. He talked as if he were the master of the universe. Did he really believe these words? What was there to say? A few days before, my father had thought the worst was behind him and yet here was a young man, reciting the same old doggerel. Just when he was beginning to feel like an ordinary villager, he had to fight their lies again.

"I am not rich... I am not a *chiabur*," he managed to say, a sense of injustice and anger rising in him again. Then, "How am I damaging the community? I am providing a service to the community."

"Who do you think you are, Mr. Flonta? That is not for you to decide. The Party decides, is that clear? You are using other people's labour for your selfish interest and that's the end of it," said Vidu curtly. He knew he had to intimidate, to crush, to confuse this man's mind, before he came up with things he couldn't argue against.

"But Comrade Vidu, I use two men for less than three months a year. I give them a job, I pay them."

"Understand one thing, Mr. Flonta. Anybody, who exploits somebody else in our society, is an enemy of the society itself. That is no longer tolerated!" Vidu shouted and pointed his long thin finger in my father's face. "And I am not your comrade!" Then he ignored my father and asked Mititescu, who had joined them, "What do you have for him?"

"Ploughing Colibi tonight," Mititescu answered.

"You heard Comrade Mititescu?" Vidu asked my father.

"It's not the ploughing season yet," my father said. He knew it was pointless to argue with Vidu but he tried. He told him that tampering with the land irresponsibly meant breaking its life cycle. His land was his life and, like every peasant, he knew what his land required of him and when the various jobs were best done. He knew, in his heart, that Vidu would not listen to his words; but he was going to tell this young man what he thought anyway.

"Don't make it harder for yourself. Tonight, from 8 o'clock to 6 o'clock in the morning, you'll plough Colibi!" said Vidu. "And then?" he asked, turning towards Mititescu.

"Then, early in the morning, he has to go to Ginta and buy a postcard."

My father couldn't restrain himself in the face of such nonsense. Ginta was 10km away and there were no means of transportation other than walking.

"Why Ginta? I'll buy it here if you need one," he said with some indignation.

Vidu stepped closer and looked straight into his eyes.

"You are hard-headed, aren't you?" Then he paced around my father, enunciating the words sternly, "You go to Ginta as you're told, there you buy a postcard, then go to the Council Secretary, have it stamped and before evening you bring it to me, directly. Is that clear?" he shouted.

My father finally saw that idiocy would prevail and bent his head in resignation, sighing deeply. He had heard news of people in other villages being shot for not obeying these kinds of orders or being taken away during the night and thrown over a cliff from a speeding car. He thought of his wife, of his son, of his youth. He thought of life. He thought of death and then he thought of life again.

"Yes, sir," he said.

"Go!" shouted Vidu.

My father went out as fast as he could.

"Why all this? Why...?" he said, without noticing Zoltan and Iosive crouched on the bench outside Vidu's office.

Mama was sitting on a small stool by the stove, peeling potatoes, when my father came home from the Council. I was doing my homework at the table.

"What did they want?" Mama asked.

My father told her. She froze, with a potato in her left hand and the knife in the right, then opened her mouth to say something but couldn't; she just stared at him. Afterwards they stared at each other and I stared at them. My father sat on the bench but did not look at me. He extended his right arm and draped it over the back of the bench, moved his head backwards, stretching his neck to the limits, and stayed like that for a long time. I looked at his Adam's apple, moving up and down, at his gaunt unshaven face and I thought he was an old man. After a while, Mama said she wanted to go with him to Colibi.

"You stay here," he mumbled.

She was going to ask Grandma Saveta to stay with me, she insisted.

"Your place is in the home," he said. "Why should we all suffer?"

"Can I come with you, Daddy?" I asked.

"No, son. You go to bed, sleep well and study a lot. Okay?"

"I want to come," I insisted.

"May God help us," said Mama, crossing herself and taking me in her arms. She buried her face in my chest so that my father would not see her tears.

That night, we heard the sound of the Militia cart passing on the road. Mama peeked out of the window to see it going to Colibi. They were checking on my father but they didn't go too close and stopped in a gully to have a smoke. My father saw the light of their cigarette butts and cleared his throat, making as much noise as possible. They heard him alright.

They couldn't stop him drinking. He drank with gusto, slurping loudly. To spite them.

They couldn't stop him singing. The flow of air out of his lungs was powerful. His *doina* was a mournful ballad telling of suffering and endurance.

The melody was as old as music itself.

The words were as old as language itself.

The two elements combined, becoming a powerful emotion that overwhelmed his soul and brought out courage, fearlessness, defiance. Never give up, never.

Ce rău am făcut la lume (How did I wrong this world)
Că nu m-aud vorbe bune (That I can't hear good words anymore)
Numai rele şi minciuni (Only bad things and lies)

De la prietenii mei buni (From my good friends)
Lume nu mă pedepsi (Oh, world, don't punish me)
Lasă-mă să pot iubi (Let me love a bit more)
Că nu știu cât oi trăi (As I don't know how long I'll live)

It was the song of an innocent man in a world full of lies. It shouldn't be like that: life was short and love, not hatred, should prevail.

"Come and have a drink, comrades," my father pressed the militiamen, throwing his arms wide in a welcoming gesture that was more a dare than an invitation.

They were on their way back to the village. They couldn't stand defiant people. They couldn't stand Pavelea and his oxen.

I was asleep when my father came home that morning from Colibi. He took off again for Ginta, unshaven, tired and resigned to his fate. The tiredness confused his reasoning and he saw himself just like his oxen, doing things because he was forced to, without any apparent sense of purpose. He knew they had more in store for him. What was even worse: he couldn't expect to receive food or recognition for his useless toil, which made his position worse than that of his oxen. His food was stolen from under his nose and that was now legal. Legal? The highway brigands never had pretensions of legality. They stole, sometimes they killed; and then hid away until the next robbery, demonstrating some decency. But these people, the new masters, didn't even bother to hide. They just ordered. They took freedom and food without remorse, without compassion, without any reasonable explanation except their empty, silly words. He had great difficulty in understanding their arrogant, criminal ways. They tried to kill hope, the last thing my father thought he had left.

The trip was long, the rain poured and he stopped a few times on his way to take a short rest. Only for moments. He would have liked to lie down. That's what he needed, after walking behind the plough all night, but he pushed on regardless until his strength was at its limits. When Ginta could be seen from the Holod plain, he crossed the river and met a woman who couldn't speak Romanian but soon he found the Post Office. He bought the card and went straight to the Council. There, he had difficulty persuading the Secretary to stamp it.

It was midday. The sky was clearing and the rain had stopped. Soaked to the skin, he took the road back with some sense of accomplishment. It could all have gone wrong. If a seemingly normal person like young Vidu could become so ruthless, they could do anything to anybody. His life was in their hands. His family was in danger. What about his dreams for his son? What about life? He was only 33. He hadn't harmed anybody. He was screaming inside but he felt helpless, and nobody else could help him either. How long was this going to continue?

In Holod, he stopped at the railway station well and drank greedily, his head under the water jet, before marching the final 2km to Lupoaia. He was happy for a moment because he had made it, which meant that he had bought more time for himself and, more importantly, for Nuța and Teodor.

Vidu took the postcard, looking somewhat disappointed. He handed it to Mititescu.

"You made it," Vidu said. "Good." Then with a commanding tone, he added, "From now on you will report to me every morning. Understood?"

"Yes, sir."

"We have plenty of jobs for people like you."

"Yes, sir."

"You may go."

As my father was leaving, he heard Vidu say to Mititescu: "You wake him up at ten o'clock tonight and send him to harrow the plot he ploughed last night."

"Yes, Comrade."

That evening Mama was worried about my father's health. Two nights in a row, without sleep, and the whole day on the road were going to kill him.

"You need a rich meal," she said, "you need to stay strong in body and in mind, God help us."

She prepared a big pot of beans with lots of pieces of lard in it. She insisted that my father eat a full plate with a big loaf of bread. He had a choice of onion or sauerkraut as a side dish, she said. He did not answer. She looked at him, wiped her hands on her apron. Not to be put off, she went to the veranda and pulled out a whole sour cabbage from the barrel, dripping smelly, sour liquid all over the floor, before cutting it into strips on a plate which she put in front of my father. He took a forkful and mixed it into the beans and lard. Than he took another one and put half of it into his beans and returned the other half to the plate.

"If you eat this, I will bring you a quarter of *pălinca*," Mama said.

"C'mon Nuța, can I have a glass now, please?" my father raised his pleading eyes towards her.

She put her hands on her hips and gave him a serious look.

"Promise to eat everything?"

"Promise," my father said and started eating. I followed his lead and began to eat, while Mama pulled out a bottle of *pălinca* from the cupboard, poured out a quarter into a quarter bottle and brought it to the table. She poured a glass for my father but did not sit with us at the table as usual. My father invited her to sit with us but she said she had to feed the pigs.

"I've fed them already," my father said, but by then she was out of the door, hurrying away with her shoulders bent forwards. I was sure that she was crying. My father and I ate in silence. I eventually told him I was going out to look for Mama. He did not acknowledge my words.

As I approached the stables, I heard Mama sobbing. I found her sitting on the rock in my father's workshop. When she saw me coming, she wiped her tears on her black apron, straightened her shawl and got up, before I had a chance to say anything.

"Let's go inside. Dad is alone," she said.

My father had finished eating and was looking towards the window when we entered the room. He did not say anything as he started to place his clothes around the stove to dry.

Mama and I said a prayer and asked God to give my father strength and to protect him from the evil men who were tormenting him. I went to bed but couldn't sleep.

I heard Mititescu coming for my father at ten o'clock.

He went to Colibi to harrow the land.

Then they asked him to go back to plough the same plot the night after.

He did.

The village heard his sorrow pouring out in his song:

Cântă trist săracu cucu (The sad, poor cuckoo sings)
Că i-o spart duşmanii cuibu ('Cause enemies destroyed his nest)
Lasă cuce nu cânta (Don't worry, cuckoo, don't sing)
Că tu altu cuib ţi-i fa (You'll be able to build another nest)
Cucule, cucuţule (Cuckoo, little cuckoo)
Mută-ţi cuibu de-acole (Move your nest from there)
Că-i fi iară supărat ('Cause you'll be sad again)
Când i-afla cuibuţu spart (When you find your nest destroyed)

Stakhanovists and Silkworms

Before the summer vacation the Principal, Comrade Picu Petroi, assembled all grades in a square formation in the courtyard and introduced to us the Party activist from Beiuş, responsible for agriculture. He came to tell us that the Party, following the successful example of the Soviet Union, had decided to make corn our staple food. In order to obtain better cultures of the precious cereal, we were going to use the square sowing method. We would still sow the corn as before, in rows, but the secret, as ordered by Comrade Khrushchev, resided in eliminating waste by sowing fewer seeds, at a distance of 80-120cm apart. We would also eliminate the considerable work of thinning out the superfluous young plants, that were too close to each other to produce record crops. After all, Communism was about records and productivity; and we all had to become Stakhanovists of agriculture – like the Soviet Comrade Stakhanov, who set new records in coal extraction every day. The Principal and his visitor took us to the Principal's garden and showed us his neat rows of green corn. The two of them had a hard time controlling us, because Comrade Picu Petroi's corn gave us perfect cover, as we ran about, deliberately breaking sheaves. At the end we were again assembled in square formation and told that, with this method, we would not only catch up with imperialist America but we would overtake it.

Our Pioneer Organization was assigned the task of growing

silkworms. This was to follow the example of another great
Communist country, China, which was the best in the world at
growing silkworms and beating the American imperialists by far.
This, Comrade Petroi told us, was our personal contribution to the
construction of the new Communist society.

I couldn't understand why we always followed somebody
else's example. Were we so dumb that we couldn't come up
with anything on our own? It was like me and Mircea, where he
always copied my homework. I knew he was doing this because
he was a bit lacking in the brain department and that made me
feel pity for him; that's why I gave him my exercise books. Was
this the case with all of us Romanians too? Were we lacking in
the brain department? How could we create a new man with a
luminous future with other people's ideas? It was beyond my
comprehension. Didn't that make us thieves? My father said the
Communists were thieves and Stalin and his gang were the worst
kind, as big as they come. On the other hand, Comrade Petroi said
that, while the children of the imperialists squandered their time
playing, we were becoming trustworthy, new men of tomorrow
and everybody in the world was going to join us, in our struggle
against the imperialists.

Although I was not a pioneer, Comrade Petroi gave me a tray
with little white worms, resembling caterpillars, which we had
watched hatch from tiny black eggs at school. I was to take them
home and make my contribution by feeding them mulberry leaves
twice daily. That was easy because we had two mulberry trees in
front of our home, one white and one black; but we also had to
take turns feeding the school silkworms, which were stacked on
a scaffold in our classroom.

The silkworms were interesting, to start with, and I enjoyed
watching them move their little heads up and down the blade of
the leaf and munch until they reached the stem. Their precision
work in cleaning out the leaf mesmerized me but, after a while,
the pleasure became a chore. The chore soon became a bore.

Peering menacingly over her huge glasses, Comrade Petroi
told us sternly that we shouldn't give the silkworms wet leaves.

The day Mircea and I had to feed the worms at school, it was raining heavily. It was so bad that we had to skip feeding them in the morning; but in the evening we managed to collect enough leaves to take to the worms. We dried them with towels and even put them close to the stove.

That evening in the pouring rain, Mircea and I went from the Hill to the Valley with our leaves in a basket. By the time we reached school we were soaked to the skin – our blue trousers rubbing our legs uncomfortably – and so were our mulberry leaves. We shook them one by one and fed them to the silkworms. We didn't see the harm in it, and the worms couldn't tell on us.

The next day Comrade Petroi was waiting for us with a cane in her hand. The silkworms had died and, with them, our chances of becoming trustworthy, new men with a luminous future.

"What could you expect?" Comrade Petroi shrieked. I was the son of a *chiabur* and a *chiabur* will always sabotage Party policies, and Mircea was a no-gooder who did not show any application to learning. I asked myself why, then, had Comrade Petroi given Mircea the red scarf in the first place? Mircea and I received four lashes each and our parents had to pay for the dead worms.

However, in Comrade Petroi's opinion, a true pioneer did not accept defeat; and in a year's time, we were going to show the imperialists what we were made of.

I was not a pioneer and Comrade Petroi's nonsense made me smile.

The 1ˢᵗ May was approaching and this year we were told we had to celebrate the Workers' festival properly. We had to start with red placards on which slogans in white chalk were to be written. Comrade Petroi chose a writing team: Gusti, Aurora, Dorel and me. We had to think hard and come up with the best slogans. My inspiration failed me; but I came up with two ideas: "Long live the Romanian Workers' Party!" and "Long live and flourish the alliance between the workers' class and the peasants' class!" I was pleased when Comrade Petroi gave them the nod.

Gusti came up with "Long live Comrade Stalin, the father of

all the people!" Comrade Petroi said we had to stick to Romanian themes. I thought she made the right decision, as Stalin was dead anyway.

Aurora put forward "Long live the Soviet and Romanian friendship!" Comrade Petroi passed it.

We needed another slogan, but Dorel had some inspiration issues. In the end, he looked at the wall behind Comrade Petroi's desk, squinting as if the answer were written on the wall, and came up with "Long live Comrades Marx, Engels, Lenin and Stalin!" Comrade Petroi thought for a moment then told Dorel to take out Stalin. I wondered why she accepted slogans that wished a long life to dead people.

We cut the roll of red paper in four and started writing our slogans. I couldn't fit peasants class in and managed to write only *p*. It couldn't be erased, so Comrade Petroi said we would put it up on the wall anyway, for the people to see how silly I was.

All the others managed to fit the words in, but with some mistakes, the missing letters being written above in a smaller size. Comrade Petroi said their writing looked like traces of chicken feet in the mud.

I told my father that Comrade Petroi did not let Dorel and Gusti write Stalin's name on the placards.

"I told you Stalin was the biggest criminal on earth," he said. "Now even the Communists don't like him. They realise that so many innocent people died because of that beast." My father's jaw clenched, when he spoke about Communists.

He said he had heard, on Voice of America, that Khrushchev did not like Stalin and that he condemned him for what he had done, so now we were all going to be better off.

Learning Russian and Fighting the Imperialists with Wooden Guns

In grade four we started learning our first compulsory foreign language, the language that conveyed the rule of the dictatorship of the proletariat: Russian. I hadn't paid much attention to other languages until then, although I knew two gypsy words, *mucles* and *mishto*, meaning 'be quiet' and 'beautiful', both of which were bandied about by everybody in Lupoaia. I also knew one word and a rude expression in Hungarian, *igen*, and *lófasz a seggedbe*, 'yes' and 'a horse's prick up your arse', which were also used by the villagers.

This was the first time I'd seen a foreign alphabet and that did not impress me at all. I asked Comrade Petroi how come the Soviets spoke a language called Russian. Didn't they learn the Soviet language? She explained something about the past and something about the present and that the Soviets are the new men of the new Russia, with a luminous future and a new name. It did not convince me, because we were Romanians and we spoke Romanian, and I knew that the Hungarians spoke Hungarian. The gypsies exposed a flaw in my logic, as they did not speak Gypsian, but everybody knew they were peculiar people and from peculiar people, you could expect all sorts of strange things. Why should the Soviets be different? Then, the funniest thing of all was the way they wrote B for V, P for R, C for S and H for N. They seemed confused to me. And how about having a number 3 for letter Z? What language did not distinguish its numbers from its letters? Plus, they had strange letters, like Г, which seemed to me a flipped over L, but for them, was G and looked like a gallows. I could almost picture a body dangling from its end. Their J was Ж, like a spider and far more difficult for us to write than the hieroglyphics we had seen in the history book. Mircea had more fun with F, in Russian Ф, as it looked comical, just like two nuts on a willie, he said. And he told everybody that my name started with two nuts on a willie.

When I learned to write my first sentence, Ада дома (Ada is at home), I was so proud, because everybody in the class had difficulty and even Comrade Petroi smiled at me. At home I wanted to impress my father and wrote it down for him but, for the first time, he did not praise me.

"May they and their language rot in hell for all the suffering they are causing us," he said, spitting out every word with bitterness and contempt.

That squelched my enthusiasm for Russian forever.

I moped through dinner, sad that I had disappointed my father. Finally, he said that I should learn Russian well, to get good marks but that the Russian language and those people who spoke it were our worst enemies; they were liars and they couldn't be trusted any more than you could trust a hungry wolf in a sheep's pen.

Some peasants, who had fought on the Russian front, began teasing me, asking me to translate Давай часы (Give me your watch), Давай папиросу (Give me your cigarette), explaining later that the first thing the Russians did when they came to Lupoaia in 1944, as liberators, was to ask for their watches and their cigarettes. The peasants laughed, telling me that nobody in Lupoaia had a watch and they smoked either pipes or cigarettes, made with cement bag paper or with wrapping paper from the local shop, glued with their own spit. Some just chewed the tobacco without the need to burn it, saving them the work of collecting and drying the tinder for their flint and steel.

I had never seen an imperialist before, but Comrade Petroi was always talking about them. I wondered if she herself had met one. Going once or twice a year to Beiuş was not the way to meet any of them, as far as I knew. One thing she was very strict about was that we had to fight them at all times. We had to be ready and equipped, because the imperialists were planning day and night of how to destroy us. We had to be organized and enrol in the patriotic brigades, of our own free will, but without exception. Our weapon would be a wooden gun, which we had to procure ourselves.

My father made a beautiful gun for me, determined to provide me with the best he could. It looked just like the one Comrade Mititescu carried on his shoulder. My gun had everything – a barrel, a trigger, a gun sight and a shoulder belt, cut by Mama from a pair of old trousers. My father couldn't find a brown dye in the shop – you could hardly find anything in our village shop anyway – but Mama boiled walnut leaves for a few hours and soaked my gun in the water overnight. When the gun was dry, my father gave me a piece of lard and told me to rub it in vigorously and then polish the gun with the cloth he used for his leather boots. My gun was as shiny as Comrade Mititescu's and the envy of all my companions at school. Mircea had something primitive cut out from a board, which did not even look like a gun.

I was so pleased to have that gun and to be on Comrade Petroi's good side for a change, bravely fighting the American imperialists, who were plotting day and night to destroy us. Let them come, I was ready for them!

My father laughed when I held my gun. He said that if I had a uniform, I would look like a little soldier, but with that gun I could not harm anybody more than a flea did, let alone defend myself or my country. War was terrible anyway. You go in and you don't know if you'll come out of it, just like Aurel, my cousin Viorica's father.

This was a bit of a let down but my father saw things for what they were, I thought, not for what people like the two Comrades Petroi claimed. Even I could spot some of their lies now.

Turkeys, Fire and a Funeral

Mircea and I chased the turkeys in their pen next to our stable, just for the fun of making them gobble and cluck. After a while we got tired of this game. Mircea had another idea. He said he could reach the beam in his house, where his mother kept their matches. We went to his house next door, which was a carbon copy of ours, although a bit more disorganised; and I held the chair he put up on the bench close to the stove, while he climbed up and threw down a box of matches. He said he aimed to light a fire in our garden, then he climbed over the fence and started running around the straw rick in Vantica's garden, challenging me to catch him.

When he was out of breath, Mircea fell down at the bottom of the rick and pulled the match box out of his pocket. He lit a match and pulled a handful of straw from the rick. I told him to be careful because the rick was catching fire. Temptation lured me into his game and, before I knew it, the rick was ablaze. Within seconds, red and orange flames jumped everywhere.

Before the women from the neighbourhood came running, we fled in horror and guilt. Their buckets were half-empty because the water in the waterholes was scarce. The water did not help, and in a few minutes the rick was gone. Mircea got a severe thrashing with the rolling pin and I was scolded by my parents.

Vantica and his wife, Saveta, now had one more justification for their hostility towards my father. For years, they had been nibbling at the *mununa*, the 20cm wide strip of land that divided our two properties. A week after the fire, they saw me in the garden and started jumping up and down like two puppets on a string, pointing the finger at me, saying that I was as bad as my father, because the apple does not fall far from the tree. I was an apple that should have been given to the pigs to eat. They knew Mircea and I had set fire to their straw rick; but Vantica was not brave enough to enter our house and complain to my father.

The *mununa* was a point of contention between neighbours and caused many fights, creating enduring enmities, that sometimes lasted for life or even into later generations. In their greed, some people cut into it, to gain 8-10cm of land, while accusing the other neighbour; and this was what Vantica did year after year to my father.

Others went even further and pushed the boundary onto their neighbour's land with their ploughs, thus appropriating even more centimetres of land.

Vantica had another bone to pick with my family. His son, Aurel, who was married to my Auntie Puica, lost his life in the war in Crimea, leaving behind my cousin Viorica. When Vantica got the news about his son's death, he and Saveta started hating Auntie Puica for two reasons: she had not produced a male heir, so they were left with a girl instead; and she was not the kind of daughter-in-law they wanted, because she had a big mouth and scolded them too much. They turned their anger from her and started venting it on my father.

Any time Vantica was outside arguing with my father in his wide-legged *gaci*, Saveta would come out to give him a hand. She was unstoppable.

One day, during one of these arguments, my father, who was holding a hoe in his hand, lifted it in the air and ran towards Vantica, telling him to stop or he'd end up with a cracked head. Vantica, who was a coward, ran for his life with my father in pursuit, dived straight into the house and slammed the door behind him. He shouted insults at my father through the windows, with Saveta yelling even more. The neighbours, who witnessed this, laughed and joked. Soon Vantica and his big mouth became the talk of the village. Still the quarrels did not stop but Vantica was careful to keep his distance from my father and sought refuge in the house, like a rat in his burrow, whenever he felt threatened.

He mellowed only when Saveta died. My father made the coffin for the old woman and sent Auntie Puica to organize the funeral. Vantica did not bother him anymore. He did not leave the house very often after that and Auntie Puica took food to him from time to time.

When he died I was allowed to go to his wake, which went on for two nights before the burial. Auntie Puica and Grandma Saveta prepared him for burial by washing his elbows and his knees and dressing him for the final voyage. Grandma told me that after a person dies, he or she has to be clean to go to heaven. When I asked how come they washed only his elbows and his knees, she said that Vantica would present himself in front of the Lord, prostrated on his elbows and his knees, so they had to be clean. It did not convince me. In short, only the parts of the body that were going to be dirtied were supposed to be washed, while the rest of the body was supposed to be left dirty. On top of that, if the dead Vantica were going to kneel in front of the Lord, those parts of the body would not be seen anyway.

At the wake, the men played cards on the coffin and drank *pălinca*. I loved the idea of being with them late at night – it meant I was growing up fast – but I did not fancy the idea of getting too close to the dead body. From time to time some men left and went home and others came in to replace them, as the wake was a big thing that had to be kept going until the burial. As usual, I had a question. What would happen if Vantica were left alone at night with nobody in the room? Modru told me that the soul would wander around, seeking company, and if it did that, it would not find rest in death but would return from the dead to torment the living. That notion prompted me to stay very close to my father, until I fell asleep.

Burdened by the thought of Vantica's wandering soul, I returned to the wake with my father the second night. This time, the lid of Vantica's coffin was placed on two stools and the men were playing cards on it. Vantica's dead body was covered by a hemp sheet – so it was not visible – but the smell was foul. Oanca told the men to put the lid on the coffin, as the odour of the dead body was getting stronger and stronger. Modru got up and sprinkled Vantica's body with half a bottle of *pălinca*.

"Here you are," he said, "his odour is that of a living man now, no better and no worse. And he enjoys it. Hear how he laps the *pălinca*."

A few minutes later, the women's chattering and the quietness of the men's card game were interrupted by a sharp cry.

"Vantica is rising!"

The women stampeded for the door.

I was so petrified, when I saw the top half of Vantica's covered body rising, that I wet my pants.

Modru told me not to worry, as it was only a prank; Vantica was as dead as a doornail. He had passed a rope under Vantica's back and around his armpits and tied it above his chest and, when he pulled the rope, the body rose. The prank had scared me so much that I did not dare go around at night for quite a while.

I was given a role at the funeral – that of starting the oxen.

When the priest finished Mass in Vantica's courtyard, the oxen were brought in and yoked to the cart, loaded with the coffin. A basket of four big, round loaves of bread with shiny, brownish crusts was brought by two women and Modru. My father spiked a loaf on each of the horns of the two oxen.

I had to start the oxen, signifying the final separation of Vantica from his earthly abode and his departure for the other world. As I was considered a pure child, in spite of my adventures with the older girls on the pasture fields, I was given a green plum stick split at the end where a small coin had been inserted. I hit one of the oxen on the rump with my stick and both of them took their first step towards Vantica's final resting place. Before the oxen reached the gate out of Vantica's courtyard, my father and Modru took a handful of corn and threw it over the oxen, the cart and the coffin. The procession stopped eleven times before reaching the cemetery, which was the twelfth and last stop. Every time I used my stick to start the oxen, I noticed Mircea's envious glances and felt important.

Modru told me to keep the coin, instead of throwing it inside the grave, because Vantica did not stand a chance of using it. He had committed so many sins on earth that St. Peter, who was waiting for him at the doors of heaven, could not be bribed with such a small coin. I was also given one of the four loaves from the horns of the oxen. Two loaves went to the gravediggers and one was broken at the cemetery, after the funeral, and distributed in small pieces to all present, as alms for the soul of Vantica, so that he would not go hungry on his way to the other world.

Modru told me that the bread, which was as white as angels' robes, was supposed to be used by Vantica to bribe the angels to shorten his waiting time for an audience with God. He concluded that angels were not so stupid as to lead a sinner, like Vantica, into the presence of God. Only a few were chosen. The rest of us were just specks of dust that counted for nothing.

So Vantica had only my stick to go to heaven with. Modru said the stick would serve as a bridge over the river that everybody has to cross. Otherwise, if they follow the river without crossing it, they end up in Hell and, in Hell, the river water turned into flames. That was not a place to find yourself in; but Modru was sure Vantica would end up there.

Multilaterally Developed

Comrade Petroi often punished or reprimanded me for asking questions. She threatened me with the cane many times, her menacing, ugly face showing how much she enjoyed threatening me.

My father told me to always ask questions because that's how you learned things.

"How about the cane?"

"The cane leaves a mark on your flesh for a few hours, a day or two. The good answers to the questions leave a mark on your brain for many years, sometimes even for life," my father said.

A bit tricky for a boy to understand maybe, but my father was always right.

When Comrade Petroi once again talked about the new man with a luminous future, I couldn't resist asking her what this new man was like. I could see from her grumpy face that she did not expect the question and that she did not like it coming from me. She sighed, planting her hands on her hips, and said that the new man was a multilaterally developed man, who was ready to give his life for the ideals of Socialism and Communism.

Multilaterally developed?

No. I dared not ask. I was too afraid she would punish me again.

I could hardly wait to get home and ask my father. He was cutting up a board in his workshop and when he saw me, he stopped.

"How was school today, son?"

"Well, do you know what multilaterally developed means?" I asked, standing in the door frame.

"What developed?" he asked, perplexed and intrigued.

"Multilaterally developed," I said impatiently.

My father thought about it for a while, but he had left school in fifth grade, having spent more time on Hurupa than in the classroom. So he called Mama and asked her – after all, she had left school in grade six – but she didn't know either and looked as perplexed as he did.

After a while my father worked something out. He said this 'multilaterally' word was made of two words, *multi* (much) and *lat* (wide), but then he scratched his head and said it can't be 'much wide' because it didn't sound right. I said 'fat' like Vuṭa, our neighbour, whose one leg was thicker than my whole body. It can't be like that, he said, and suggested that *multi* could be many and lateral sounded like *latura* (side); the new man is a man with many sides to him, he said triumphantly.

"We all have many sides," I retorted.

He thought again and said that they were referring to the man's mind, the man's thinking. How could it be otherwise? Ever since Adam and Eve we had been born the same way, with the same number of sides. No matter what these Communists did, they wouldn't be able to add sides to human beings. Now we think differently from Adam and Eve, though, meaning that we have added something to our minds. So the Communists wanted to take credit for what has happened to our minds. In other respects, not much has changed in man. You might not find a man in the whole of Lupoaia, Holod, Hodiş and Forosig taking an apple from a serpent today but if you gave him *pălinca*, yes, he would take it alright, Dad said and laughed.

I was confused. In the end, he told me that the Communists wanted everybody to think like them, to do what they wanted. They just confused you with these silly words. He couldn't tell me anything more, he said.

"How about women?" I asked.

"What about women?"

Comrade Petroi talked only about the new man, never about the new woman.

"When she says new man she also means woman, that's what I think," my father said.

"But I never heard anyone calling Mama or Grandma Saveta a man," I said.

He laughed again. "Well, son, we are peasants and we are ignorant. You should learn as much as you can and read as many books as you can, because books know more than people. You will find all your questions answered by them. If they tell the truth."

Bricks for a New House and a Happy Farewell

Between arrests by the Securitate and hiding from them for five years, my father did not spend much time at home. One thing we almost took for granted was that he would be at home for the *pălinca*-making season – October to December. Although his new *cazan* had been nationalized in 1952, he was allowed to manage it, either for lack of qualified people or because he had a good relationship with the State Wine and Spirits Company managers. The quotas every peasant paid on his annual *pălinca* production were important for the Communist authorities, so my father made the most of it. He was paid a decent salary for those few months of the year and, as in the past, he took a percentage of the total production from each individual – he shared this with the inspectors and the managers of the Wine and Spirits Company. This was common practice and those, who did not conform, weren't appointed as *cazan* manager the following year. His workers were happier too, because they got a modest salary as well as being paid in kind, as before.

The quota on the *pălinca* was established at the beginning of the season by an inspector from the Company. As the Party did not trust the new man it was trying to forge, it based the quota on the output of *pălinca* per hour. The lower the output, the lower the quota and vice versa. There were a couple of tricks employed to artificially lower the output, such as using slightly green firewood and adding a few buckets of water to the fermented plums. Once the output was set, the inspector went away and, as the surplus of production was not subjected to any quota, everybody gained.

What the State took with one hand – all our wheat as quota – the State gave back, unknowingly, with the other hand – the surplus of *pălinca*. Each year my father bought back all our wheat, and the remaining *pălinca* was hidden under the ground.

Now that Stalin was gone, my father decided to build a new house, a solid brick three-bedroom house with a big cellar. He hoped that the Communists would disappear and that, as a *pălinca* maker, he would be able to put the cellar to good use, with no need to hide anything anymore. And no need to hide himself all the time.

Bricks were expensive and the transport was costly, because the nearest factory, the one in Ceica, had been closed by the comrades.

Our backyard was big and had clay soil, which was good for making bricks. My father brought the slag from Holod station, the sand from Vintere and the lime from Oradea.

Gypsies were renowned for making mud bricks, stacking and drying them in Dumbrava. My father made ten rectangular brick-size forms, invited his friend Ciotu over and put a bottle of *pălinca* in front of him. They reminisced about their time in the army, the hard times of the past few years, and they talked about bricks.

Soon our garden became a gypsy encampment, with children running all over the place and stripping the trees and the cultivated area of anything edible. My friends Dolea, Mircea, Domnica, Floarea, Petrica and I joined in. At night, our mothers reprimanded us for the bad deeds of the day.

"It won't last long," Grandma Saveta used to reassure Mama. "They'll calm down soon."

We did; but the little gypsies continued roaming our neighbours' gardens until the neighbours started threatening to put a pitchfork through their dirty gypsy bellies and feed their entrails to the pigs. Their mothers got scared and established some order.

My father killed a pig and there were eggs from our hens. The gypsies were happy with Grandma Saveta's cooking, because they said the lard in the soup gave them sustenance. My father's *pălinca* helped them digest the lard and sleep well at night. The children went particularly crazy for my grandma's *pancove*, licking the sugar off before eating them.

We kids were also useful. Every day, as the bricks were made, our garden expanded into a glistening grey pavement, which we had to defend from the dogs, cats, hens and other domestic animals; and we did so with enthusiasm, as proved by our dirty trousers. We did not want our bricks decorated by animals' paw prints or soiled by their poo.

When the bricks were dry enough to be handled, we stacked them into triangular heaps like bee hives. We stacked the bricks close to each other so they could be covered in case of rain; but there was no need for that, as the summer was hot and dry. Later on, when the rain started, the big hole the gypsies had dug to make the bricks became a pond, relished by the geese and ducks and hens and pigs. By the time the twelve thousand bricks were made, our garden looked like an archaeological site.

When the bricks were finally dry, we stacked them on top of each other in a 5m high furnace. The fire went on for a week, with the smoke visible all over the Valley. The mouth of the furnace was walled in and the wood inside smouldered for forty days. After the furnace's mouth was opened, it took a couple of weeks to cool down.

We had our bricks.

After the long and tiresome journeys bringing the slag, sand and lime, our oxen grew weaker and crankier. It was as if they were trying to tell my father that their burden was too heavy. I loved those oxen. They had accompanied me through my formative years: from the age of four I often took them to pasture. Later on, as they got older and slower, I felt for them and, in late spring, when my parents were not watching, I would cut clover and juicy green hay to comfort them.

In summer, I would pull Mama's carrots from the ground or

the beetroots, destined for the pigs, and take them to the oxen. They liked my gifts and ate them, while watching me with such interest and tenderness in their eyes, that I interpreted the dribble falling from their mouths as their way of showing how much they enjoyed the juicy, sweet vegetables. But after the latest hardship, Mojar developed the habit of charging at people. I thought that was his way of rebelling against humans, who were careless and demanded too much from an old ox who had given so much throughout his life. I sided with him. They were both tied to a pole with a long rope; but one day Mojar pulled up the pole and roamed freely through the garden, churning up the mud with his oversized hooves and ending his journey in the cabbage patch, munching our delicious, green cabbages. The men cutting timber in the garden called me to chase him away. He obeyed for a few metres and ran in front of me, then suddenly turned and, disturbed by my stick tickling his nose, he charged. The next minute I was flat on the ground, with Mojar at my back, preparing for another attack. I was saved by the men, who came running with their arms outstretched and their deep voices ringing through the air. I respected Mojar more after that.

At the end of fourth grade, our primary school cycle was completed. The two Comrades Petroi had us on the People's House's stage again, reciting poems about the grandiose work our Party and our leaders were doing so that we could be the beneficiaries of that luminous future they promised us. Other poems dealt with the Soviet-Romanian friendship, the generosity of our big brother from the East, while my father was saying that it was just the opposite: the Russians or Soviets, as they liked to call themselves now, were the worst bloodsuckers on earth. He'd seen it with his own eyes as he worked for them in Băiţa and had seen train after train, full of uranium ore, leaving for Russia. It was estimated that some hundred thousand tonnes of uranium ore were transported to Russia from Băiţa. Some other poems were about a woman tractor driver working from dawn to dusk alongside men to improve productivity, just like the stakhanovists in Soviet factories and mines.

The Principal, Comrade Picu Petroi, violin in hand, conducted our choir singing the national anthem and songs about the achievements of our Socialist system, all to the rhythm of Soviet marches.

I was in a play again; but this time not as a *chiabur*. Instead I was Klestakov, the Inspector General, from Gogol's play by the same name. Comrade Petroi said that we had to show our parents how greed and corruption, traits of the bourgeois society, defined the old man (i.e. the Inspector General) as opposed to the new man, who was selfless, honest and totally devoted to the struggle for the new Communist society.

Again, my father said Comrade Petroi should see how eager these so-called new men, in command now, were to grab a bottle of *pălinca* from him, when giving him what he asked for. That was greed and corruption, he said, because in a normal society, those things he asked for would have been his by right.

The ceremony ended with another prize-giving. Everybody in my class thought I deserved the first prize; but again Comrade Petroi bestowed only a mention on me, even though the pressure on *chiaburs* had now slightly dimmed. She just couldn't bring herself to such generosity.

My father, smiling proudly and dressed in his best shirt and trousers, told me to be glad that I was now a big boy and was going to move to the Middle School in Holod, where they would do the right thing by me. Comrade Petroi, he said disapprovingly, was as corrupt as they come for not giving me the prize, more corrupt than the Inspector General and the Mayor in the Russian play.

I was glad to see the back of the two Comrades Petroi and hoped I would never cross paths with them again. Mircea did not continue with school. Lucky arsehole, I thought.

A Revolution and America

All of a sudden, in autumn 1956, two Lupoaia militiamen began patrolling the street. They puffed out their chests self importantly, as they marched up and down the dusty street in their clean uniforms. It would have been funny, had it not been for the violence and repression that we had already endured. The villagers saluted them with due reverence, watched them with some circumspection and gossiped a lot about the reason for this new routine. In the past, they had patrolled at night or, if they came during the day, they had taken shortcuts through orchards, gardens, and the ravine of Hurupa to avoid being seen. Now, such a change, showing themselves to everybody in daylight and even stopping to chat to each other in the middle of the village, just below Hurupa, was strange and unprecedented. Why did they start patrolling the Lupoaia road? Why did one of them start his walk from the far end of the Valley and the other from Dumbrava, the opposite end? And why did they scrutinze everybody they met with such insistence?

Something was brewing, but what?

Voice of America was talking about some revolution in Hungary; but we were forbidden to speak about that. We were also forbidden to listen to the programme.

I found out that my father listened to the imperialist radio station on his wireless, every night. He had dug a hole under the oxen's manger and he hid there, cramped but warm in the straw, to listen to the forbidden news from our enemies. In the past he had used this hole, for short periods, to escape the Securitate. He had covered the entrance with the straw the cattle slept on, and I saw him hook the antenna onto nails on the stable gutter. One day I caught him unawares with headphones on his ears and intense concentration on his face, looking like the phone operator in Holod. He later told us he heard that Stalin's statue had been ripped down in Budapest and that the Russians had deployed thousands of tanks and soldiers to crush people's thirst for freedom. He told me how the students collected petrol to make bombs, with the names of Soviet leaders on them, and greased the paving stones to make tanks slide, so they could take a better shot at them. He understood that the West was amassing troops in Austria, to invade Hungary and set its people free once and for all. He hoped we would have our freedom back too.

One day he let me try the headphones. Men with funny voices that seemed to ripple through water spoke into my ears. My father told me that was Voice of America, addressing us in Romanian from across the seas and the oceans, which interfered with their voices. It was like when I had a bath in the wooden vat and the water entered my ears and I had to press my palms against them for the water to come out. The Romanian these Americans spoke was a bit different from the language we spoke at home. At times, I did not understand what they said. One thing I understood clearly, though, was that they spoke ill of our leaders, whom we were taught to revere. I asked my father how come they did not like any of our leaders. We were not allowed to say that sort of thing at school, where we were made to learn the strange names of all the men on the wall. One had two surnames, something that I had never heard of before. One had a Hungarian name and there were a few with Russian names.

My father said there were more Russians among the men on the wall but they had changed their names into Romanian ones. He told me that these men were a curse on the country, because they had sold us to the Russians. Who knew if we would ever be free again? The voices from America were voices of free men and they told the truth. At school, Comrade Petroi was telling us lies.

I was confused. These radio voices from America made me pay more attention to what my father said; and I realised I was confronted with two different ideas about the same world, or with two worlds, very far apart in every respect. Suddenly I felt the urge to get far away from Comrade Petroi, the Party activists, the Party secretary and the militiamen, all of whom lied to us and made us lie to ourselves. I wanted to be in America, the land of the free, and say what I wanted to say, when I wanted to say it, without fear of being punished.

My father said I shouldn't tell anybody that we listened to Voice of America, because it was not allowed. This was our secret, he said. He also insisted that I was not to tell anybody about his hiding place.

"I was born in the stable," he said, "and that brought me luck, because people born in a stable are good people."

I didn't understand why people born in a stable were good people. What about the rest of us who were not born in a stable? Certainly Comrade Petroi was not born in a stable. My father also told me that he felt free in that little hole in the ground, much freer than he felt outside, where he was always being chased by the criminals of the regime. That freedom came from inside, from his thoughts, from his soul; and nobody could take that from him.

Then he told me about Manasia and Vasalia, both of whom went to America and made a fortune. It began at the turn of the century, when there was talk of a railway being built to Oradea. It was an exciting time for villagers hoping to find work and improve their meagre existence. The railway was going to link Lupoaia, Ceica, and Drăgești with Calea Mare and Oradea; but the project was derailed by the rich Jews from Rogoz and Sâmbăta, who bribed the railway officials to build the railway near their homes. This allowed them to deforest their land for the railtracks and make money out of the timber; and left Lupoaia without a direct link to the big city.

While my great-grandfather, Pavelea, was making his fortune in Lupoaia, many men decided to take the 3-4 week boat trip to a new life in America.

Only a few migrated permanently. The majority lived there for
6 years at most, enduring a desolate existence, eating only once
a day, to save every cent they earned.

One of the first to return was Manasia, who had taken his wife
with him. While he worked in the factory, she cooked for migrants
and made good money too. On his return, he bought land, a thresher
with its own locomotive and a tractor as well. For the villagers the
thresher and the tractor pulling a plough seemed miraculous. In
their uneducated minds, only strong, resilient oxen and buffalos
were capable of dragging a plough through the soil.

Manasia was very successful with his new machinery, so much
so that he married off his four daughters and left a good inheritance
for his two sons, Dragoş and Licu.

Vasalia came back from his American experience with vast
wealth, by Lupoaia's standards. Not being able to count, he had no
idea how much money he had. Legend has it that he brought back
more money than Manasia and his wife put together. He did not
eat much during his stay in the New World, saving every penny
to bring home. Once he came home, the village women asked
his wife, Veta, how much money Vasalia had brought back. The
silly woman went around with her apron full of dollars, to show
everybody how rich they were.

With their riches on constant display and word of it spreading
around the neighbouring villages, Vasalia's new-found wealth
haunted him. One day he received a visit from Dinca, a young
man from Duşeşti. Dinca asked about life in America and chatted
to the couple for a few hours, all the while checking out the house
and garden, making a mental note of every detail. Veta showed off
their riches, proudly bragging on and on about their good fortune.

Dinca returned one evening, disguised as a gendarme. He
inspected documents and money, and declared that Vasalia had
failed to notify the authorities about the money. He was going to
make sure that everything was made completely legal, so that they
would not have problems in the future. He promised to deposit the
money into the bank for them, according to new foreign currency
laws. Veta packed the money into a couple of thick hemp towels

and tied them with a double knot, before handing everything they had to the gendarme, grateful that he was saving them from jail. Dinca left hurriedly through the back door; and this aroused the suspicion of the neighbours. They started running after him, but caught only a glimpse of his shiny uniform buttons as he hurtled into the forest.

Vasalia and Veta were left in the same situation they had been in before their journey to the United States: poverty and ignorance. Dinca, on the other hand, made his way to Italy, took a ship in Genoa and later surfaced in America, where he did very well for himself.

When Micula came with his drum, calling the villagers to a general assembly at the People's House, my father asked him if the militiamen's new patrol was due to the events in Hungary. Micula looked around warily and nodded. He had heard the militiamen and the Party activist discussing Russian tanks passing through Oradea into Hungary.

My father rejoiced, saying that one day he would not be a *chiabur* anymore and that the Communists would get their due punishment: a kick in the pants and a stick up their arse. Too many people had paid the ultimate price because of them. And, apart from the men of straw, everybody suffered now.

With hope in his heart and the bricks ready in his garden, my father went to Ginta to talk to Fekete, the Hungarian bricklayer. When he entered the village, a militiaman appeared from nowhere, sneaking up on him like a rat up a drain pipe, and asked for his identity card. Seeing that my father was a *chiabur*, the militiaman began to mock him: "What do we have here, a *chiabur* and Hungarians, an unhealthy union..."

My father pretended to not understand, adopting a look of confusion. His strategy seemed to work. The militiaman asked him a lot of questions – about the person he was visiting, the reason for the visit and the duration of the visit. He let him through with the injunction to leave the village within an hour. My father hurried, as he knew that he had to keep that deadline. Fekete agreed to build our house and to bring other two Hungarian bricklayers with him. The only condition he made was to be fed beef for lunch, twice a week.

My father stopped at the Ginta shop and bought the two newspapers, Scînteia and România liberă.

The militiaman was waiting for him and, this time, he was friendlier, telling my father to avoid passing through the village of Holod and instead, to follow the railway toward Dumbrăviţa and then the road leading straight into Râturi.

Later Fekete told my father that the militiaman had questioned him to verify his story in detail.

When he arrived home, my father handed me the two newspapers and told me to look for articles that mentioned some revolt or revolution in Hungary.

"And look also for news about Russia," he said.

I looked and looked. There was plenty of news about the Soviet Union and the conquests of the Communist Party, the cultivation of the hybrid corn and the increase in productivity, in every sector of the economy, that made our brothers there look as if they were feasting on sausages every day. The successes of our working class in the struggle for the creation of the new man, the new society, the luminous future for all citizens, following the wise guidance of the Party, took up the remaining space.

"No news about Hungary," I said.

"You see, son," he said, "if you don't want people to know what's happening around them, you just don't tell them anything. Nothing at all. And the working class is supposed to be happy with that. Don't believe it. Man is by nature a curious animal. You can hide the truth from him temporarily, but not for ever. Remember that."

I nodded. I thought about man being a curious animal. Was it because of this, that the activists and militiamen called the *chiaburs* swine and pigs?

"Ah, but on the other hand, do you see a luminous future here for us, in this new society? Oh, yes, you can see the new man, the activist, the militiaman, the Party secretary… these are the new men – liars, torturers, well-paid instruments of this regime. They are men of straw, spines bowed to their masters."

I listened, not knowing what to say. Things did not look good, but I did not know anything better. Yes, I could see the clothes on the militiamen, on the activist, on the Party secretary… they looked new and clean but, then, they didn't work the land. Everybody else in Lupoaia was dirty, going around in rags and patched clothes, eating lard and raw onions for breakfast and drinking litres of *pălinca*.

The New Principal and His Wife

The novelty in the Middle School was that we had more teachers: some who taught two or three subjects, like Comrade Abrudan, and some who stuck to one subject, like Comrade Balan. As in the primary school, though, the Principal, Comrade Hulea, was married to one of our teachers.

Comrade Hulea was a tall man, strongly built like those soldiers in the Soviet films, defending the revolutionary conquests of the new society, with hair cut short and thinning on top.

His wife, the slightly built Comrade Hulea, taught French, a new subject altogether. I liked the idea of learning a language that did not have the word *tovarisch* in it; that is, until the day she punished me and the whole class. She asked us how we said watch in French. I put my hand up. Nobody else did. She repeated the question with the same result. Nobody else knew.

"Flonta," she said.

"*Montre*," I said.

She stood there waiting, her eyes peering over the rims of her glasses as if boring a hole right through me.

I did not know what else to say.

"The article?"

I had to think fast. It was neuter in Romanian but in Russian it was masculine.

"*Le montre*," I said.

"Wrong!"

She must have had a bad day before coming to the class. All the students who did not raise their hands had to stay in detention after school for two hours, write *la montre* in their notebooks a hundred times and study French for the rest of the time. As for me, I sulked all the way through detention – for one hour – and writing *la montre* fifty times. I still thought she was wrong to punish me for the article that made so little difference.

"To teach you a lesson," she said. "From now on you learn the nouns with their article."

She was cross with us because we all had better marks in Russian than in French. Little did she know that, in the Russian class, we were given good marks for mumbling and that the teacher completed the words for us. As for the home work in Russian, most of the class copied mine in a hurry. On the days we had Russian, my exercise book became the source of strife between my classmates before the lesson. Everybody wanted to get to it first.

Comrade Hulea, the Principal, saw me in the corridor, stopped me and asked where my red scarf was? When I told him I was not a pioneer, his expression became stern. I was down there, with the worst students he had in the school. With those who failed and repeated the year.

Two weeks later, he called me to his office and told me that, being a good student, I was to be made a pioneer in a special ceremony, the following week.

I told my father. He stopped driving nails into a door frame, paused for a while, then looked at me with a strangely blank expression on his face and asked what I thought about it. I just shrugged my shoulders. Then he smiled and said that the scarf could come in handy, as I could always use it as a handkerchief. We laughed.

The big day arrived. I was not looking forward to the ceremony because all eyes were going to be on me. I was uncomfortable with the idea of being singled out again, even if this was a good thing in everybody's opinion. I simply did not like being the centre of attention. You never knew how things would turn out, when you were the centre of attention in our school. The *careu* was the place where you faced criticism and got your punishment for improper behaviour, for being slack, for having a speck of dirt under your nails or wax in your ears. You had to step forward and become the target of all the other students' and teachers' glances and feel unworthy, humiliated and crushed. You had to blurt out your *angajament* – solemn pledge – that you would mend your faults and would become a role model pioneer, an example to be followed by everybody. So, with that in mind, I did not care about being a pioneer anymore. However, I wondered if this could mean that I was going to be treated like everybody else. Whatever happened, I had learned by now how to make everything more bearable, when I was singled out through no fault of my own. In my mind I simply blamed those in control and I felt better. Although I couldn't speak out, I spoke to myself and they couldn't do a damn thing about it.

Comrade Hulea called the teachers and students to the *careu* at 8am. The red, yellow and blue flag was brought in by Luminiţa, the seventh grade girl from Vintere, followed by Horga and Solomie with their shiny red scarves. Comrade Hulea was behind them and, when they reached the centre of the *careu*, he stepped forward and called me to the flag, to make my pioneer pledge. I was blushing all over, fidgeting uneasily and playing with the hem of my shirt, as I looked at the sea of red scarves around me, some of them faded by time, others crinkled from never having been ironed. My red scarf was going to be the newest and brightest in my class.

I touched the tip of the red flag and looked at Comrade Hulea. He nodded.

"I, Flonta Teodor, solemnly pledge …," I started with a shaky voice. I knew everything by heart. Words rolled off my tongue at a quick pace. I pledged that once a member of the Pioneer Organization, I would be a trustworthy son of the People's Republic of Romania. I would be faithful to the people and to the Workers' Party. I would study hard. I would be disciplined and I would honour the red scarf and the duties that came with it.

Then Luminiţa passed the flag to Horga and tied the scarf around my neck, pinning on a little badge with red flames sticking out of its top and wheat ears on both sides. "TOT ÎNAINTE!" (Always Forward!) was written on it.

Now I was a pioneer, like most of the arseholes in my class who, in spite of copying my homework, had often made fun of me for not having the red scarf and the badge.

I had to perform my last act, reciting big words – for the glory of the people, the development of the motherland, the cause of the Party. Then I gave the pioneer salute, my right hand to my eyebrow.

"Înainte!" (Forward!)

"Tot Înainte!" (Always Forward!) said the assembly.

The day after I was made a pioneer, I saw Eugica, the lanky gypsy from Lupoaia, cleaning the toilets in our school courtyard. He pulled the yellow stinky stuff from the hole in the ground in a bucket and spread it on the Principal's vegetable patch. Then he went into the hole with his boots which, being too short, immediately filled with shit. He appeared not to mind and continued to do his work, from time to time cleaning his nose on the sleeves of his jacket, until his face looked yellow too.

When I went up to him and said hello, he gave me a big grin and carried on without saying a word. He was always meek and silent. The most you could get from him was a subdued hello.

Other kids noticed the smell. The girls giggled, as they covered their faces. The boys were pointing at the man. They laughed and pushed each other towards the hole. Then Horga said:

Țiganu când e împărat (Even when the gypsy is an emperor)
Pân la brâu stă în căcat (He is still up to his waist in shit)

12 and 13 year old children can be cruel, and in this case, a group of them joined Horga to form a chorus.

Țiganu când e împărat
Pân la brâu stă în căcat...

Eugica looked at them, smiled and continued his job.

The mob of impertinent, boisterous boys did not relent until Comrade Principal, surprised by this new initiative of singing so loud in the courtyard, came out of his office. The mob broke up and they all turned into angels.

Suspecting some mischief, Comrade Principal asked Eugica what they were saying. Eugica smiled broadly and shrugged his shoulders, which meant that he did not understand.

On the way home, I saw him walking behind me, so I slowed down. I asked him if it was true that he did not understand what the kids were saying. He smiled at me with his eyes and continued munching on the lard and bread the Principal had given him for lunch. I walked with him for a while, thinking how little he had and wondering if his life was ever going to change.

Zero in Maths

Comrade Abrudan was my maths teacher in grade five, as well as my class teacher. He was a short man in his thirties with pointy bones that made his face triangular, his chin forming the acute angle. His lips were constantly red from smacking and licking and he had the habit of coming down from his platform and stopping at one of the desks in the front row. While asking us about homework, he would rub his groin against the corner of the desk. The girls saw his arousal, blushed and struggled for words. During the break, the boldest boys did the Abrudan act and girls ran away, threatening to tell the headmaster. They never did.

Abrudan was the only locally born teacher and the only one who had not completed his degree. He came from a poor family and rumours circulated that he was unkind to his parents, particularly his father. However, he was the School Party Secretary and knew everybody, even people from the villages around Holod.

One day he took me aside and said he had heard that somebody in Lupoaia was keeping bees and was making good honey. Could I ask my mother to investigate this?

I asked Mama.

She said Uncle Doanea kept bees but the honey was very expensive because of the shortage of sugar on the market. She had bought a kilo of sugar from Oradea market, or so she thought, but when she came home had found that only the top two-centimetre layer of the packet was sugar, the remainder was salt. She had been cheated.

I told Abrudan about my Uncle Doanea's bees and he said to get him a litre of honey. Mama asked if he gave me the money for it.

"No," I told her.

"Then he'll have to wait a bit. I don't have money right now."

Abrudan asked me again after a couple of days. He didn't take it well. The morning after he came into the class very gloomy and asked everybody to put their hands on the desk for hygiene control. Dirty hands, dirty nails and soiled ears brought blows from the triangular ruler on the offending part. He gave me a painful blow on the nails with the angle of the ruler, leaving its mark on my fingers. Now he wanted us to place our maths notebook on the desk, to see if we had covered it with brown paper for protection. A few of us hadn't, but mine had the cover torn and detached from the notebook. He went red in the face as he shouted at me, calling me stupid, lazy and dirty before getting the class registry and marking me with a zero in maths. Zero was rarely given, but here I was with high marks in every other subject and a zero in maths. How was I going to tell my father that I'd got a zero in maths? What was I going to get as a final mark? Was I going to pass maths at all? I felt helpless and scared. To make matters worse, he wrote the mark on my report card to take home to my parents. He threatened me further. If I did not come to school the next day with all my books covered in brown paper, things were going to get worse.

Worse than getting a zero, without being tested at all? Nothing left for me to do but cry.

Once home, I told Mama about my zero mark, tears running down my cheeks. She couldn't believe it. She blamed herself for not having sent Comrade Teacher the honey he wanted. We went to the shed together where my father was tinkering around a half-assembled cart and, when he saw me, he wanted to know what had happened to my face.

As I sobbed, Mama took over the explanation. My father couldn't believe that I'd got a zero for the miserable, uncovered notebook. He wanted me to confirm that the Comrade had not asked me any maths question whatsoever, which I did vehemently.

A Sunday's Parents and Teachers meeting was scheduled in the Holod People's House, a month later. When that Sunday came, my father began preparing himself for the meeting from dawn. While he was feeding the oxen and the cow, he chugged a mouthful of *pălinca* from the bottle resting on the windowsill after each pitchfork full of hay.

Mama kept a close watch on him but could do no more than shake her head.

"Don't drink too much, if you are going to the school meeting. You will only say stupid things and make matters worse for your son," she said.

My father looked at her but seemed to be staring into a vacuum.

Then he walked away, his right hand raised and a finger stretched out as if proving a point, the neck of the bottle sticking out from his jacket's pocket. As he descended the slope to Valea Ştefani, we saw him drinking from the bottle.

"It doesn't look good," Mama said.

On the People's House's stage was a long desk where the Principal and some teachers were seated. There were not enough chairs in the room for all the parents and some were standing. Comrade Hulea was talking, when my father entered the hall.

My father heard only half of what was said but he remembered his reason for being there. He raised his hand. With the boldness given to him by the *pălinca*, he caught the Principal off-guard by asking him what sort of school he ran, where bad marks were given without testing the students.

Everybody in the room stared at my father with interest and curiosity. He certainly had guts. The Principal jumped to his feet, surprised and irritated. He asked for my father's name.

"What do you mean, Comrade Flonta? I don't believe any of our school teachers could do such a thing."

"Why then is Teacher Abrudan not here? I would like his opinion on this matter."

"Comrade Abrudan asked to be excused; but I will send for

him if you think he did something like that."

"He did it to my boy, he did it alright. He's got some explaining to do."

Then, between hiccups, my father told Comrade Principal and the other parents the story about my notebook cover. After a while, a nervous Comrade Abrudan arrived and got onto the stage.

"Comrade Abrudan, Mr. Flonta is saying that his son, who is in the fifth grade, has been given a Failure in maths, without being tested. Is that true?"

"With a zero mark," my father said loudly. "I was an ass at school but I did not get a zero mark. My boy is tops, I know that," he added.

"I don't remember the circumstances. I would need to see the register," Comrade Abrudan said.

That sent my father raving mad. Stretching out his right arm with forefinger pointed, he shouted, "You remember bloody well. It was only a month ago. Are you persecuting my son because I am a *chiabur*? What happened to your teachings about this wonderful egalitarian society of yours?"

"Please, Mr Flonta, calm down. We don't want to get into that, do we? For everybody's sake! Let's hear Comrade Abrudan's version. We will settle it, don't worry. If any wrong has been done to your son, it will be remedied. Soon, very soon."

The Principal showed Abrudan the register, and told him that it recorded a zero in maths.

Comrade Abrudan tried to make amends. "Yes. Well... I am sorry I've been too harsh, perhaps... I will definitely look into the matter, no later than tomorrow, Comrade Principal."

My father couldn't hold back and raised his voice even louder as the strength of his conviction grew.

"You had bloody better do that. I am sick and tired of seeing my son suffer unjustly. Isn't it enough that I am suffering unjustly all the time!"

"All right, Mr Flonta, all right. I promise that tomorrow we will fix this, no need to dwell on it further. Calm down, the mistake will be corrected, you have my word," said the Principal.

The next day the Principal, followed by Comrade Abrudan, entered my classroom. We were all frightened because the Principal's appearance meant trouble most of the time and we had to be on our best behaviour. As maths was the first lesson of the day, we had first to sing the national anthem, the two teachers exhibiting all the solemnity they could muster.

The Principal sat at the back of the classroom while Comrade Abrudan opened the register and called me to the blackboard. I was scared stiff but the equations Comrade Abrudan gave me to solve were rather easy. I passed the test and my zero mark was changed into a five, the top mark. It was countersigned on the register by Comrade Hulea.

My parents were pleased, and Mama decided to buy a litre of honey from Uncle Doanea. As Uncle Doanea was at the end of his year's supply, he gave Mama just three quarters of a litre in a litre container. Mama filled the rest with sugar and mixed it in for a few days. I took it to Comrade Abrudan who accepted it, no questions asked, and did not even have the courtesy to thank Mama.

Being my class teacher, he took his revenge on me at the end of the year, when the prizes for the best students were assigned. As usual, we had our school festival, where we presented a program of poetry and drama for the parents. That was followed by the prizes award ceremony. Mama was there alone and I told her I was going to get a prize.

Surprise. The first prize Comrade Abrudan called out went to Burca, a boy from Dumbrăviţa. I exchanged devastated glances with Mama. The second prize was awarded to Floarea, my neighbour, and the third prize to Ioan, a boy from Hodiş.

I was given a mention and, with it, my illusion of being given credit for my results was again shattered, just as it was in the primary school.

Mama went to Comrade Abrudan at the end of the ceremony and told him about my marks and that I should have been given a prize. Comrade Abrudan was not interested and fobbed her off, showing her the list he had concocted with all the names and prizes, where my marks were artificially lowered. Mama insisted that he check the register and he said he would do that and let her know. He never did.

My father decided not to make a fuss about this, but told me to never mind, because what I put up there, in my head, nobody would be able to take from me. He always said that. "My riches," he said, talking about himself, "are the *cazan*, the land and the cattle, but yours are the knowledge up there in your brain. They could take away my cattle, my *cazan* and my land, but they'll never be able to take the stuff from your brains, the stuff you know." That was going to be my power over these thieves, he said. He insisted that knowledge was going to be my salvation. His words began to make sense to me; but I was still angry, a lot angrier still, when I saw the kids showing their prizes to their parents, as if they deserved them. Yet again, all I had to show my own parents was a meagre mention and that hurt.

My paternal grandfather Teodorea
(Teodor Flonta), circa 1933

My maternal grandfather Toderea
(Teodor Andor), circa 1950

A touched-up professional photograph of my parents after they finished
building their new house, circa 1958

Mama and myself in Oradea, circa 1952

Auntie Floritza, Dad, Mama and myself, circa 1957

Grandma Saveta and the *cazan*, which was the official reason why the communists declared my father a *chiabur*

Mos Cule, our neighbour, with whom   Myself at the tender age of 15,
Grandpa Teodorea fought in Italy   1961
during World War I, circa 1970

The main road through the Valley, Lupoaia, with the Church I was
baptized in

Teacher in Hodis at age 18, 1964

With my family
in 1961

Student at
university, 1968

My wife, Ariella, in the courtyard of my parents' house in Lupoaia

Loveless Child

After Stalin's death, my father's *pălinca* business went well. He continued to be a *chiabur* and suffer the consequences, such as paying more taxes and, from time to time, being subject to temporary detentions, but he was allowed, every year, to install his *cazan*, now nationalized, and to employ the same two seasonal workers. They were paid by the state and my father gave them the same amount of *pălinca* per shift as before. He learned fast how to cope with the misfortune of being a *chiabur*, often ending up greasing the palms of officials and people in command, who in turn, would help him out of difficult situations. There was no other way, if he wanted to survive. His life was like that of a sea creature subject to the waves of high and low tides. During the high tides of repression, he was detained and sometimes tortured for incomprehensible reasons, while during the low tides he got some respite and could take care of his family and his business. Fortunately, my father used to say, his youth has prevented him from being crushed against the rocks by the tides, as happened to many people who lost their lives during those turbulent times. What tormented him most was that he never knew exactly when the next high tide was coming in; but sometimes he was lucky and went into hiding, just before it started. When the low tide returned, he resurfaced and was subjected to interrogations by the Militia, nonsensical chores like forced, voluntary work – spreading gravel on the road between Lupoaia and Holod was a Militia favourite and second best was cutting trees in the forest. He could take that as, after the initial bouts of cruelty, the repressive system gradually grew tired, perhaps because everything was decided at the top and so, the enthusiasm of the executors grew less. Then a period of relative calm was established, until the next order from the top.

The drawback, for my father, of having been declared a *chiabur* was that it stigmatized him in the eyes of some villagers, who did not get enough free *pălinca* from him, or had some other bone to pick, often for trivial reasons. They referred to him, in a derogatory way, as *the chiabur*, but only behind his back, as they were cowards who secretely envied his strength and ability to deal with the authorities.

There was none more unhappy with my father than his greedy half-brother Mitru. For years he had been saying that there was no place for two *cazans* in Lupoaia and that my father should have moved to Dumbrăviţa or Forosig. Izvor, where he was located, was a bit out of the way, while my father was established on the Hodişel creek. This was on the main road and customers would rather go to him. Mitru was also a bit heavy-handed with the quota he took from his customers and there was talk that his *pălinca* was of a poorer quality.

When my father told Mitru that he did not intend to move, Mitru resorted to all sorts of tricks to wreck my father's business. One morning my father discovered a strong petrol smell around one of his tubs, where the plums were fermenting. Overnight, somebody had poured a canister of petrol in it and now the whole lot was useless: *pălinca* made from those plums would retain that strong smell and couldn't be sold. My father knew it was Mitru but couldn't prove it.

A few days later when my father met Mitru and told him about the tub, Mitru denied it was him and repeated his advice that my father should move to Dumbrăviţa or Forosig the next season. My father told him that he would consider moving, if Mitru paid him everything he owed him from the time of Grandpa Teodorea's death. Mitru threatened to kill him and made sure everybody in the village knew it.

One day I felt very sick. By the time we left school, I had little energy left. Floarea took my bag and carried it until we were on the road to Lupoaia. I could barely walk and told her to leave me behind. I sat in the ditch in the warm sun. She said she was going to tell my parents to come and pick me up.

I must have fallen asleep or fainted because, when I opened my eyes, Grandma Saveta was stroking my forehead. She wanted to carry me home on her back. She said she was used to carrying firewood and I would not be a problem for her. Her determination made me smile, as I could see myself, taller than she was, on her back, dragging my feet and spurring her on like a horse. How could I be seen, at 12 years of age, on my grandmother's back and not be teased by all the kids at school for the rest of my life? So I walked slowly behind her. After we crossed the Hodișel, she asked me if I had seen Mitru and his cart on the road. I had not and, even if he had passed me, I wouldn't have been able to see anything from the ditch. Just as well, she said, because you never know what that man is capable of. She told me that Veta Ioani had heard that Mitru was waiting, with his axe, in the cart on the road for my father to come from Beiuș. Fearing the worst, Mama had sent Modru to Vintere to alert my father and travel with him.

I asked Grandma what was wrong with Mitru, why he always threatened my father and didn't give him a break. My father didn't do anything to him.

"He grew up as a loveless child. Perhaps that's what is wrong with him," Grandma said. She told me that his mother died when he was very small while Grandpa Teodorea was busy fighting for Franz Joseph. When Grandpa came home, Mitru did not recognize him as his father. When Grandpa married again, Mitru remained with his maternal grandparents. Then they died and Mitru was alone. He was taken in by his father but did not feel any affection for his half-brothers and sisters; he felt the odd one out. "He feels he needs to have more than others, as he was deprived of love as a young child. And he hates anybody who is competing with him. This is very dangerous because he becomes blind with hatred and could harm people."

My father came home with Modru, who had walked as far as Răbăgani that night, to meet his cart.

Mama, a worried frown casting a shadow across her face, told him that he was not to go anywhere alone, while his mad half-brother roamed the roads threatening to kill him.

Mitru was a man of his word. My father was coming home from the *cazan* on a rainy day in November, just after midnight, when he was attacked from behind by two men. He couldn't see their faces but could feel their weight as they bore down on him. He couldn't move or protect his head from being bashed against the hard gravel road, clumps of his hair pulled out. His back was cracking under those huge knees. A large hand squashed his face, stopping him from breathing. A finger went into his mouth and pulled hard, tearing his mouth wider and wider open. One eye was pushed deep down into his skull. His head was like a bouncing ball, up and down, up and down, and with each blow the excruciating pain diminished in proportion to the numbness spreading through his lacerated forehead. He bit with all his might, feeling a warm liquid in his mouth, blood, and he spat out a piece of the attacking finger.

A prolonged, agonized shout, then nothing. He was left lying there in the mud.

After a while he found the strength to get up. He knocked on Auntie Puica's door. She took him in, poured *pălinca* on his wounds and tore a piece of cloth from a bed sheet to bandage his head. My father told her that it was Mitru who had done this to him. Puica did not accept that and said that he must have other enemies.

Mitru was seen with a bandaged hand during the days after the incident. My father did not report him. He was his brother after all, he said.

A Transistor, a Lovely Language

My father was happier than I had ever seen him. In March 1959, the Great National Assembly had announced that the exploitation of man by his fellow man had been resolved, eliminated from our new society along with the *chiabur* class. A stroke of the Party's pen meant my father was no longer a *chiabur*. Now he could look much further than his problems with his silly brother – to a better future. As I was finishing middle school, he decided to send me to study at the *Şcoala Medie Nr. 1*, the High School in Beiuş. This school had a good reputation. It had been founded long ago by Samuil Vulcan, a bishop whose name the school had borne until a few years back. I asked my father why the name had changed. He said that the Communists tried to erase anything of value from people's memory, so that they could take credit for everything. They were the worst thieves on the face of the earth because they stole your name and gave you a new one, in order to demonstrate that they were doing something. "They are like a swarm of locusts that destroy everything in their way; and it will take a long time for things to come back again," he said.

In July, Comrade Hulea took three of us to the High School to sit the entrance exams. We waited to be allowed in, watching other principals arriving with their students in the entrance hall. One of them recognized Comrade Hulea and they started talking to each other. Then Comrade Hulea introduced his boys. I was standing the closest to him and he told his friend that I would eliminate 7 candidates, Horga would eliminate 5 and Buda 3. This made me think of the Securitate, always wanting to eliminate my father. I felt strange listening to Comrade Hulea talking about my being capable of eliminating 7 other students. I did not want to eliminate anybody and I did not want to be eliminated by anybody, just as I did not want my father to be eliminated by the Securitate either. Why did somebody always have to eliminate somebody else in our society of equals?

After my successful exams, I went to Oradea with my father. I saw a portable radio, that ran on batteries, in a shop window. I liked it so much that my father bought it for me, which was fantastic because we had no electricity. That radio kept me happy for many years to come, particularly during vacation time, when I took our cows to pasture. I took the radio with me everywhere I went. I kept it in a red nylon net and everybody knew where I was, because the volume of the radio was up to the maximum. I started listening to music from neighbouring countries and I grew particularly fond of Bulgarian and Serbian music. I listened to the news too, without understanding a word of what was said; but I liked being transported into another world, even if only linguistically. I worked out the Hungarian news fairly quickly, thanks to the few words I heard in the village and to what I picked up during my rare visits to Oradea. Bulgarian and Serbian were more problematic because they were similar to Russian; but soon I worked them out too.

One late afternoon, as the sun was sinking in the sky and casting shadows over the undulating fields of Dumbrava, I came across a radio station in a language I had never heard before. It was so beautiful that I could hardly wait to listen to it again the next day. I discovered that the same program was broadcast each evening. I loved the sound of that language and, when I began to understand a word here and there, my excitement was such that I had to work out what language it was. The words *italiano* and *italiana* popped up often and I assumed it was Italian. I took the radio with me to the bench outside our porch, wanting to share that sound with everybody.

Micula, who had been a prisoner of war in Italy with my Grandpa Teodorea, asked me if I understood Italian. That was Italian alright. He started telling me about his time in Italy with my Grandpa during World War I, about the battle of the Piave River where he and Grandpa were taken prisoner and about the Italians shouting *Kaput* at them, because they were soldiers of the Austro-Hungarian army. Their epaulets, the stars and all the decorations were stripped from their uniforms and their pockets were emptied. The kids grinned at them, throwing biscuits and saying, 'Austria *kaput*.' Although the kids did not know it, the Romanian soldiers, particularly those from Transylvania, were all happy that Austria was *kaput* – they hoped for annexation to Romania. After their initial shock subsided, they had a good stay in Italy. Taken to Cittadella, then to Ferrara and from there to Asinara, the Island of the Asses, they did various jobs for the Italians and even got paid for the work they did. They started understanding a few words and repeating them to the Italians, who shook hands with them and declared that they were brothers. Now old Micula was happy to show me that he had not forgotten his Italian. From then on he often kept me company and told me the few words he still recognized. We listened to Italian songs and he laughed at himself saying *amore, cuore, ti voglio bene, anima mia, ti amo* and he encouraged me to repeat them. Then he said I was better than he was. I loved those words, those expressions and played them again and again in my head, long after Micula had left. They were so beautiful. They filled my mouth with their crystal clear vowels, all the endings pronounced clearly, nothing missing, which gave the words rhythm and rhyme unparalleled in other languages I had heard. From then on I absorbed Italian words quickly.

Micula said that my Grandpa knew more words than he did because he could read and write – and it was a pity that he'd died before he could teach me some Italian himself.

Who Is Going to Look After Our Oxen Now

Autumn arrived in Lupoaia in all its glory. It was the best season of all. The fruit trees in our garden – apricots, plums, pears and cherries – began to shed their yellow-brown leaves, covering the earth with a soft carpet that masked the muddy ground churned up by the rains. The plums had almost finished fermenting and were ready to be turned into *pălinca*, while the insatiable villagers were hoping for better prices.

I was 13 now and, for the first time in my life, I was going to live away from home, at Beiuş High School No. 1. I did not know how many candidates I had eliminated and I did not have the courage to ask Comrade Hulea.

For days Mama prepared the things I was going to take with me. She washed and ironed my new blue-grey uniform, made from recycled material, then she sewed a square black patch on my left sleeve with an inscription embroidered in yellow: "High School No. 1 Beiuş" and underneath "No. 183". This was my identification number and every student at our school had one. Its purpose was to enable teachers and willing citizens to keep us in check by complaining about our bad behaviour outside school, by reporting those students who were seen in town during class time, and those seen holding hands in the street or at the cinema. We were to be strictly controlled and prevented from straying from the path that would lead to our becoming the new men required by the society with a luminous future.

It was a Sunday, September 13, 1959, when I left home. The night before, I checked my heavy wooden suitcase to see that everything was packed. I helped Mama fold my new cotton sheets – I had never slept on cotton sheets before – and my new feather-filled cushion and roll them into the equally new, feather-filled doona, which my father tied with strings at both ends and in the middle. My father tied another piece of string from one end of the bundle to the other, to make a handle.

In a separate bag, Mama stuffed a freshly baked round loaf of bread, a piece of lard wrapped in newspaper, three onions from our garden, the last piece of dry garlic sausage, kept specially for me, four apples and four *pancove*. My father added a bottle of *pălinca*. For the doorman of the college, he said.

I went to bed early but I couldn't sleep until late, excited and nervous about my new adventure. Only a few days earlier, the thought of leaving home had been wholly exciting. My head had been filled with dreams of what it would be like, away from our new, cosy, three roomed house and muddy courtyard. Not anymore. When I heard Mama sobbing, I started crying quietly, tears spilling down my cheeks. I did not want her to hear me.

My father woke me before 2am to catch the train that left Holod station at four o'clock. It took me a while to wake up and only Mama's tearful voice got me out of bed. I did not want to go to school anymore. If my parents had said I could stay home and forget about school, I would not have hesitated. I would have abandoned school altogether.

My father and I began walking, he with the wooden suitcase in one hand and the doona roll held on his shoulder with the other, I carrying the food bag. Mama and Grandma hung behind so that I would not hear them crying. We stopped at the Colnic crossing and embraced, tears streaming down our cheeks, but my father strode on, his steps getting bigger and bigger, as he descended the slope towards Râturi. It took me a few minutes to catch up. We walked silently and, at the entrance to the narrow valley opening onto the Raturi plain, he sighed and said with a broken voice that belied his proud swagger:

"My dear Teodor, my dear son, who is going to look after our oxen now?"

This was just what I needed, after leaving Mama and Grandma crying at the top of the slope. I started sobbing, all the while trying to keep pace with him. And, as he didn't want me to hear him sobbing too, he walked faster and faster.

Those were our last words until we reached Holod station.

I was sad, very sad and, although the darkness hid my tear-drenched face, it lit up the thousand memories of this road, along which I had trudged on my way to the Holod Middle School over the last three years. I remembered the torch Dolea and I made that scared the Valley kids on their way to school, the serpent Dolea and I killed, an act for which we were meant to obtain the forgiveness of seven sins, our falling in the icy Hodişel rivulet in winter, my trips with Mama and Grandma Saveta, taking our hemp to soak in the creek water and later to check that nobody had stolen it, picking blackberries before our long vacation, lying sick in the ditch, waiting for Grandma to come and rescue me, my fear that my father would be killed by Uncle Mitru, climbing to the top of the cliff with Dolea to chase hares, which we never caught.

We walked down the road leading from Beiuş train station to the High School.

My father continued to walk briskly, although there was no reason to hurry now because the dawn was only just breaking, bathing the wide, tree-lined street in front of us with swathes of reddish orange light; and there would not be anyone to open the door. He kept marching on, passing other boys and girls and their family members with their own bundles. I wondered how my father could take such a long step each time, much longer than my steps, even though I was already taller than he was. He had explained to me once that he was forced to do lots of chores as a young boy and learned that one long step was better than two quick steps. It saved you energy and made you less tired. Over time, this would become a habit for me too.

As for my steps, he said, they were short because he had never asked me to do any heavy chores. All I had been required to do was take the cattle to pasture and read the newspapers to him. They looked more like games than chores, because when I took the cattle to pasture, I had fun playing with other children. He also loved to see me reading so well and so quickly. He couldn't read, in a whole day, what I could read in half an hour and that was one of his greatest joys in life, perhaps the greatest, he said.

The Crişul Negru river bridge came in sight and I realised our journey was coming to an end, or at least my journey, as my father would be returning home in the afternoon.

Then I saw Beiuş High School No. 1. I was going to spend four years in that place. It was a solid, old-fashioned, two-storey building, erected a century and a half earlier, with thick walls and many windows. It looked more like a fortress than a school. A heavy, brown door was the only breach in the wall. I had seen this door during my entrance exams but was too busy to worry about being confined behind it. Now, suddenly, I worried about how I would cope in a courtyard enclosed by high walls, without the freedom to roam the fields of Dumbrava and watch the flight of the cranes, or listen to the wolves' howling, or explore the ravines of Hurupa, or just get out into the garden and watch the butterflies and the bees flitting from one flower to another. I felt sorry for myself and the realization, that there was no way out, hit me harder than I expected. So hard, in fact, that I had to pull my cap down to cover my teary eyes and keep a distance from my father. This was neither the time nor the place to cry, as we did earlier, on the plain of Râturi.

When my father and I sat on the wooden suitcase in front of the brown entrance door, a smallish boy of my age appeared from nowhere. One of his shoes was flapping, as its sole was unstuck and his poor clothing matched a sad countenance. He was alone and was carrying only the doona bundle with him. He greeted us and stood next to me. My father asked his name and where he came from. He told us he was Ion Pantea and he came from

Roşia, a village not far away. My father told him he knew where his village was and Ion Pantea smiled. We told him our names and the name of our village, but he did not know where it was. Even when I told him that Lupoaia was next to Holod, he did not have any idea. I told him that Holod was a train station halfway between Beiuş and Oradea. Then he nodded. In the meantime, the few boys and girls, who had come on our train, reached the school door and we all studied each other, feigning indifference.

At seven o'clock, a short man with a limp, wearing a long, heavy coat over his shoulders, crossed the road, with keys dangling from his hand. He stopped to talk with my father. They seemed to know each other. He opened the big door and disappeared inside. After a couple of minutes he opened the door again and invited my father in. My father took the food bag from my hands and entered the building.

When he came back, I asked him how did he come to know the doorman. He told me that it was a long story and that, one day, I would find out for myself that, sometimes, it is more important to know the doorman than the many bosses above him. I noticed the bottle of *pălinca* had found its new master.

A tall, young man with a pointy head, just a few years older than I was, made his way in through the main entrance and, in no time, was back again, telling us that we could enter the building. He called us in alphabetical order and the doorman pulled in an iron bar through which he controlled the entrance into the rectangular courtyard, which was enclosed by two-storey buildings. The canteen was in the basement on the right hand side, below the dormitory for girls. On the left side, an L-shaped building was the boys' dormitory. The smaller side of the L wing was used as storage space for the canteen. There was a well a few metres from the boys' dormitory.

At the lower end of the courtyard was the infirmary and, between the infirmary and the canteen, there was just enough space for a truck to pass through and bring in weekly provisions. Right at the bottom end, beyond the infirmary, stood the high external wall, which separated the school from the marketplace on the

Crişul Negru River. The young man, who introduced himself as Comrade Dragnea, took us to the top floor and showed us into a huge dormitory with twenty-four beds and a terracotta stove.

After thirty minutes we were back in the courtyard surrounded by those high buildings. I realised I was going to live there, day in day out, and I felt sad. I could see myself like the little sparrow my grandpa had caught in the pumpkin trap when I was a boy. When he opened the pumpkin, she lay down on the bottom, crouched and motionless, without reacting or trying to escape. As long as she was kept in the dark, it seemed that she had accepted her fate. When she glimpsed the light, the wide open space from Grandpa's hands, she started yearning for freedom by fluttering her wings; she was longing for what she knew, for what was natural to her. Was I going to be like that little sparrow? Was this college, with its high walls, going to be my pumpkin trap? How well would I cope with the darkness projected by those walls bearing down on me? I was going to miss my Italian broadcasts for sure, particularly the songs. I was already fond of Nilla Pizzi, Claudio Villa, Domenico Modugno and Tony Dallara. I recalled my father's hiding place, that hole in the ground under the manger in our stable. In proportion, his hole was much smaller than the sparrow's trap and yet, he told me that he felt freer there than outside. Suddenly my own situation looked more bearable.

Little Soldiers

That evening, when we were allowed to go to the dormitory, Pantea and I chose beds next to each other, not too far from the stove. These metal beds were different from the one I had at home; they were low and you could sit on them comfortably, while at home you were so high up you needed to get onto the bench first and then get into bed. The mattress here was still hard but it did not have straw in it like the one at home, where you could hear the rustling with your every move. I noticed Pantea was good at making his bed and I tried to copy him, surreptitiously watching him with my tongue sticking out of the side of my mouth in concentration. Seeing my inexperience he smiled, then told me to wait as he would give me a hand. I told him Mama always did it for me.

"She should have taught me, as your mother did with you," I said to him.

His smile was replaced by sadness. "My mother died."

I was shocked and did not know what to say. I mumbled a sorry and Pantea said it was okay. How could that be okay? In Lupoaia all my friends had their mothers. Some were quite bad, I thought, remembering the beatings Mircea used to cop from his mother, but some were good, like Mama who would have given anything to see me happy. I pitied Pantea but I didn't know how to express it. I remembered being so afraid, when I was small, that the Securitate might kill Mama. I used to cry by myself, out of sight of the other children. Mircea saw me once and he couldn't understand how I could cry about Mama's death when she was alive and well. Now I considered myself so lucky to have a living mother and a wonderful Grandma. After a while I asked Pantea if he had a grandmother. He shook his head and my compassion for him grew. I had never imagined life without Mama and Grandma. Pantea's family situation moved me deeply and, so as not to let him see my tears, I left the room and went to the lavatory. When I returned, my bed was made.

That Sunday night there were only the two of us sleeping in the dormitory. Other boys were scattered in other dormitories. I asked Pantea why he had come one day early and he said that anywhere was better than home. His father had remarried and his stepmother was mean and vented her anger on him, beating him for no reason, and his father always took her side. But he got along with his four year-old half-brother, he said. How lucky I was not to have these complications in my life, I thought. While we had the Securitate against us, intent on killing us all, I pitied Pantea for not knowing what motherly or fatherly love was and what a family should be.

Most students arrived the next day. I told Pantea we should go and meet our companions from the Middle Schools. He was not very enthusiastic and told me that his cousin Vasalica, an arsehole who always dobbed on him, was among them and he did not want to see him. We'll have plenty of time together, he said, because we are in the same class. He preferred to come with me and meet Horga and Buda from my school and show them the dormitory and storeroom.

On Monday morning we had our first unpleasant experience. Comrade Dragnea came at six o'clock sharp to wake us up, shouting and beating a metal rod against the bed frame. He wanted us ready in the courtyard – and within thirty minutes – for the *careu*. Pantea and I rushed out of our beds as if they were on fire, reaching for our blue-grey clothes, but some boys stayed behind. He helped me make my bed and, after washing hastily, we made it in time for the assembly. Those who did not get up straight away were hurled down the stairs by Comrade Dragnea, with half their clothes in their hands. Little soldiers at the mercy of the Commandant.

A few minutes later we saw grade eleven students coming down at their leisure and asked ourselves if the rules were not the same for everybody. We assembled in a *careu*, just us boys, and were told that at seven o'clock sharp, we were to line up in pairs in front of the canteen, for our breakfast. At 7.30 we would have to assemble again in the bigger courtyard for the school *careu*, where the Principal would talk to us. At 8.00 sharp we were to be at our desks.

Just before seven o'clock the girls came down and lined up in front of us for the canteen. They did not take part in our *careu* and were accompanied by Comrade Mornea, a young lady with big front teeth and a red scarf around her neck. I noticed the girls holding hands while standing in front of the canteen. There were two shifts at the canteen and the girls were always in the first. We were counted by Comrade Dragnea and Pantea and I got a place in the first shift too. The veterans from higher grades did not seem to hurry up and looked as if they preferred the second shift. Later we learned that, after they had their normal breakfast, they finished off the leftovers too, or at least, those that the kitchen staff couldn't hide in time.

That first day they gave us cumin soup for breakfast, which was yellow water with not a hint of fat in it, and a piece of bread with a little slice of solid red jam. The soup tasted dreadful and, after smacking my lips and pulling a face at the first mouthful, I couldn't eat anymore. Pantea asked me if he could have it, and ate it right away, gulping it down as if he had never eaten before. I munched on the bread and jam, longing for the sausages in my suitcase; but the storeroom was closed in the mornings. I went hungry until afternoon, when I would have eaten rocks if they had been put on the menu. What a difference from my typical breakfast at home – with fried lard and raw onions, or sausages, kept by Mama for me in jars with melted lard, that would not go bad even in the heat of summer. I had not drunk milk since I was little, when my father had forced me to and I vomited. The doctor told him to let me be. Sometimes Mama kept the cream for me and I liked that. When I was really hungry, she spread melted lard, with all the cracklings, on slices of bread. If I did not feel like lard, she would spread sunflower oil on bread and put sugar on top – and I liked that too.

For lunch we had cumin soup again – most probably the leftovers from breakfast – and cabbage with fatty meat. I forced myself to eat half of the cumin soup and, being hungry, I devoured the cabbage. I then went to the storeroom and cut out a chunk of sausage and bread and savoured it in the dark, like a thief. For dinner we had fettuccine with cabbage. The cabbage tasted like the one we had for lunch. We also had rice pudding. This meal met with my taste buds' approval more than the previous two. I was still hungry and again had to resort to my suitcase provisions.

The next day we had tea for breakfast – red tea with a strange taste. For me, all tea would have had a strange taste, as I had only drunk linden tea before, which was made with the flowers and the leaves I used to gather from Auntie Sofia's huge tree, next to the waterhole behind her house. Again, we ate bread and red jam but there was vegetable soup and beans with sausage for lunch. I finally thought that I had a chance of surviving in that place.

Unanimous Decision, the Egghead

A few weeks into the school year, Marton, the year eleven student and secretary of the School's Youth Communist Organization, came to our class, just before the last two lessons of the day, Latin and Music. He had been raised by the local orphanage and had achieved good results at school, and this combination made him the perfect candidate for the position. He was robust, tall, sporty and muscular, fitting the image of the new man of tomorrow. He told us we had to elect a class secretary for the Organization, who would report directly to him. As we had all received our membership cards, a name had to be put forward. Everybody looked at me.

I pretended not to see, keeping my head low whilst a blush spread over my face. They said my name, but I said no. Marton said I couldn't say no. Then I told him my father was a *chiabur*. I had found the best excuse, I thought. He said that there were no more *chiaburs* in our society. Wasn't I going to the Political Awareness lessons regularly? There was no more exploitation in our People's Republic and the Decree of March 1959 spelled that loud and clear. I felt trapped. The Party had me cornered, just as it did my father. They had cornered him, for having the *cazan* and now they had cornered me, for having a better brain than some others.

So, by unanimous consent, I became the secretary of the youth Communist organization for my class. I would have to meet Marton and the other class secretaries to prepare for the school general meeting, where I would have to make the solemn promise, on behalf of my class, that we were going to become new men – vouching for the girls too – and fight for the luminous future towards which the Party was guiding us.

Marton left and everybody congratulated me. Little did they know how much I hated what they had done to me. My first thoughts went to my father. I could see the sneer on his face. I could hear his words ringing in my ears, just like those he used when I told him about my prowess in Russian in grade four. Most of all, I couldn't bring myself to utter all the lies I would have to tell the class, in front of the whole school. I was not made of the same material as the Comrades Petroi, as some of my teachers, as this Marton fellow. I had to get out of it.

First, though, I had to face a new subject, Latin. It should have been easy for me, as I was doing fine in both Russian and French. The first class was a bit of a disappointment. Comrade Trifa, a short man with narrow shoulders and broad hips, dragged his left leg into the classroom, making a scratching noise on the floor, and went straight to his desk. He wore thick round glasses on his pale, oval face, and his bald head looked like an egg sitting on its wider end. Students of higher grades predictably called him the 'egghead.'

He called our names from A to Z, in a slurred, monotonous voice, with his thick glasses almost glued to the register, which made us laugh. Some of the more mischievous students tried to mimic his tone when answering 'Present' to the roll-call. In the middle of the roll-call, Comrade Trifa banged his fist on the desk and said he could see what each of us was doing. He went into a tirade about what was acceptable behaviour and what was not, all the while frothing at the mouth as if he were having a fit.

Then he went back to the roll-call until he finished. After that, we opened our books and he tried to explain grammar rules to us. He got lost in between the words and missed others, so we couldn't understand much. We put more effort into playing games and talking to each other, rather than listening to Comrade Trifa and his precious Latin. He couldn't bear it any longer and shot from behind his desk, dragging his left foot as quickly as he could.

He reached for Borza, took him by the sideburns and lifted him up in anger, frothing at the mouth and spilling incomprehensible words. Borza, the bully, cried in front of the whole class and his reputation was tarnished.

After a few weeks, Comrade Trifa, who had put up bravely with our lack of discipline and our cruelty, demonstrated how one should behave with vicious, little creatures without compassion for anybody but themselves. He gave us an *extemporal*, an instant, half-hour, written test that counted towards our grade, and we all failed. By the end of the term we had improved a bit, in both Latin and in our respect for Comrade Trifa, who, I thought, had made a big effort not to strangle some of us. We began greeting him more loudly each morning, when he entered the school courtyard dragging his feet.

Comrade Moghioroș was our music teacher. His name always reminded me of the man, whose portrait had been on the wall ever since I saw him in first grade, but he was a skinny man and appeared much taller than he was. He liked making us sing the Internationale and the national anthem, as well as trying to spot those who lip-synced, like me. When he came closer and listened to my singing, he stopped the choir and shouted that I was singing like a farting donkey.

He failed me in music in grade eight, but he was overruled. The school's policy had him review my mark and turn it into a 7 because I had good marks in the important subjects. After that, Comrade Moghioros, who spoke with a mild Hungarian accent, was careful when he marked me.

Sinusitis and the Fish with a Missing Tail

November was a very cold month. The ground was already frozen and our blue grey uniforms barely kept out the chill. The frosty air rose up my nose and straight to my forehead. I felt I was going to freeze from the inside out. A throbbing pain, just above my right eyebrow, was becoming unbearable. During my visit home, Grandma had made a polenta hot patch, very hot, she had insisted, because it was going to melt the rot and drain it out. It did not work. So she crushed a big, raw onion, wrapped it in a towel and tied it around my head, with the onion right over my eyes. It produced tears but did not cure my pain. She tried garlic and then, on the off-chance that it might work, she remembered that raw cold potato slices, freshly cut, were good for warts and, who knows, they might be my cure; but nothing could relieve my suffering.

The infirmary nurse sent me to the hospital to see Dr. Racota, the ear, nose and throat specialist. He was married to my French teacher. A robust man of a few words, he intimidated me with his white coat and that round mirror fixed on his head.

"Sinusitis. It has to be operated on," said Dr. Racota.

Well, puncturing my right sinus to clear the inflammation.

For me, the sinusitis cloud had a silver lining. The day I was to go to hospital I was due to meet Marton and contribute ideas to the general meeting. He replaced me with Vasalica, Ion Pantea's snivelling little cousin, who was only too happy to become his puppet.

Long live sinusitis, I thought. I would have been sicker if I had been forced to do what Marton wanted me to do.

My father came and took me to the hospital, just 200m away from the school. He told me that he had visited Dr. Racota's home and left two bottles of *pălinca* for him. He was impressed by how nice Mrs. Racota was as well. He said he had found out that Mrs. Racota taught English too, and wanted me to study English with her as a private student. I did not say anything but I was worried about her two daughters. At 14, I was excessively self-conscious. How could I, a peasant boy, go once or twice a week into my teacher's city house with my dirty shoes, with access to a shower only every second Saturday, and be around girls a couple of years younger? I told my father I had a lot to study anyway and I did not feel well, as he could see. I couldn't tell him about my apprehension at finding myself in the presence of the teacher's daughters and I think he accepted the latter of my reasons, because he did not believe that anybody could ever be too busy. He expected people to work hard because work never killed anybody, only gave you more freedom. While I did not see his point about work and freedom, I was happy that he did not insist too much on my learning English. It was a decision I came to regret in later years.

Dr. Racota smiled, the round mirror attached to his forehead, and sat down on the swivelling chair in front of me. Behind him stood a waist-high cabinet with lots of small drawers, which might once have been white. On top of the cabinet lay syringes of different sizes, scissors, pinchers and shiny rods with round tips. I looked around, wringing my hands nervously and breathing hard through my mouth, in an attempt to be a man and calm down. He pushed a cotton stick with anaesthetic up my nose. Not for long, though, because he picked up a huge syringe as thick as a salami, with a needle like a pencil. I began to panic.

"Never mind. It's big, but it's not going to hurt," he assured me.

The nurse gripped my head from behind.

He pushed hard. I could see the veins in his neck popping out and his face reddening. I heard the bone cracking, but he did not stop and kept pushing until he met no more resistance.

My feet, under a white sheet, went wobbly and the nurse's grip on my head made me uncomfortable.

"When you feel cold in the cavity above the eye, you blow your nose very hard. Right?"

Then he pushed the piston of the syringe and I heard a gurgling sound above my eyebrow and it felt cold. I blew my nose as hard as I could.

A stream of yellow pus, mixed with little patches of clotted blood, squirted out of my nose into the kidney shaped bowl, onto the sheet covering me and onto the doctor's white coat.

"Never mind," he said. "Here we go again."

This time the stream was clearer, more clotted blood than yellow pus. He repeated this operation again.

The nurse changed the full bowl and the doctor detached the syringe from the needle and attached a smaller syringe to it.

"This is medication," he said and pushed the piston to its limit.

I closed my eyes and felt my head pulled down by the doctor forcing the needle out. When I opened my eyes I saw a yellow cream dripping from my nose into the bowl.

The nurse stuffed my nostril with cotton.

I stayed in hospital for a week. Ion Pantea came to visit me a couple of times. He said he would have liked to come more often but Comrade Dragnea would not sign his permit. He tried to sneak out once but was caught by the doorman and reported to Comrade Dragnea.

My father came every second day and once brought Mama with him. Her bright smile made me feel better. Mama had cooked a big fish for me, five or six times bigger than the little fish we used to catch in the Hodişel. This was a fish without a tail.

I asked Mama about the missing tail.

"This is a new kind of fish," my father laughed. "Only for hospitalized people."

Mama blushed and told me that she was given the fish by Solomie, a friend of my father's from Holod. She had put it on the table as she was preparing the frying pan, flour and oil. By the time she turned around, the cat had dragged the fish down to the floor and was feasting on its tail. Mama chased her away, cut the fish tail off, washed the fish many times and cooked it for me.

Tail or no tail, this was the best fish I had eaten in my life and it made Mama happy, seeing me eating with such gusto.

My father bought a new *cuşma* for me, a black sheepskin cap for winter. It was not the usual cheap, pointy, black *cuşma* that most kids and men wore during winter. This was a round cap with a flat top, which could be pushed inside to achieve a nicely-shaped form, like the ones seen on the heads of generals or Party officials. I don't know where my father found it because you couldn't see such a thing in a normal shop. The *cuşma* also had a double brim that hugged my head and kept it warmer than usual. I loved it and could hardly wait to strut around the boarding school courtyard.

It was cold outside when I left hospital, colder than when I went in.

My father was there waiting for me to get dressed, holding his bag on his knees, with another bottle of *pălinca* for Dr. Racota.

I did not have cotton up my nostril anymore and I felt the chilly air freezing my forehead from the inside again. No more throbbing or pain though.

Some kids from grade ten and eleven saw my *cuşma* and were intrigued by it. They admired it, they said, and were taking turns patting my head a bit too hard for friendliness. My forehead was throbbing with pain. After they finished patting, Moga from grade eleven grabbed my *cuşma* and ran away with it, calling others to play football with it. My beautiful *cuşma* was ruined in the mud of the courtyard.

I ran from one to the other, trying to grab my *cuşma,* but the hooligans were having too much fun. Then, hardly able to stop myself from crying, I went straight to Comrade Dragnea and reported them. I saw them that evening cleaning the toilets, with gloom on their faces and hatred in their eyes.

An Olympiad, Showers and Girls

Comrade Caimac, the history teacher, was a caricature of a man – short, with a round belly protruding from under the colourful Chinese-type jacket he always wore, and the funny 'r' he couldn't roll on his tongue. We were not impressed with his long explanations of every mistake we made. On the other hand, when he latched onto one of us, the rest of the class were sure not to be interrogated and made as little noise as possible, so as not to distract him from his ramblings.

When I was in grade nine he organized a History Olympiad and, surprisingly, I won. I was a quiet boy as opposed to the more flamboyant Alexandru and Popovici from town; and Comrade Caimac looked long and hard at me and asked me if I had cheated. We were not allowed to take any books or papers into the room and I told him that. He accepted it and started a long speech about the value of history in society, how the Party viewed the work of historians as central to the building of the new man, and how history will tell generations to come about our struggle in building a luminous future for them. As I was listening, a smile spread over my face at the thought of what my father would have told Comrade Caimac, who must have interpreted my smile the right way and commended me for my attitude. I blushed and he said I was modest too. That term, I could do nothing wrong in Comrade Caimac's eyes. It put pressure on me to try to keep up with history. In the end, when I did a little worse, he expressed his disappointment but gave me the benefit of the doubt, because he wanted to show that we got good marks as a result of his excellent teaching.

Every morning at 6am, Comrade Dragnea raged into our dormitory, cane in one hand, a bottle of water in the other.

"Wake up!" he would shout, beating the cane against the metallic foot of the bed.

Twenty sleepy bodies, with eyelids drooping, sat on the bed waiting for him to pass through into the next dormitory.

This was a cold morning, wintry cold; and the fire in the terracotta stove had died early in the night. When Comrade Dragnea left the room, twenty bodies fell flat onto the beds and disappeared under the covers.

The next round was due in ten minutes. This time Comrade Dragnea did not make any noise but started uncovering everybody's feet. Some of us jumped out of bed and hit the lockers, to dress. For those who remained sleeping in bed, he had a nasty surprise. He opened their toes and placed pieces of paper in between, then he took a match and set fire to the paper. Screaming and disoriented, the small group of students left their beds faster than rats abandoning a sinking ship. Ion Popa's doona caught fire. Terrified, he jumped out of bed, bellowing like a wounded beast, dragging the doona onto the floor and dancing on it to put the fire out. In the meantime, the smoke had filled the area around his bed and the smell of the burned feathers had spread. Unperturbed by the event, Comrade Dragnea shouted his orders.

"You have five minutes to be ready, naked torso and towel, in the corridor!"

We left Ion Popa to clean up the mess and marched briskly from the first floor to the courtyard. Comrade Dragnea made us do twenty warm-up laps, before giving us 5 minutes to wash our faces at the well, in the freezing cold. It was often like this – a violent start to our school days.

Washing and hygiene were not a high priority for our administrators. We were given clean sheets and a clean pillowcase once every two weeks and, if for some reason you did not collect them at the prescribed time, you had to wait until the next round, in two weeks' time.

As for showers, they were every Saturday afternoon, for girls and every second Saturday, for boys. The shower room was in the basement of the boys' dormitory and had ten showers, on one side and ten, on the other. At the end of the room there was the coal water boiler.

Comrade Dragnea strutted up and down behind us, his face obliterated by steam.

"Hurry up! You have five minutes left, you have two minutes left, you have half a minute…"

If he saw anybody getting aroused by the hot water, he sneaked from behind, swift as a tiger, and let his cane fall on the offending organ, leaving a trace not only on the organ itself but also on the boy's brain.

The girls had their showers before us and, giving free rein to our fantasies, we watched them from our first floor. They walked in a line, with their soap and towels, flanked by Comrade Mornea. We clapped our hands in unison and shouted questions about which girl wanted to have her back scrubbed. In spite of Comrade Mornea's warnings, one or two girls in the line always smiled at us, so we placed bets on the names of the girls most likely to favour us with their smile. The winner was going to shout the question alone, to the next lot of girls.

"Would you like me to scrub your back, baby?"

They looked even more appealing after the shower, coming back in the same Indian file, with their hair tied in a ponytail or spread over their shoulders.

Mares, Party Activists and Free Will

The Party activists became relentless in their pursuit of peasants to join the collective. My father knew, in his heart, that his land would be gone some time but he was too strong-willed to accept it. So, realising that his faithful oxen were old and tired, he decided to replace them with horses. With angst in his heart, he took Iambor and Mojar to Holod one day and had them loaded onto a truck heading for the Salonta abattoir. Mama told me he came home crying.

In the 1960 school holidays, the three of us went to Tinca market and checked out the horses. There were only a couple of mares that caught my father's attention and captivated me. Mama conceded they were nice, but were they good for the hills of Lupoaia? Will they draw a full cart up the Colnic slope, during the muddy season, without slipping back?

"Let's find out," my father said.

He convinced the owner of Boaba and Doina, as they were called, to allow him to put them to the test. The three of us got in the cart and walked the horses, then trotted and then galloped them in the empty field nearby. Mama was scared during the gallop but she was impressed.

The most difficult of all tests was to block the front wheels of the cart and see if the mares would still draw it. It was known that some horses, under severe strain, would refuse to draw a cart and no amount of whipping would make them move forward. Even when some peasants used hot irons to burn their flesh, the horses would refuse. Only my father stayed in the cart. After the first hard pull, the two mares had no problem in raising dust behind the cart as they drew it through the market, to the admiration of the onlookers.

My father was not content with that. He blocked all four wheels, but the cart was still being dragged at speed by Boaba and Doina. His mind was made up. And mine too. Mama did not commit herself, and that meant a yes.

I was in love with the two mares, particularly with Boaba's supple body and slender legs, which were fit for a race horse. Her chestnut-red head with its white patch in the middle was always held high with pride. Mircea and I began to take the two of them to the Hodişel to give them a good wash, with a bunch of soapwort and dry them with straw.

One afternoon, just after sunset, Modru and I decided to try the mares by galloping up the road to Dumbrava and back. I was more cautious on Boaba's back, because we did not have a saddle and stirrups, only a bridle without the bit. On our way back, I kept Boaba behind Doina and, as we approached our home, I set her into a light trot. Suddenly, Doina bolted. Modru couldn't stop her. Afraid of being taken to the stable at that speed and having his head chopped off by the door beam, he jumped off and broke his left arm. Doina galloped into the courtyard like a bullet and slowed down, only when she reached the stable.

For those living on the Hill, the Colnic was the only access by cart to their homes. One rainy April day, my father had Doina and Boaba carry sand from the Vintere cave. For the first and longest part of the Colnic, the two mares did a good job but, when they reached the great curve at the intersection with the Râturi road, they stopped pulling. The road was full of small stones and my father had difficulty finding a rock to wedge under the cart's wheels, and it began to roll slowly towards the precipitous edge. He whipped the mares and shouted at the top of his voice, trying to spur them on; but they were dragged backwards by the cart. My father tried to stop the cart rolling down the cliff' but, once one wheel was over the edge, he stood no chance. The horses were dragged down and fell on top of each other, with the cart smashed in half. My father cut the harness off Boaba and she sprang back to her feet, then he cut Doina free and both mares came out of the accident unscathed – but they were mentally scarred forever. Whenever they saw that slope, no matter whether the cart was full or empty, they would quiver and stop, and my father would have to untie them from the cart and ask Norea or Pilea to come with their oxen to rescue him. Once the cart was 10m past the curve, the mares were happy to pull it again.

Four Party activists, one of them a woman with a bad reputation, arrived by train at Holod station, where a cart and horses were waiting. They were taken to the Lupoaia Council and received by the newly anointed Party Secretary, Comrade Picu Petroi himself, along with the Young Council Secretary, Ilie, two militiamen and Collectivization Committee members. Their mission was to beat the villagers' brains into submission and make them sign the application to join the collective. Collectivization was now the Party's highest priority. It had to happen at any cost. Their first task was to instruct Comrade Picu Petroi, Comrade Ilie, the Collectivization Committee members and the two militiamen on how to go about their business in order to achieve maximum success in minimum time.

The militiamen were asked to bring the peasants before the committee. Each husband and wife were made to sit down together. The woman activist was the most vicious and, if they refused to join, she became so furious that the two people left the room totally bewildered and humiliated. Nonetheless half of the village signed, mostly those classified as poor peasants, because they were intimidated by the committee or because they were told that, at last, they would be sitting at the same table as the richer people of the village.

My father was found at home by Mititescu and brought in. Mama refused to go. He was grilled by the committee. They told him that many people in the village were following his example, refusing to sign, which in itself amounted to subversion. They tried to persuade him that it was in his best interest to join the collective. Other villages had been collectivized for ages and their production had increased considerably. The Soviet Union flourished and the Stakhanovists popped up like mushrooms, in agriculture and in the factories. The new man was successfully forged there.

My father told them that he had heard, from the war returnees, that the kolkoz was a disaster in the Soviet Union and life was miserable there, much worse than in Romania. He went on to say that, if you deprive a man and his family of the basics, such as food and freedom, then the likelihood of his becoming a so-called new man was nil. The man was condemned to use all his energy to look for those basics, essential to his survival. He also argued with them that Lupoaia shouldn't be collectivized, because it was hilly, susceptible to erosion by rain, and the land, being clay, was not very fertile. To cut my father's arguments short, Comrade Picu Petroi, with his elephantine subtlety, suddenly brought my future into it. He thought I should be given a chance to study, as I was a good student; and it seemed that my father did not understand that. What would the son think of a father, who couldn't overcome his own selfishness, who was prepared to deny his only son a luminous future?

My father squared his shoulders, defiantly raised his chin and told him that my future did not depend on his joining the collective. It depended on my brains.

He did not sign. He was playing for time. He left – without asking permission – and the committee were fuming because they couldn't keep him in check.

More peasants entered the room and some came out crying. They had signed their land over, the land of their forefathers. Whenever the members of the committee saw a weakness in the peasants' arguments or any indecision, they pounced on their prey with the rapidity of a venomous serpent. Every time they were successful, they congratulated themselves. It was a gleeful and wicked conspiracy of predators.

Once this first phase finished, they allowed the recalcitrant peasants breathing space of two or three days. Everybody hoped the activists had left. They had not; and the peasants were paid a visit by all the committee members on the third day.

Our turn came. They entered the courtyard, went to the veranda – where some wheat was stored in a big wooden box, went up the ladder into the attic and poked their hands into a mound of grain. They found pears, apples and walnuts, corn still on the cob, and sunflower seeds; but they looked irritated, when they saw the lard of half a pig hanging from a beam and dripping onto the attic floor, which was made of oak boards plastered with clay. A couple of committee members got their hands and clothes dirty. My father refused to have anything to do with them. Mama had to give them a towel and I poured water from a pitcher for them to wash. They saw the stables and complained that the cow, Joiana, was not clean enough, as she had patches of dung on her rump. The biggest complaint of all was that the stable was not freshly painted. They moved onto the garden and found the toilet unhygienic. They also found the straw pile and the haystack too close to the house and proclaimed them a fire hazard.

The young Council secretary, his head bent over his book and pencil working furiously, recorded their complaints – which in the meantime, had become infringements of the law. A fine was imposed for each infringement.

My father refused to sign the record.

They asked Mama to sign. She declined, saying that she was not the man of the house.

All the peasants visited were asked to sign the record, like the one they tried on my father. Some refused to sign but others did, to avoid paying the fine. Those who signed the minutes were called to a meeting at the People's Council a few days later, and Ilie congratulated them on having signed the application to join the collective, of their own free will. They did not know that, under the sheet they had signed, was carbon paper with an already typewritten application to join the collective; their signature was now impressed on that application.

Some protested, saying that was not the way to treat decent people, and some asked why they were treated worse by Romanians than they had been treated by the Hungarians during the Empire, and what luminous future could they have, when they were cheated openly, as if they were blind and stupid or both?

Comrade Picu Petroi, perhaps fearing a rebellion, jumped to his feet and, choosing his words carefully, asked them if they opposed the great work of the Party, aimed at improving the peasants' conditions, and if they had anything against the great mass of peasants, who saw benefit in joining the collective.

The peasants knew that, if they said the wrong words, they would be accused of anticommunist behaviour and be considered rebels to the cause of Communism. That meant condemnation by the People's tribunals or even deportation to Bărăgan. They accepted their fate. Nonetheless, the Party Secretary asked them, now that they had signed – of their own free will – to persuade other peasants to join the collective. After a few days, they were again called to the Council and told that the Party, in its wisdom and magnanimity, had waived their fines. The others had to pay the fines under duress; they were threatened that their children would suffer at school and they would not be authorized to sell their produce in the markets.

On a Mission with a White Envelope

It had been a warm spring day. Evening was already showing through the windows of the reading room. Comrade Dragnea was pacing up and down, cane in hand. I was thinking of supper and the free hour before the dormitory doors opened. I had finished my homework for the following day and was keeping my political information notebook open, to give the impression that I was keen to memorize the guidelines and the directives of the Party. It always worked with Comrade Dragnea.

Comrade Mornea, the female students' tutor, tiptoed into the room and made straight for Comrade Dragnea with a smile on her face. They were lovers, everybody knew that, and her arrival was a feature of almost every session Comrade Dragnea had with us. He bent his tall body towards her, as he always did, and she whispered something in his ear, pushing her breasts up towards him. There was no smiling after that. She just left – and we thought something was brewing between the two lovers. 15 year-old boys like us paid close attention to relationships between the sexes.

Comrade Dragnea came straight to my desk and told me that I had to go to the Vice Principal's office. I wanted to ask why but one did not ask questions when summoned by Comrade Berbec. As I did not get up immediately, Comrade Dragnea looked at me with a question mark on his face.

"Now?" I asked.

"Yes, right away," he said with a sense of urgency.

He followed me and I became very worried as we crossed the courtyard, towards the east wing of the building and the Principals' offices. I thought about my behaviour over the past week, trying to find something I might have said or done, somebody I might have talked to, what marks I got, anything that might have caused this sudden invitation to Comrade Berbec's office. I was preparing my autocriticism just in case, but nothing stood out in my mind.

I took a deep breath and knocked on the door. "Come in," said a voice.

Comrade Dragnea pushed me in and closed the door behind me.

Comrade Berbec stood as I entered his room, which was almost as large as our classroom. A cigarette was smouldering in an ashtray full of butts. The window behind him was half-opened and the breeze made the gray curtain flutter its torn fringes. He circled his cluttered desk, came to the front, then leaned his backside on it and crossed his arms. His gaze moved over me as he appeared to scrutinize my posture, my clothes, my grooming, my face. I saw the portraits of Marx, Engels and Lenin on the wall over his head.

"So, you are Flonta Teodor," he said with a half smile.

He was a small man with a baritone voice and a forest of curly hair on his head that made him look as if he were wearing a dense wig. He was a primary school teacher from Vaşcău, without a degree and the only staff member who did not teach a class. He dealt with all the behavioural and administrative problems of the students.

"Yes, Comrade Principal."

"The two of us have a problem to solve – a big problem," he said.

"I didn't do anything, Comrade Principal."

"I know, I know. You are not the problem, we all know that. You are a very good student," he said in a conciliatory tone. "How were your results last year?" he asked.

"I took the second prize for my year," I said.

"You see, you are not the problem. And let me say that you are a very bright student, with a great future."

He looked me straight in the eyes and suddenly asked, "Is

there a collective in your village?"

"Not yet, Comrade Principal."

"You know there's going to be one, don't you?"

"Yes."

"In fact, my sources are telling me that many citizens have already joined."

He paused to gauge my reaction. I didn't know – and my face must have conveyed that, because he soon pressed on.

"This is the only way towards a real Communist society and, as we teach you here, the only way forward for our nation and for the whole world. By the way, do you regularly attend the Political Awareness lessons?"

"Yes, Comrade Principal."

"Good, good. I heard you took the first prize in the History Olympiad. Congratulations."

"Thank you, Comrade Principal."

"What do you think about collectivization?"

I did not answer. I knew I had to say something.

"Tell me. Don't be afraid."

"I don't know."

"You don't know what? What collectivization is? Or what it will do for our future?"

"I know what collectivization is."

"And you know that the Party teaches us, that the only way to become masters of our destiny, is to renounce our selfish aspirations and create the common good, don't you?"

I was trapped, nothing else to say but yes, although I tried to keep this realisation from crossing my features.

"Good. Why is your father so stubborn? It seems that he doesn't want to understand our Party policy. As a young and bright member of the Youth Communist Organization, we put our trust in you."

Trust? I was glad the Comrade could not read my thoughts and find out how eager I was to get out of fulfilling the position of class secretary.

He asked point blank, "When is the first train to your village?"

"Today?" I wondered.

"Of course, Flonta, of course."

"At 8.05."

He looked at his watch.

"Now it's 6.40pm. You pack your things and go home immediately and try to convince your father to join the collective."

"But Comrade Principal, I don't think I will be able to convince him," I almost begged him, my arms moving sidewise from my body.

"I don't believe that. You are a clever boy and I am sure, if you use the right arguments, you will convince him," he said unimpressed, clearing his throat in a clear dismissal.

"He is my father and I have to listen to him. After all, he brought me into this world, not the other way around. You are teaching us to obey our parents and our teachers," I dared, almost choking.

"I know, Flonta, I know," he replied calmly. "But there are things more important than our teachings and our individual aspirations – they are the Party teachings and they require our total obedience because they go beyond you and me or your father. They're aimed at constructing a better future for all society, for all of us, and one of the steps to be taken, to reach that goal, is the collectivization of agriculture, the elimination of inequality," he continued, stretching his right hand for emphasis. "You remember the cardinal rule at the basis of the Socialist society, that says that everybody should give, according to his ability and everybody will receive, according to his work. You remember?" He waited for my answer, his brows arched and his forehead wrinkled.

I nodded.

"The peasants give their land and work it together with others in a collective, thus eliminating the bourgeois sense of ownership; and they will be paid according to the work they put in. Exactly like the workers in a factory. This alliance between the workers and the peasants can be sustained only on a parity basis."

He got my attention when he put the factory workers on a par with the peasants. We were taught that the working class – the factory workers – was the leading element in this alliance.

"There is no individual ownership, only common ownership.

Everything belongs to all and everybody gets the just reward for his work. It's a new type of society which relies on a different kind of man, the new man." Comrade Berbec continued his lecture, stretching out his hand again, higher than before. "Tell your father this and he will understand. He must be made to understand, if he wants you to go on with your life and create an even better society, the Communist society, which will ask everybody to give and perform, according to his own ability; and in return everybody will receive according to his own needs. That is the ultimate, and we all have to do our bit to achieve that stage."

We were periodically given this type of lecture and most of us did not pay attention anymore. We had reached saturation point but we had to put up with it and pretend we understood. The worst of it was that we were made to repeat this stuff and made to take a solemn oath, an *angajament* – a pledge – in front of the class that we would fight for the creation of the new society – as new men ready to build this eternal, luminous future of ours. We would be the envy of the capitalistic societies, where the workers would revolt and do exactly what we had done. Communism would be the only ideology and socio-political system in the world, where inequality and the exploitation of man over man would be a thing of the past.

"Now you go home without further ado and let your father know that you are expelled from school until the day he joins the collective. He will listen. He cannot go against our Party, thinking selfishly only of himself. As a former enemy of the people – he was a *chiabur*, wasn't he – he should count his blessings that our Party still wants him to become a dignified member of our new society. Remind him also that he is playing with your future too. And tell him about the History Olympiad."

I was shocked and struggled hard to block my tears. I was expelled from school. The worst thing that could happen to anybody. It was not a joke. It was real, just as it was when Comrade Abrudan gave me zero in maths.

"Do you have any brothers or sisters?"

"No."

"Well, this is it. If he doesn't agree with our ideals and thinks that joining the collective is a sacrifice, he should make this sacrifice for his only son. My word, I know he will. Go now."

"Good evening, Comrade Principal." I struggled to remain respectful.

I turned my back to him and walked towards the door, my feet heavy, my heart in my mouth, and my thoughts black.

"Oh, I almost forgot. What's the name of the school principal in your village?"

"Comrade Picu Petroi."

"Yes, yes, I remember now. Picu and Elena Petroi. First thing, when you arrive home, take this letter to them and give them my regards." He handed me a white envelope.

Comrade Dragnea was waiting for me. He took me to the dormitory and made sure I cleaned all my stuff out of my locker. Then we went to the store room, where my suitcase was, and he made me fill it with the contents of my locker. After that he told the doorman that I could leave the premises but I would not be allowed back in without his permission. The doorman wanted to know what I had done.

"Not now, Comrade," Dragnea silenced him.

I walked the few metres between the doorman's room to the main door, Comrade Dragnea in tow, and I found myself in the street. He dismissed me with a gesture, pointing to his watch to indicate that I must not miss the train. I crossed the nearby bridge on the Crişul Negru and was on my way to the train station, some 700m down the main road – the same road I trod with Comrade Hulea when I came for my entrance exams and the same road I trodden with my father when I came to the college.

I was in a no-win situation, remembering my father's convictions and his toil on his land and his father's toil, on his own land. It was a chain of sweat and toil and strife and hope, which couldn't be broken by this situation. It had all started from almost nothing with my great-grandpa Pavelea, who came to Lupoaia penniless from Duşeşti, the village across the forest. Although he had had a reputation in his village for being a bully, he started understanding that in life, as in history, you must be tough but you have to know when to compromise.

I asked myself how can one compromise, when the most precious thing is asked of you, the thing which makes your life possible – the land of your fathers – and nothing is given in return? Compromise, from what I knew, was give and take on both sides.

How could I ask my father to give up his land to strangers? For what? For promises and shallow words? So he could be like everybody else? Why couldn't he just be himself? Why should somebody have the right to come into your home and tell you what to do? That's what we did to animals. They had to obey our orders. Just as I had to obey Comrade Berbec's order now. It was as though I had been placed on the donkey bench, like my father in his school days. There was a reason for doing that to him, a reason that had to do with his own actions. He knew that. He accepted that because it felt right. How could I ever accept the donkey bench spot Comrade Berbec had prepared for me? The donkey bench was for the arseholes. I was not one of them. The whole thing was not right. Not right at all.

On the train to Holod, I took the white envelope out of my pocket and turned it over. Only the addressee's name on it. I wished I could read its contents. The more I looked at it, the angrier I became. I put it back in my pocket after a little while and a surge of emotion took hold of me as I looked out through the dirty windows of the train, trying to make sense of what was happening to me. Students were expelled from time to time but for things they were guilty of, like Carțiș who was caught in town several times, when he should have been in class, or Vasile Popa from grade eleven, who was caught by Comrade Harbagea, the biology teacher, making love with a girl from grade nine, in a dark corner of the chemistry lab. I had not done anything wrong and I did not deserve this.

A young couple who shared the carriage with me got off at Căpâlna, so I was left alone and could cry without being seen. There was nothing worse, for a boy of 15, than being seen crying.

The ticket controller asked to see my ticket.

"What's the matter, young man? Somebody died?"

"No," I said, trying to smile, hoping to divert his attention from me.

It was dark when I left the train in Holod. I looked around for somebody from Lupoaia for company, because I was a little afraid of the dark. There was nobody, so I did not take the shortcut through the fields and instead, stuck to the main road through Holod, where some light from the houses illuminated my path of shame. When I reached the uninhabited road between Holod and Lupoaia, I walked very fast and looked over my shoulders at the slightest sound. I felt relieved when I passed the first house in Lupoaia. I crossed the creaking bridge over the Hodişel and, next to the People's House, just across the road from school, was Auntie Puica's house.

Their dog barked with excitement. The light from the house dimly lit the porch.

"Uncle Mihai! Auntie Puica!"

Uncle Mihai opened the door, asking who was calling.

"It's me, Uncle, Teodor."

He came quickly towards me. "What are you doing here at this hour? How come you are not at school?"

"I've been sent home, Uncle." I said, looking down.

"Sent home? What did you do for goodness sake?"

"Nothing." I looked into my uncle's eyes. "I didn't do anything."

"Come in and tell us."

Auntie Puica was as astonished to see me as Uncle Mihai. Cornel, my 10-year-old cousin, asked me what was going on. The light of the old lamp hanging from the ceiling was dimmed, so Uncle Mihai turned up the wick, making the room a bit brighter and hurting my eyes, after the crying and the dark journey home.

I told them the story and showed them the letter to Comrade Picu Petroi.

"Give me that letter!" Uncle Mihai ordered, anger rising in his voice.

He took a knife and slowly opened the letter along the seal.

"I am sure the bastard has something to do with it," he said, referring to Comrade Picu Petroi.

"Uncle! Don't do it, they'll punish me," I begged.

"Stop it, Mihai, listen to the boy," Auntie Puica said.

"They've punished you already. What a disgrace, taking it out on a young boy for his father's ideas. Don't worry, I will fix it and they won't notice anything."

He continued opening the letter with the knife, taking care not to rip the paper.

"Here you are. Read," he said.

"Dear Picu,

I was very happy to hear from you after so many years.

Congratulations on your appointment as Secretary of the local Committee. The Party needs people like you. As per your request, I sent the Flonta boy home and he will hand deliver this note to you. I agree with you that once Flonta's case is solved, you will have nothing left to do, apart from happily reporting the mission of collectivization in your village concluded. I will not take the boy back until his father gives in; he would not like to see his only son's future destroyed, as you said. It always works. It won't take long, you'll see. You can count on an old friend.

I trust Elena is fine.

Looking forward to happy news from you,

Yours, Traian."

"That miserable bastard! I had a hunch it was him," said Uncle Mihai. He hit the table with his fist, taking his anger out on the wood.

"Now how will you mend the envelope, you fool?" Auntie Puica asked.

"I told you not to worry, woman, didn't I? It'll be like new."

He poured water and flour into a bowl, mixed them well, and sealed the envelope with the paste. When he finished, he pressed the edges of the glued lines with a knife so they would stick together, and wiped off the excess paste with a damp cloth.

"In a few minutes it will be dry," he announced with a grin on his face. "Cornel will take the letter to the Comrade tomorrow morning when he goes to school."

Then it was time for Uncle Mihai to take me home.

Destroy Your Only Son's Future

My parents and Grandma Saveta were distressed about this turn of events. My father said he had not expected Comrade Picu Petroi to stoop so low, but then he seemed to drift away, as if lost in thought and said we were going to talk tomorrow.

In the morning, I found Mama preparing breakfast and my father sitting at the table, with his head in his hands. Mama was arguing that they should sign the application to join the collective. My future was out of Lupoaia, not working the land of others.

"We have to sign. You can't be so stubborn as to destroy your only son's future. If he did not do well at school, I would understand," she was saying, her hands open and palm up, as if she were imploring him to see sense.

"Destroy your only son's future, destroy your only son's future, Comrade Picu Petroi, Comrade Berbec and now you!" my father yelled at the top of his voice, punching the table with his fist.

He jumped to his feet.

"I am stubborn, I am stubborn? You have already forgotten what we went through? I can't have these damned, evil creatures telling me all the time what's best for me and my family! I know what's best for my son, I know!"

Then he slammed the door and went out.

Mama sighed deeply and raised her eyes to the heavens before she told me to go and see what my father was up to.

I saw him wandering around the garden for a little while.

Then he walked towards Valea Ştefani's well, pulled up a bucket of water and poured it over his head. He continued on the road towards Râturi, moving his right hand up and down with the index finger extended, pointing somewhere in the air, as I had seen him doing when he was planning something. Suddenly, he knelt on the ground, his palms firmly pushing into the soil, his head slowly bending down until his forehead touched the grass. He remained there for a long time, his grey trousers gathering dirt.

I returned home thinking about my father's words. Mama was saying to him what the two comrades were saying too. The difference was that Mama was saying it out of the goodness of her heart, thinking of me, only of me with love, unlike the two comrades who did not care about me at all – they cared only about themselves. For those two I was just a toy that could be sacrificed, in the blink of an eye, if they couldn't win over my father. How could they hate him so much? Did they hate me too? How twisted was the situation I was in, I thought, where Mama and the two comrades could use the same words, from two different angles, to force my father do what he felt was wrong? And why should I be in the middle of all this? I had learned about Hitler gassing millions of Jews, obliterating families, just because they were Jews. Were we, the enemies of the people, the Jews of Communism? I was very confused because I had just started to forget about Comrades Petroi's and Abrudan's interfering with my results in primary and middle school. Here we were again: in spite of my good results, my winning the History Olympiad and my overall good behaviour, my future could take a different turn altogether. Not a luminous future at all.

Mama told me not to worry; I'd be going to school soon. We both decided to go and see what my father was doing. From the bottom of our garden we could see him, still in the same position. I saw tears running down Mama's cheeks, as her hands fiddled nervously with her apron strings, but I pretended not to. She took me by the hand and told me to give him time. Everything was going to be alright, everything.

I couldn't stay in the house, so I went back to see my father.

He was getting up and looking around, perhaps to see if he had been spotted by some villager. He went back to the well, pulled up another bucket full of water, drank a mouthful, splashed his face and started walking slowly up the slope. I hid behind a straw rick and heard him saying at short intervals:

"No. No. No."

Comrade Picu Petroi gave my parents a couple of days to convince themselves not to destroy the future of their only son, before he called them in front of the committee again. My father refused to go but told Mama to sign. She did sign her name alone on the application. The committee accepted and soon rumours began to circulate that Pavelea had joined the collective.

After seven days I returned to school. I felt apprehensive, embarrassed and scared about going back. I knew I hadn't done anything wrong; the teachers and students knew it also but I felt nobody cared. I was different from everybody else, but didn't want to be seen as being different. I wished with all my heart that I could stop being treated unfairly. I hated being the centre of attention on account of my family, a family that was making a huge effort to send me to this school. As if expulsion weren't enough, I now faced the humiliation of questions from Comrade Berbec, the teachers and my fellow students. The thought of facing this on my own gave me stomach ache and made my shoulders and my head twitch.

My fears were unfounded. The teachers did not comment on my return, almost as if I had not been absent at all. While relieved, I found it so abnormal that I suspected something else was going to happen to me. Most of my classmates asked me how my vacation had been; but the look in their eyes told me they knew the reason for my sudden disappearance.

I was expecting Comrade Berbec to summon me to his office. He did not. Nevertheless my expulsion from school and my readmittance left their mark on my body and my soul.

Stalin's Sosia, Witches, and the Crossing of Seven Rivers

Comrade Fazekas was a sturdy man with a moustache resembling Stalin's, but he was taller, his face unblemished and his shoulders straight. Rumour had it that his wife committed suicide because of his harshness. A former boxer, he fitted his discipline – Physical Education. He would make us run behind the main building until somebody collapsed with exhaustion. He was rude and uncompromising, particularly with girls that tended to make excuses and invented sick days when they were fine. Comrade Fazekas would scream, "C'mon young lady, run faster, don't be a weakling." When the young lady couldn't run anymore, he would force her to continue until she cried. The girls plotted to denounce him to the Principal but they didn't, for fear of retaliation. They had to put up with him.

He saw me exhausted by the run one day and, observing my head movement, he pulled me to the side.

"Look at me," he commanded, "and stay still."

Panting and unstable on my feet, I tried to obey his orders. My head tilted left sharply and the muscles in my neck twitched at regular intervals.

"What's this head movement about?" he frowned.

"Nothing," I said, trying to stay as still as I could; but my head gave another jerk. I had noticed it doing that, of its own accord, for a few days but, fearing I'd be labelled a freak, I ignored it in the hope that it would stop. It didn't. I was becoming a bit of a laughing stock.

"Go and see a doctor," he said, dismissing me with a wave of his thick hand.

Instead, I went back home that Saturday, three weeks after Mama joined the collective. She knew I was coming and was at the bottom of the garden, watching me and my wooden suitcase crossing the Hodişel and walking through Râturi into Valea Ştefani's. She was so happy to see me, took my head between her hands and kissed me on the cheek. "What's wrong, my son? Is school going well?" she asked, her head tilted to one side, as she studied me intently. She held my head again and tried to keep it still, but that seemed to make the tic worse.

"Yes, everything's fine, Mama. Don't worry," I said.

It wasn't true. I felt depressed, embarrassed and annoyed by my inability to keep my head still. Later, I saw Mama crying on Grandma's shoulder.

Auntie Sofia came to visit, as she always did when she knew I was home from school. "Where is this nephew of mine? I haven't seen him for a while. I've brought him some apples," she said.

"He is in the shed with his father," Mama told her.

"I'll go and see him."

"Don't go yet, Nuţa wants to talk to you," Grandma Saveta said.

"Anything worrying you, little sister?" Auntie Sofia inquired.

"It's my Teodor. He has a terrible tic. He jerks his head and cannot control it," Mama explained, grimacing as the worry lines settled across her face once more.

"God forbid!" exclaimed Auntie Sofia.

"You wait here. I'll call Teodor, you pretend not to see it," Mama begged. She opened the door and called me.

I liked Auntie Sofia, so I immediately left my father in his shed and went to greet her. Auntie Sofia, who always complained about her varicose veins, was a delightful woman with more grace about her than a nun. She was caring and ready to help out. She had one phobia which made me laugh: dogs. Whenever she saw more than one dog on the street, she got so scared that she ran straight back into the house. I laughed and tried to comfort her, before going into the street myself, to show her that the dogs ran away when I shouted at them. Nonetheless, she couldn't summon enough courage and would hold onto my arm tightly, looking about her while I accompanied her home. She continued to be on the lookout for dogs all her life – because she believed they were out there, trying to get her. In her youth, a witch had told her that she was going to be mauled to death by seven dogs.

"Auntie! How are you?" I asked.

"You big boy, look at you, how tall you are."

She embraced and kissed me and handed me an apronful of apples. "Take them with you, when you go to school, so you'll remember me for a while."

"I always remember my favourite auntie. How could I forget you?"

"How is school? Grandma says you are not getting good marks anymore," she teased.

"Don't believe her, Teodor, don't believe her," Grandma retorted.

"Come to visit me and I'll give you some more apples," Auntie Sofia said, squeezing my cheek between her thumb and her forefinger.

I returned to the shed to help my father.

"Did you notice?" Mama asked Auntie Sofia.

"Yes. Poor baby. It is not good at all," she said, shaking her head in a mixture of pity and disbelief. She told Mama about a woman from Râpa that cured people. A witch called Lina. This woman had been arrested a couple of times for her practices; but she had been out of prison for a year. Sofia offered to take us to her.

The following afternoon, I found myself walking alongside Mama and Auntie Sofia through corn stalks, sunflower stems and wheat fields from Lupoaia to Hodiş, from Hodiş to Mociar and from Mociar to Râpa. I was thinking about witches the entire way there, a bit put off by the idea. However, with the exuberant Auntie Sofia there was not even a remote chance of calling off the visit.

I recalled Micula's story of a young couple, Saveta and Petrea, who had lived at Colibi, my Great-Grandpa Pavelea's property, at the turn of the century. They had a girl and two boys. Micula swore on his ancestors that what he told me really happened. In olden times, witches flourished in Transylvania. Each of them had a spirit or a demon who acted as a servant, through whom they performed their deeds. The spirit could be bad, performing only bad deeds, or good, performing only good deeds. The spirit couldn't be created or just appear out of thin air – it had to be passed on by a dying witch and, according to old wives' tales, the spirit was rather choosy. If it did not like the woman it was to be passed on to, then it denied the dying witch the sweet release of death. It prolonged her suffering and pain until it was completely happy with the choice.

"Saveta had a demon-servant for sure," Micula insisted. "Nobody knew how she received it. I was there one evening, when a peasant woman from the village asked her to help her clean some wheat, which was to be taken to the mill. In the morning Saveta went to help the woman and, while she was helping her, Saveta's husband Petrea went to look for a shirt in the dowry chest at home. His attention was drawn to a dirty, useless-looking bundle of rags. He threw it in the stove. The stove exploded and something – resembling a small whirlwind, flew into the attic. Who or what it was, I don't know, but it flew up into the attic, screaming. At that precise moment Saveta, who had a sieve full of wheat in her hands, fell to the ground. Minutes later she got up and continued as if nothing had happened. About an hour later, she came home with a bowl full of flour. As she put the bowl on the table, her husband demanded to know what was in the bundle of rags that he had tried to burn. He explained that he had thrown it into the stove but it had exploded in front of his eyes. "I know that," came Saveta's reply, "now we are both going to die and leave our children alone in this world." Petrea yelled at her, cursing and conjuring up demons and every saint he had ever heard of, but she just repeated her previous words: "Now we will both die and leave our children alone in this world."

Micula paused for a moment, as if casting his memory's eye back 80 years, then looked at me, nodding his head. "I remember as if it were yesterday. I was 12 at the time," he said sadly. After a while, he continued the story.

"Saveta took off her heavy jacket and got into bed. Not long after, some soldiers came but I couldn't see them. I only heard the noise of their boots and their blows on Saveta's face. She was crying to me – "Come my young Micula, lie down beside me and hold me tight, because otherwise they will beat the life out of me." She said I was chaste and pure and the spirit couldn't harm her, when she was in contact with me. I went and lay down next to her and the beating stopped, but every time I got up, either to put more wood on the fire or to feed the animals, they started beating her again. They kept on beating her throughout the night. This continued until the next afternoon and then the slapping and the thumping blows on her body grew louder. So did her wails. Suddenly she stopped. There was no more life in her. Petrea was in bed too, being visited by unknown creatures dressed in military uniform. The night after Saveta died, he asked me to help him go out. The men present in the house did not want me to do it, offering to help him themselves. However, Petrea insisted. He did not want anybody else but me. I took him out but he stopped in the doorway and refused to go any further. Instead, he raised his head and looked at the stars. Then he asked me to take him back to bed. The men helped me get him into bed and shortly after we heard a terrible blow. He did not say a word, only gasped heavily and the life soon fled his body, just as it had his wife's hours earlier. We laid him on boards on the floor, next to his wife, and spent the night in their home for the wake. We buried them both the next day, but without a priest, because women who were possessed by a demon were not allowed to have a Church funeral."

All of us were tired, particularly Auntie Sofia who complained about her varicose veins, so we stopped to have a drink at a common well before entering Râpa. Auntie Sofia told us that we were going to walk through the orchards at the back of the houses, so as not to be seen by anyone and create suspicion and trouble for Lina.

We reached Lina's house and waited in silence for a while at the back of her garden, listening for sounds from the nearby houses. When everything seemed to be clear, Auntie Sofia entered the courtyard, constantly checking that the coast was clear, and knocked on the door, which we heard open. Shortly after, Auntie Sofia came back and beckoned us to follow her.

We found ourselves in a dark room. Ioanea, a tall man in his mid twenties, invited us to sit on a bench next to one of the beds. Opposite, on a low stool at the end of another bed, sat a corpulent woman in her seventies. It was Lina. Auntie Sofia, who seemed to be on familiar terms with the old woman, explained our reason for visiting and her belief that Lina could do something about it. Lina listened with her head bowed and I could see her profile. From time to time she grunted a monosyllabic "Hm."

Then, with some difficulty, Lina started talking. It was as if her voice came from a chest being squeezed by a millstone. Her speech had a rhythm of its own. I had never in my life heard anything like it, with some sounds stronger than others and fluctuating between sharp and flat.

"The mother should get one of the child's garments, a shirt or something that only he has worn, then cut a lock of the child's hair. Put the hair together with 300 *lei* in the shirt, tie it in a knot and have the child throw it in the oven just outside this room. Only then, will I be able to invoke my servant. Don't be afraid of any noises you hear. My servant doesn't harm anybody. He does only good things."

Mama had come prepared. She pulled from her bag an old shirt of mine. Auntie cut a lock of my hair with the scissors she always carried in her bag and gave it to Mama. The three of us went out to the oven, a normal bread oven no different from that in every peasant home. I took off the lid covering its mouth and flung in my bundle, as far as I could. Mama and Auntie Sofia checked, just to make sure. Many questions passed through my mind. What was the money for? What was the purpose of the shirt that only I had worn? Why throw the bundle in the oven?

As we returned to the room, Ioanea left. Lina told Mama and Auntie Sofia to go and wait in the adjacent room, but to leave the door ajar. I was to stay with her. I felt very scared by now. She got up from her stool and opened the window.

"Whatever you hear, don't be afraid. My servant does only what I tell him. He is always instructed to do good things and he won't harm anybody. Whatever happens to me, don't intervene because he is very protective of me," Lina told me solemnly.

When she mentioned her servant, I thought of Micula's story about Saveta and Petrea and their tragic end. It was getting scary and I almost wet my pants. When Lina came towards me, I shivered with fear. She placed both her hands on my head and muttered something. Then she said to me, "Oh, yes, you are a tormented boy, but you are defending yourself bravely, very bravely. Don't be afraid, you are going to be well again."

She lifted her hands from my head and stepped backwards. Then she backed off more, watching me attentively. She took a broom from the corner of the room and leaned on it. I watched her every move, mostly out of fear of what was coming next. I was also thinking about her words, about my defending myself, but I couldn't understand what she meant. How was I defending myself? I still felt compelled to do the odd thing with my head, right there in her presence. What defending did she see me doing? And what about the broom? I knew that witches had brooms on which they flew and I expected to see Lina, heavy though she was, fly around the room or even out of the window.

Then, all of a sudden, she spoke:

"Oh, you Almighty Lord of Darkness and the Abyss! I beg you! Oh, you Almighty Lord of Darkness and the Abyss! I beg you! Oh, you Almighty Lord of Darkness and the Abyss! I beg you! Send my servant to me, over seven hills, seven clouds, seven waters, seven fires and don't let him stop for hunger or thirst, for tiredness or fear, until he reaches me, his beloved one, his spouse. Make him walk only on the edge of the roads, on the air, over the water, over the fires, so that he won't harm any living soul..."

A hissing sound, louder and louder, came through the open window and stopped with a thump, somewhere very close to Lina. She said it was her servant who was standing on her shoulder and she felt he was too heavy for her. He refused to sit on the broom because he had missed her a lot. I trembled at Lina's grimaces.

The servant called Lina his spouse and talked to her in a screeching voice, at times playful but wise too. He prefaced each sentence with *abunăsamă*, which meant something like 'by all means', then paused before continuing. Lina asked him to go and search everywhere for people who, knowingly or inadvertently, could be the cause of my pain and ask them to free me from my suffering. She asked him to go to all the places I had been to, throughout my life, and destroy all the demons, who might have performed mischievous acts against me. Then, at midnight sharp, he was to take the bundle from the oven and the illness from my body and carry them to an intersection of seven rivers and throw them in the waters, so the illness would be dispersed and would not be able to find its way back. Then he had to leave the way he came, without harming anybody, and not come back until I was healed.

At about the time Lina finished giving instructions to her servant, Grandma Saveta, who was in the courtyard at home, heard a terrible noise, as if the terracotta tiles on our roof were rising, one by one, in a quick succession, and falling into place again. She was so scared that she ran inside and prayed.

That night I slept in one of the two beds of the room, squeezed between Mama and Auntie Sofia, while Lina slept in the bed opposite. We tossed and turned, with Auntie Sofia complaining about her varicose veins again. Eventually I fell asleep. Early in the morning, Auntie Sofia told us that she had fallen asleep after us and in the middle of the night she had felt something, or somebody, lift one of her legs, which was over me, and push it towards the wall. She couldn't sleep any more after that.

Lina said that it was her servant at work and it should have happened at midnight when he took my illness away. I wondered how long it had taken her servant to get from her house to the confluence of seven rivers. She said that he travelled as fast as the wind and that, if he put his mind to it, he could go as fast as a thought.

We left with Lina's reassurances that I was innocent and brave in defending myself from evil, and that I would soon be healed. It was early in the morning and the sun was still high in the sky as we walked towards Mociar. I walked fast, at times 20m in front of Mama and Auntie. They would shout at me to wait for them. I did, but soon started the game again. On the stretch between Mociar and Holod, I noticed Mama and Auntie whispering to each other instead of talking normally. I asked what the secret was.

Mama smiled. "All the way from the Mociar church to here, your head did not twitch once."

"Really?" I asked, and suddenly the tic gripped me again. "You see," I said with a tone of reproach.

"Don't worry, nephew, don't worry, you'll see that you'll be over it in no time," Auntie reassured.

I lengthened my stride, making my long legs work for me for once and trying to get control over my tic – but I was not very good at it. We decided to take a shortcut through Hodiş rather than Holod, and again Auntie told me I had long periods when I did not make that silly movement.

I had mixed feelings about Lina and her servant. I was there and heard all that stuff, but I did not see anything or anybody apart from her, a corpulent old woman bent by age, marked perhaps by the time she spent in prison, and who spoke in a peculiar way. Her voice, intonation and rhythm seemed to belong to another world, the world of the fairy-tales and stories of devils and wolves, that Grandma told me. Lina's servant was there but only in sound, not as an image or shape. I did not see him at all. I had seen only Lina's left shoulder bending further down after the thump, when the servant landed on it. I was impressed by Auntie Sofia's story about her leg being lifted from me at midnight, and later, by my Grandma telling us about the roof tiles. All these elements made it eerie and, because of that, perhaps more believable.

Ulcer and Bromide

After I returned to school my tic slowed down, but the stomach ache that had bothered me for a while grew more insistent and acute. One evening, before Comrade Dragnea started the rounds for the night curfew, my companions had a pillow fight. A pillow hit me but I couldn't move. I was curled up in bed, cradling my abdomen and trying to ease my pain. The students laughed at me, thinking that I was on another planet, dreaming of home, but I kept on writhing with my knees up to my chin, moaning and crying. The boys stopped laughing.

The following day Comrade Dragnea sent me to the infirmary. When the nurse heard my story, she told me I had to see a doctor straight away. The hospital was nearby, a couple of hundred metres from the school, she said. She gave me a note for Comrade Dragnea who wrote a permit allowing me to leave the college premises. Permit in hand, I went to the doorman who said, "What's this? Shouldn't you be in class?"

"I don't feel well," I said, indicating my abdomen.

"All of a sudden?" he asked.

"Well, sort of," I said.

"Oh," he wondered aloud. He left his cabin and accompanied me to the main door, then walked with me up to the church in the square and pointed to the hospital.

The doctor said he didn't want to believe it was what he thought it was. The symptoms suggested a stomach ulcer, but an ulcer was rare for a boy of 15 to have. He sent me for an x-ray. I had to drink a creamy, thick, white, chalky barium milkshake. After the first sip my instinct was to choke and vomit, but my gagging did not impress the tall, dark-haired doctor. He placed me under the machine and told me to drink it all. I did, but then it came out of me, like a projectile, right into his face. He was quick to swear at me, at Mama and all my relatives and, after cleaning himself and his rubbery apron, he tortured me with another half-full glass of barium. He kept shouting and cursing me as I drank it down.

Duodenal ulcer was the verdict.

My father came to visit me at the weekend and I gave him the bad news. He just said, "God forbid. It can't be," and then stood there in silence for a few minutes. I saw his chin trembling and the tears running down his cheeks. I did not like seeing my father crying. I wanted to reassure him that I was going to be fine – one of those things you say, when somebody is crying for you.

The doctor did not give me any medicine but said to take sodium bicarbonate and to follow a low fat diet. My father found the sodium bicarbonate for me; but the low fat diet became a big problem. The menu at our canteen was based on the extremes: tea or cumin soup in the mornings and everything fat and gas producing for lunch and dinner. Beans and fat sausages, cabbage and fat pork meat-cum-lard, or cakes made with lard were not the ideal food for my condition. The chicken and the beef, when available, were cooked in fat too. The justification for this was that we were young and growing and needed energy. The food from home was no better, because it was predominantly made with lard. Apart from the white, unsalted cheese Mama made out of our cow's milk, there was not much that could really help me. Five or six weeks after the diagnosis, my father brought me a half a litre bottle filled with a yellow-brown liquid. When he unwrapped it from the paper, a strong smell of *pălinca* hit my nostrils.

"What's this?" I asked.

"Grandma Saveta sends it you," my father said.

"What? *Pălinca*?"

"Honey, garlic and *pălinca*, fermented together. They say it's good for ulcers," my father said.

"It can't be good, it's alcohol, Dad," I retorted, with an air of superiority.

"Yes, but it's been buried in our manure for a month and they say it performs miracles on ulcers."

"Who are they?" I asked.

"People, women in the markets, somebody in Tinca. Grandma knows the names. They've been cured," my father insisted.

I did take a sip from the smelly concoction but it did more harm than good. After my father left, I threw it away.

As I was queueing at the canteen, my ulcer acted up. There was not going to be tea this morning, but the smell of the bromide in the cumin soup wafted from the kitchen. The soup was just as saturated with bromide as the tea, or any other soup they served us. The bromide was to dampen our libido. Luckily, I had the milk my father ordered for me from the canteen cook, who kept a cow at home on the outskirts of the city. My father told the cook not to put bromide in my milk and, if possible, in any of my meals. Sometimes the cook could do as he asked, sometimes he couldn't. He said that bromide went into the big pots and even the teachers who ate at our canteen, from time to time, were served the same food.

Ion Popa and others were too hungry to care about the bromide, and competed for my tea and cumin soup. To prove their resilience to bromide, they sat on the brick wall surrounding the courtyard with their hands in their pockets massaging their willies, asking the girls if they would like to jump on their tumescent bump, chanting the verses Eminescu improvised for his lover, on a romantic night on their boat ride on Herăstrău Lake.

Uite luna, uite faru (Here is the moon, here is the light)
Uite sula mea ca paru (Here is my prick, hard as a stake)

As I had given them my bromide contaminated food, the boys were grateful and stood up for me when the bullies in grades ten and eleven wanted me to retrieve their ball from awkward corners of the quadrangle, or to shine their shoes, just for the fun of humiliating us. They were trying to assert their cockiness and dominance over the mob and to show others that muscles and age were more important than brains in the quadrangle.

I often wondered why the authorities bothered stuffing us with bromide, as we were not bad at all and they already controlled us in so many ways. I thought bromide would have been more appropriate for some people in Lupoaia than in a school of young boys, whose time was controlled, from dawn to dusk, by everybody around them.

The Party Paper and Teachers

Most students at our high school came from the surrounding villages. It couldn't be otherwise, as the only town in the area was Beiuş, which was little bigger than a village itself. Only one of its streets was asphalted and most were crowded with carts drawn by horses or slow oxen. The carts carried people, piled up on top of bags of flour, potatoes, beans and seasonal vegetables, to the little market on the bank of the Crişul Negru.

Some of the women from the mountain villages looked different from the women of Lupoaia. They were wider and rounder and were said to wear seven petticoats under their skirts. Their aprons and head scarves were strikingly coloured and not just plain black. They wrapped everything they sold in old copies of the Party's official paper and, when that was finished, in old, used exercise book pages. That reminded me of the toilets of Lupoaia – little enclosures in the garden, with a thatched roof and walls made of mud plastered over tree branches. The round hole in the high wooden seat was always encrusted with brown matter. The children's used exercise books ended up here, each page torn into two or three pieces, into which a hook, sticking out of the wall at head height, was driven. When school ended, the exercise books replaced the more abrasive materials such as maize husks, straw or hay. It was a luxury to have the finer paper of books in the toilets because, apart from the one Bible in Teleac's possession – which was given to his ancestors by their

Hungarian landlord who said that he needed Romanian brawn to work for him, not Romanian words to confuse him – there were no books in the peasants' homes and it did not take long, if one accidentally entered a home, for it to find its way to the hook in the toilet. Modru used to say that our toilet paper was coloured knowledge that ended up down the shithole.

The official Party's newspaper was the toilet paper for those few peasants, who could read and afford to buy it, on their trips to the markets. In bad times, we did not have any toilet paper at our school, but the toilet was often the destination of the school's copies of the Party's newspaper. Our best journalists racked their brains to produce pieces of high propaganda, which we had to study today and flush down our squat toilets tomorrow. The irony was not lost on us and we often joked about how pitiful it was for our Party, to come to the realization that it couldn't create the new men it wanted us to be, by working on our heads. Rather, it had to stoop so low as to work its propaganda up our bums. We were sure the Party did not stand a chance, though, as we convinced ourselves that our bums had become bullet-proof with all that lead from the ink.

We had our own ways of using books for unintended purposes. All hard covers were ripped off our text books and used as ping-pong rackets, during the breaks between classes and after hours. The girls also used them to defend themselves from sudden attacks from us boys, as Cristina did with Lucian, who used to jump on her back to simulate sex. Once she hit him with a hard book cover right in the eye and he had to wear an eye patch for weeks.

Some teachers left their mark but most didn't, especially those who infused their lessons with Party propaganda. We had already had enough of that, being obliged to submit ourselves to a set hour every Wednesday afternoon, when we were already tired after a full day of lessons. The grey walls provided more interest than those lessons did. The propaganda hour was called "political awareness lesson" and stifled our spontaneity and curiosity. While it was easier to understand the life of microbes in biology or the chemical reactions in chemistry, or even to memorize Russian or French sentences, it was impossible to grasp concepts relating to the society we were supposedly building, when around us nothing changed. If anything, what we witnessed in our own lives or in those of our own families, was more hardship and more restrictions. Day by day, we saw people resorting to more lies and more subterfuges in order to survive. That's what we did in our school too. Those in charge believed us less and less, even when we told the truth, and often punished us when we did tell the truth. The only hope of escaping punishment was by telling an even bigger lie. So, we were always caught between our truth and the official truth and lived our student life expecting our teachers to punish us regardless. Some of them were gloomy and we stayed away from people like that; others with some elements of a sense of humour, did not take anything seriously, including us. Those who were not directly involved with Party propaganda were lifeless, incapable of infusing any enthusiasm into us. There was no fire in them to inspire us to greater things. We soon learned how to take advantage of some of them.

I was good at chemistry but not so good at physics. This was partly to do with the teacher. A giant of a man, with a matching stentorious voice, the physics teacher had previously been an army officer and appreciated obedience far more than the learning of his discipline. The overweight Comrade Bala, with his protruding belly, had a penchant for minimalism, starting with his little wife who barely reached his armpit. He rode a rusty old woman's bicycle that screeched, with the tyres flattened under his heavy weight. He wore round glasses and had a prisoner's crop. His tight shirts were always open at the belly because the button had popped off at the first wearing. His shoes were worn-out and his trousers a few inches too short, revealing powerful calves and fatty ankles. He read the lesson to us, line by line, from the textbook and, when it came to solving physics problems, he was regularly off the mark. Nobody learned much from him. Being a man of the Party, he did not even need a degree to teach in a reputable high school like ours; some sort of diploma put him on an equal footing with his colleagues, and they did not respect him. He was immune to serious knowledge and succeeded in immunizing his pupils as well.

We had more affinity with young Sorin, our chemistry teacher, fresh from university and more taken by his new wife than the Party line. He was approachable and treated us with some camaraderie. Young boys like us, although aware of the risk of punishment, knew how to take advantage of people like him. At the end of term one in grade ten, my classmate, Buda, and I demonstrated how close we had come to becoming new men with a luminous future in our society. During one weekend Buda, who had become the teacher's lab assistant, got hold of the lab keys, which had been left next to the pile of our final term assignments, still to be marked by the teacher. With some excitement, he told me and Horga about it. We decided to remove our assignments from the pile and replace them with new ones to get a better mark. Buda was thorough enough; he had also found a stack of special empty booklets on which the assignments had to be written. We worked separately, to avoid being accused of plagiarism and inserted a couple of minor errors to eliminate any suspicion. We got the highest marks in the class and that helped me snatch the first prize at the end of the year.

Our biology teacher, Comrade Harbagea, also helped me achieve that goal by giving me a 10 out of 10 for two words only. He asked for the Latin scientific name of the pig and nobody knew. I had the name stored in my brain, but not the courage to stand up. He challenged us, saying that he would give the top mark to the student who knew it; but if the answer was wrong, then the mark would be 4 out of 10 and complete failure. He looked around and called us chicken. I raised my hand. He pointed his finger at me. I got up and said 'Sus scrofa'. It was easy to remember because both words meant something in Romanian, 'scrofa' meant 'scroafa', or sow, and 'sus' meant 'up'. It had struck me when I read my lesson on pigs and it stuck with me. Comrade Harbagea kept his word, going straight to the register to immortalize my mark, thus creating something of a sensation among the students of other classes.

High on the boys' preference list was Camelia, the Russian teacher. She was always smiling and closed an eye to our unwillingness to learn the language of our brothers from the East. Strangely enough, she tried to indoctrinate us less.

Every time she entered the class she said: Здравствуйте (Hello) and every time she left the class she said: До свидания (Good bye). On one occasion, when she was leaving, I said jokingly *Arrivederci*. She looked at me and nodded, "You speak Italian, Flonta." I didn't have a chance to reply, because, by the time she'd finished the sentence, she was out of the door. The next Russian class, when she called us one by one to her desk, to return the corrected home work, she asked me where I learned Italian.

"From the radio," I said.

"From the radio? Oh, that's good," she said with some admiration.

On weekends, when we had our one-hour permit to go for a walk outside the college compound, we used to pass by her house and she was often in the garden. We would say good evening to her and she would smile back at us.

Boys of 16 talk a lot about girls, particularly about more mature and experienced girls. Our favourite was Camelia; her smile, her legs, her round breasts and sinuous curves fired our imagination. I don't think I had the most fervid imagination, but one of those evenings I fell prey to Horga's game about what we would do to Comrade Camelia, if we had that chance. It was all sexual, of course, and we were all peasant boys accustomed to roughness and vulgarity. It was my turn just when we were approaching Camelia's house. I must have been very convincing in my more tender approach, telling the boys about soft caresses and slowly sliding fingers on wet skin and sensual whispers in receptive ears. The boys became aroused. I was invoking her name in a moaning loud voice. All of a sudden, Camelia's head rose from behind a bush: "Flonta, Flonta!"

For a moment I felt like sinking deep into the earth. My legs refused to carry me further and I could barely hear the boys' chorus of "Good evening Comrade Borza". Horga and Buda dragged me past the teacher's house. I tried to be brave in front of the boys over the weekend but, when they did not see me, I ran to my Russian manual and learned by heart everything that was to be learned. The thought that I could be expelled from school, this time with just cause, terrorized me. Monday and the Russian class came, and Camelia entered the classroom with the register under her arm. She was smiling as usual. I couldn't bring myself to look at her directly but I was like a hawk, watching her every move and expression from the corner of my eye, whilst a slow blush crept up my neck and remained on my face for much of the lesson. She made some people read lines from Gorki's novel *Mother*, told them they were pitiful and their translation way off the mark. Then she made me translate and, although I struggled more than usual, she said, "Good, Flonta, good."

Those three words lifted a thousand boulders off my chest and made it easy for me to breathe once again.

Cherries and Lice

At the end of May the lush, green cherry branches began to surge above the walls of the college, as if taunting us with the first cherries of the season. Ion Pantea and I decided to jump over the gate, at the back of the college and go to the market to fill our hungry stomachs. We bought fluffy white buns from peasant women from around Beiuş, and sliced salami from the smelly tavern in the middle of the market. A small stall was selling cherries, still on branches, and we bought one branch each, managing to save them while undertaking the difficult task of climbing over the gate back into the college. On the path leading to the store room we encountered Ion Popa and Laura, a girl one year younger than I, walking towards us, not hand in hand but very close to each other. It looked like the beginning of a new romance and I was jealous. I liked Laura. I found beauty in her hair, which was gathered into two thick brown plaits, tied at the end with big coloured bows that danced on her back. Her perfect smile graced her nicely shaped red lips and her slightly protruding cheek bones gave her an exotic look; but I had never had the courage to tell her. I hated seeing her with the bulky, rough, brainless Ion Popa by her side. I told Pantea what I thought and how unfit they were for each other.

As we approached them, Laura pointed at my branch of cherries and said, "Is that for me, Flonta?"

Surprised, I handed it to her. "Of course." I added hastily, "The first of the season. Make a wish and it will come true."

"I already have. You'll find out soon," she said.

Ion Popa didn't look happy with our flirting. A scowl spread over his already ugly, twisted face. Laura, on the other hand, blushed and ran away with her trophy towards the classroom upstairs, leaving Ion Popa in the lurch.

"Sorry, mate," I said and continued on my way with Ion Pantea.

"She likes you," Ion Pantea said, laughing at the dumbstruck look on Ion Popa's face as we walked away.

"Do you think so?"

"Do I think so? It's written all over her face," Pantea concluded.

As I looked back, Ion Popa was still in the middle of the path. That was the end of his relationship with Laura and the beginning of mine because, the next morning my friend Nori told me Laura had fancied me for a while now but she had thought I was ignoring her signals. She thought I did not fancy her.

I invited Laura to the cinema the next day. Boys and girls were not allowed out together on their own, only as a group, to prevent promiscuity, or so our teachers told us. We had our leave permits signed by Comrade Dragnea and Comrade Mornea by pretending to visit relatives in hospital, and we met in the cinema. I checked for teachers but did not see anybody. Laura kept her head down. It was her first experience like this, she said. It was my first too, I replied. Fearing that the ticket lady would take down my matriculation number and report me to the school, I pulled my sleeve up and twisted it so that it was illegible, wiping my clammy hands nervously on my trousers. We always lived with fear, when in town on our own, because anybody could become our enemy at any time. There were only a few people waiting to see the film. I bought the two tickets and waited with Laura in a corner of the hall until everybody had entered and the lights were dimmed. We found two places at the back, next to the exit, so we could get out first. When we sat down, I felt Laura's hand touch mine.

"Did your wish come true?" I whispered in her ear.

She leaned her head against my lips and nodded. The rose perfume from her hair filled my nostrils and the touch of her skin filled my heart with happiness. What a great thing to be 15 and able to feel the delicate skin of a girl of 14, when all your senses are on the alert and going to explode at the slightest touch. We didn't see the film at all.

We had still time left before we were due to report back to the college and decided to go to the park in front of the cinema. Laura spotted a free bench and pulled me by the hand towards it. It felt so good to be outside the walls of our 'prison' and be able to hold hands. We played with each other's hands and I put my arm around her shoulders. I started humming the latest Italian song I had been listening to on the radio and Laura was intrigued. I had copied the words of the song and handed her the piece of paper. She tried to imitate my bad humming, reading the words from the paper. I discovered she had a beautiful voice and I loved her effort to read the words correctly.

Come prima (Like before)
più di prima t'amerò (More than before, I will love you)
per la vita (For life)
la mia vita ti darò. (I'll give my life to you.)
Sembra un sogno (It seems a dream)
rivederti, accarezzarti (To see you again, to caress you again)
le tue mani tra le mani (Your hands in my hands)
stringere ancor. (To hold again.)

A few days later, as we were waiting for the teacher to come to the classroom, Nori came and sat next to me. She was a bright, short, plump girl – good friends with Laura – and asked me to tilt my head. I thought she wanted to whisper a message from Laura in my ear. I tilted my head and, in an almost motherly way for her 15 years, she took my head in her lap and started stroking my hair. I liked the sensation, but suddenly she said that I had lice. I blushed, yanked my head away from her touch and wanted to crawl beneath the earth and never come out again. She said it was nothing, shrugging lightly. She had them too and so did many other girls. She assured me the lice would go away, if I put petrol on my hair every evening, for a few days and did not comb it until the night after. I did that and everybody kept their distance from me.

The lice did not prevent me from seeing Laura during the breaks between classes and in the evening before dinner. I apologised for the petrol smell in my hair but she said not to worry. She was used to it, as that was her mother's perfume each Sunday morning when she combed her hair. She sprinkled it with petrol to keep it shiny and clean.

One evening we found the Chemistry lab, on the first floor, open and went there to avoid the supervision of the teacher on duty. We wanted to kiss without being punished. We knew it was not the right thing to do; but we took the risk and sat close to each other in the darkest corner. I reached around her waist and gently drew her towards me and she quickly twined her arms around my neck. I felt her soft lips touching mine and we stayed like that for many seconds. She withdrew her arms but I did not release her from my embrace. She looked me in the eyes and raised her hand and played with my hair and said we should go to the cinema again. Just as she was suggesting that we invite Pantea and Ilona, his red-haired Hungarian girlfriend, the door opened. We froze. Steps came closer and closer until we saw Comrade Harbagea, the Biology teacher. He was known to be very strict. Rumour had it that he was like that, because of his past as a seminary student. He had caught Vasile Prunea and his girlfriend in the place where we were, doing exactly the same thing and had had the boy expelled from school.

"What's going on here?" he asked us.

"We… we are talking…" I said. My skin broke out in a cold sweat.

"And you can't talk outside – like everybody else?" he asked.

We were lost for words and looked down.

"You, young lady, should be ashamed of yourself. You are not very bright in class, are you?"

He did not say anything to me and I felt sorry for Laura. He told us to get out and warned us that if he caught us again, in a similar situation, he would have us both expelled. We left the room humiliated. We were more careful after that and found more isolated places to go, not far from the crowd of students.

Our plan to invite Pantea and his red-haired Ilona to the cinema failed. She had broken up with him and he did not know why. He was plunged into the depths of despair and would barely eat anything for days, instead, playing with his food with a morose expression. Our classmates mocked him for having been left by Ilona and they teased him for everything else. I felt very sorry for him and stopped giving my Russian and French homework to the bullies.

Collective Farm Forever

In 1962, the Party decided that the process of collectivization had to be completed. The war against the recalcitrant peasants had to be won at all costs. It had dragged on too long. No more procrastination was allowed.

Many of the peasants in Lupoaia believed the lie told by the Collectivization Committee, that my father had joined the collective, and so they joined too. Only a handful, among them Uncle Ionica and Uncle Spirea, did not sign. They went into hiding at relatives' places in neighbouring villages. Occasionally they came home to test their fate.

On one of these occasions, at the end of January 1962, Mayor Firu knocked on Ionica's door at 1am. Ionica got up and asked who was there, at that hour.

"It's me, the mayor," Firu said.

"What's the problem?" Ionica asked, suspicious as he wrapped his arms around himself, as if for protection.

"I want to have a talk with you. Open, please."

"Not at this hour," Ionica insisted.

Another voice ordered him to open up. It was the voice of Dulău, the tall and rather grotesque militiaman in charge of the Lupoaia station. He never smiled and always looked as if he were about to plant his fist in your face.

"Hurry up, we need to talk."

Ionica did not have any choice. He opened the door and three men burst into the house: Dulău and Horea, the other militiaman, and Firu.

"Get dressed, you are coming with us."

"Where? What have I done?"

"Just get dressed. We are going to Salonta," ordered Dulău.

"Why?"

"There is a problem with your ID card," he lied.

What could Ionica do? If they said to go with them, you went with them. Auntie Raluca's cries for help were muffled by the cushion with which Dulău had covered her face, so that nobody would have a hint of what was happening.

When Ionica was ready, he himself said, "Let's go." He did not want to prolong his wife's agony or wake their daughter to see her father taken away by the militamen, like a criminal.

At 2am Ionica and Dulău took the train in Holod.

On the train Ionica asked Dulău, "Why are you taking me to Salonta?"

Dulău ignored him and Ionica did not talk anymore. He knew the bastard told lies. Everybody in the village hated him.

At the Militia Headquarters in Salonta, Ionica was pushed into a cold room and left to wait. Through the door, which was left ajar, he saw Lieutenant Mangra from Rogoz. He stood up and greeted the lieutenant, asking him if he knew why he had been brought there.

"Is it a Militia matter?" asked Mangra. "If it is, I can help you."

"I don't know, I was told there was a problem with my ID card."

"Ah," said the lieutenant with a tinge of sadness in his voice, "that is a totally different matter. I am afraid I cannot do anything in that case. Nobody can," he whispered.

After a while Dulău came back for him and took him to a courtyard at the back of the Militia building. After crossing the 20m wide courtyard, they entered the Securitate building. The Securitate buildings were always at the back, grey and unwelcoming, away from the public eye. When they entered, Dulău delivered Ionica into the hands of a young sub-lieutenant, who ordered him to empty his pockets of all their contents, money, matches, cigarettes, penknife, handkerchief and so on.

"Undress," he commanded.

Ionica took off his *pufoaica*, his heavy winter coat. He stopped.

"Go on," the subofficer told him. "Take your jumper and your pants off too."

Ionica obeyed and was left only with his shirt and longjohns in the cold.

"Comrade Lieutenant, what have I done? Am I a prisoner?"

"Shut up and turn your face to the wall."

So Ionica did what he was asked. And he waited. He waited for minutes and minutes.

A captain came in. He ordered Ionica to turn around. Ionica recognized him as being from Topa de Sus. He did not say anything. The captain asked him how his paper was going.

"What paper, Comrade Captain?"

"I am not your comrade, Mr Ionica. Understood?"

"Yes, sir."

"How about the paper?" he asked again.

Ionica couldn't answer.

"The paper you are writing and reading to your friends."

"I barely can write my name, Captain sir. I can read a bit but newspapers are hard for me to understand."

"Why do you shut your door at night and block your windows with sheets? I have news that you are organizing meetings with people who are resisting collectivization. You are waiting for the Americans to come and save you. Isn't that true?"

"I don't do such things and never have," Ionica said calmly.

The captain stared at him and then invited him to come and sit at the table.

He changed tactics. He started talking politics. What did Ionica think about the Party policy? Ionica told him he was not interested in politics and couldn't understand all those directives, orders and resolutions.

What was the difference between the State and the Party?

Here, he told the captain, he had a problem; like everybody else, he couldn't see much difference. Everyone knew that there

was only one Party allowed to function and everyone knew that
the State should be above parties, but with one Party in the whole
State that was one of the things a peasant couldn't explain. It was
a bit like having a house with only one room and only one person
living there. You could call it either a house or a room, but the
space the person lived in was the same, regardless of the label.

The captain seemed to like his answer, particularly the idea of
one person in the room. He said that even if you had more persons
in that room, they should act as one in the end. That's why the
peasants should all be in one big room – in a collective – the only
way forward towards the new society the Party was building.
Why did he refuse to do what everybody had already done? Did
he think that all the other peasants were wrong, or at least the
overwhelming majority of them?

Ionica just said he was comfortable with his situation as it was.
He couldn't give away his forefathers' land.

Then the captain started all over.

"The paper. Tell me, this time for real."

"I don't know who told you this, Captain sir."

He had an inkling. He found out later that it was the anonymous
letters written by Bombic, Tutu and Irina, the three denouncers
who harmed many people.

"I don't buy newspapers. The only time I came close to a
newspaper was when I was in the army. A Party activist came to
the regiment one day to teach us about the new political course –
Communism, Socialism, Marxism. He explained the difference
and then asked me a question. Apparently, my answer was the right
one. He put me in charge of the wall gazette. You know, the one
on which newspaper clippings are glued every day with the most
important news. For the soldiers to see. Perhaps that is the paper
you are talking about. There is no other paper, I swear, Captain
sir," he said in a begging tone.

"When were you a Legionnaire?"

"Never," he answered, with a slight tone of indignation in his
voice.

"I have information you were."

"It can't be. I was too young when the Legionnaires were in power."

"You are lying!" the Captain thundered, staring into Ionica's eyes.

"No, sir. I was a *frățior de cruce*, little brother of the cross, in their youth organization. Yes. Like we have now, the pioneers, the young students, you know," Ionica conceded, moving his back against the chair.

"You see, Ionica, now we understand each other. What activity did you take part in when you were a young fascist?" The captain leaned across the table.

"Sir, all the youth of my age in Lupoaia were *frățiori de cruce*. We simply listened to Legionnaires coming from Oradea, Beiuș and Ceica. They taught us patriotic songs. The main thing we did was to go from Lupoaia to Beiuș and change the mayors in all the villages we passed through. There was a new order, we were told, a new world, a new future, a new beginning. We were only kids. I was a minor, very young, sir."

"How did you go to Beiuș?"

"Most of us on foot, but some had carts. There were no cars then."

"Why is it so difficult for you to confess about the paper you keep and about your interest in the imperialists?"

"There is nothing to confess, Captain sir. I am not as knowledgeable as you think."

The captain frowned. He stood up and called a militiaman.

"Take this man to the basement," he said before leaving the room in a hurry.

It was dark and cold in the basement. The guard pushed Ionica into the big room, which was full of bodies and smelled of faeces and urine. He stumbled forward, trying to hold his breath and attempting to make out individual shapes so as to avoid stepping on them. One by one, the people in the room told him that they had been there for a day, for three days, for a week.

He stayed there from eleven in the morning till about three in the afternoon, when the door opened and his name was called.

A young lieutenant with a Moldovan accent started investigating him again. About the paper. About the secret night meetings in his home. About the imperialists. About the fascists. Then he asked him about raising the fascist flagpole in Lupoaia.

He did not know anything about it, because he had not been there. One day he saw the flagpole and did not make much of it. That was all. He was very young then.

The captain came back again and sat next to the young lieutenant.

"You are a peasant, Ionica."

"Yes, sir."

"Are you going to join the collective?"

"Why should I join? My life is fine as it is."

"Wrong, Mr Ionica. We should strive to improve our life. Always. And here is your chance. The majority of the peasants have understood this. Why are you so stubborn?"

"What's this collective to you, Captain sir? I just don't want to join. My land is my parents' land and I inherited it from them. When I die, it will go to my daughter. Why should I renounce it?" Ionica asked.

"You don't renounce it, mister. It becomes everybody's property, as everybody's property becomes yours. It's a selfless act. You don't lose anything. You are not a rich man, after all. You'll become richer once you join the collective. All Lupoaia's land will be yours." The vein in his neck darkened. "Don't you realise that there is no future for you, outside the Party line? For anyone for that matter. The Party helps us forge a better life for ourselves. Look at Russia. They are better off since they joined the kolkhoz."

Ionica repeated that he had no interest in joining any collective ever. He did not like the idea itself. As for the Russians, good luck to them. He did not want to be like them.

The captain stood and clenched his hands around Ionica's neck, pushing his head backwards over the back of the chair; the heavy knee on Ionica's groin inflicted excruciating pain. He was panicking, losing consciousness and started to see scenes from his life flash before his eyes.

The captain stopped just in time.

A guard took Ionica to the punishment room. Two uniformed men came in and started hitting and kicking him on the head, in the stomach, groin and ribs. Ionica couldn't defend himself – although he did try to cover his head with his arms – and became their training ball until he fainted. They poured a bucket of urine on his face and he came to, the stench filling his nostrils. He felt the cold penetrating his aching bones and, as he came to, one of them punched him in the chest so hard that he stopped breathing. Ionica felt as if he were dying.

They dragged him back to the basement. After a couple of hours they came for him again. A new line of interrogation commenced – not about his past anymore. They wanted to know what he thought about Communism. Why did he cling to old ideas about capitalistic regimes that advocated and practised exploitation? Communism was a paradise where nobody was exploited anymore. Everybody ultimately gave society what they were able to give and took what they needed. Wasn't that beautiful? After all, that was happening already in Russia. Wouldn't he like to go to Russia?

Then they asked him if he had relatives in America.

"No."

"In any Western country?"

"No."

"In any country at all?"

"No."

He had a distant relative in Hungary, but he decided not to tell.

Then they asked him about all his relatives in Lupoaia. They had a list and went through the list with him. He gave them details and they seemed happy with that.

At the bottom of the list was Flonta Pavel. He told them my father was his brother-in-law.

"The *chiabur* is your brother-in-law?"

"Yes. But he is no longer a *chiabur*, as you know. The *chiabur* class has been eliminated."

"Too soon," the captain said. "But you know that the *chiabur* has joined the collective."

"Yes."

"Why do you think he did so?"

"I don't know, Sir."

"You know, but you don't want to say. Tell me."

"It's not my business, Sir."

"Remember this, you pig, everybody's business is your business. It's our business."

"Yes, Sir."

"Any other relatives in other villages or towns?"

Seeing that the surname Flonta caught the captain's attention so much, Ionica ventured.

"Yes, I have one. In Beiuş and he is called Flonta too."

"What's he doing for a living?"

"He is a Securitate lieutenant."

The captain paused for a moment "What sort of relative?"

"First cousin," he lied.

"First cousin?"

This was Ionica's eighth day in the dirty, dark and cold Securitate basement. Each day he had been interrogated three times and beaten during each interrogation. The next step would have been prison, if he did not die during one of the interrogations. Some people from the basement were sent home in a coffin.

On the ninth day, Ionica's name was called at 1am. He was taken to a room with no windows and no furniture, just the black walls. He feared the worst. The guard gave him his clothes and ordered him to get dressed. They locked him in. He leaned against the wall, then slid down to the floor and fell asleep.

Two militiamen, guns on their backs, came in. One of them told Ionica to follow him; the other walked behind. They walked in this formation to the Salonta station where he was made to buy a ticket to Holod. They waited for the train to come. When it came, they got into a carriage and told Ionica to sit. The militiamen kept guard at the opposite ends of the carriage. When the train started to move, they jumped off.

In the dark Ionica could distinguish the silhouette of a man in one corner of the carriage. It was Dulău, watching him from a distance, his hard stare penetrating Ionica's very bones.

Ionica wanted to ask him why he had lied when he arrested him. He wanted to tell him that there was no problem with his ID card. He wanted to tell him he was a liar. The urge to talk to him soon waned, when Ionica asked himself what would be the use of talking to such a low life creature, anyway?

They got off at Holod. Dawn was breaking. Ionica walked towards Lupoaia and Dulău followed him – twenty paces behind. When they reached the Hodişel, Ionica was overcome with fear. He might shoot me and bury my body in the mud of the river bed, he thought, but he jumped over and nothing happened. When he was twenty paces ahead, Dulău jumped too. As soon as Ionica reached his home and entered the courtyard, Dulău left the main road and took the path leading to Valea Gavri, turned left and hurried towards the Militia station.

Spirea had better luck: he and his horses travelled the roads towards Beiuş at night and hid in forests during the day. He was nowhere to be found but, in his absence the comrades from the Council emptied his house of his few valuable goods – beds, table, benches, doonas and cushions – and put them into the middle of the courtyard. Spirea's wife began crying and wailing but they were not impressed, not even when the neighbours came to watch. The goods were loaded on two carts and taken to the Council annexe, never to be returned to Spirea's home. When things calmed down, Spirea and his horses came back to Lupoaia. My father helped him make new beds and a table and Mama gave his wife a doona and two cushions.

They couldn't persuade Spirea to sign because he was always drunk and could barely stand on his feet. His land was taken by the collective anyway, with the excuse that it fell within the collective's perimeter. He and Ionica were given land 50km away from Lupoaia.

Ionica did not bother going to see the land. Spirea took the People's Council paper, which gave the location of his new land, determined to salvage something for his suffering. He went to Ciumeghiu to take possession of the land but the People's Council there told him that there was no such parcel of land. That was the end of the matter. He could do nothing. By not signing the application to join the collective, Spirea kept his horses. He was the only person in Lupoaia to do that. He started transporting materials and bags of cereals and potatoes to and from the markets. On his way back from the markets he would stop at a pub and get drunk. Then he would put the horses on the road and would fall asleep on the bottom of the cart.

No matter where they were, the horses always found their way home.

All those who joined the collective had their draft animals, oxen, cows, buffalos and horses, taken away. The animals became collective property and nobody was allowed to have more than one cow, without any exception.

My father sold Doina, one of our mares, before collectivization; but I was so in love with Boaba that he kept her. He managed to keep the collective away from her for two years, warning the brigadier, the president and Traleu, the new militiaman, not to enter our courtyard, the fierce expression on his face enough to persuade them.

One day, when my father was not at home, the cowards came and took our Boaba away. She became the brigadier's horse. He would show up on the main road passing our home, riding our Boaba with the arrogance of a landlord, who wanted to show off his most precious possession. Mama suffered most because her health was deteriorating. She had lost weight and she looked like a haunted woman of twice her age. Every time she saw this man riding Boaba, she said it seemed as if one more nail were being driven into her coffin.

My father built a new cart, bought a new plough and started training our cow, together with Ghiona's, to draw the cart and follow the furrow when ploughing our garden. They wanted to confiscate the cart and to stop my father and Ghiona using the cows as draft animals.

"You just try and see what happens," my father said to them. And they tried.

They came with Traleu, who laid his hand on my father's cart. My father, as always, asked for their written authorization. He knew, somehow, that the word authorization worked. However, it did not work this time and so my father took Traleu by surprise, clenching his huge, work worn hands around his neck. He told them, through clenched teeth and with veins popping in anger, that blood would run if they did not leave his courtyard at once.

They left, threatening that they would be back. They never returned.

A Farewell

It was the end of October, 1962, and we were only a month and a half into our last year of high school. I was 16, awkward and taller than everybody in my family, but couldn't wait for the future. All of us were looking forward to finishing school and moving on to the next step: university for 5 years, a technical institute for 3 years, or maybe a job.

At five o'clock one cold morning, a female cleaner went to the first floor of the school building to sweep the classrooms, as she did every school day. She had noticed something written on the blackboard in our classroom but did not pay attention to it and, even if she had done, she could barely read even her own name. She started to sweep the long corridor between the classrooms, then turned right into the small wing that connected the chemistry and physics laboratory. It was still dark but dawn filtered through the window at the end of the corridor. Strange, she thought, it was darker than usual. She reached the end of the corridor and her broom hit something. She raised her eyes and saw a student, his face in shadow.

Comrade Dragnea came into the dormitory shouting, a bottle of water in his left hand and a cane in his right hand, just as he did every morning.

"Wake up! Wake up, you sloths!"

Some of us jumped up immediately, some didn't. The latter

had water poured on their faces and were hit with the cane. This had an instant effect. Comrade Dragnea took us to the courtyard, made us run for a quarter of an hour in our pyjamas, lined us up in front of the artesian well to wash, and hurried us back to the dormitory to get dressed.

I noticed Ion Pantea's bed was already made. I thought he must have got up earlier and gone to the classroom to study. That was until Ion Popa, whose locker was near mine, bent down and picked up a small box from the bottom of his locker. He opened it and found a razor and a note inside.

"Look here, this is from Pantea for you. I haven't seen him this morning," said Ion Popa, handing me the note.

"I think he got up early. He must be studying," I said, shrugging.

The note read, "Give it to Flonta from me. Ion Pantea."

I was puzzled as I had not asked for Pantea's razor. I understood why he put it in Ion Popa's locker: his door could be pulled open just enough to pass the razor through, while mine was shut tight.

As Ion Popa rushed to the lavatory, I was left confused, thinking about Pantea and his razor. I heard Comrade Dragnea warning us that we had to leave the dormitory in five minutes. Instead of lining up in front of the refectory for our breakfast as usual, we had to position ourselves in a square and wait. The tutors could control us better that way.

Comrade Principal dashed through the courtyard towards the teaching wing. Teachers began arriving one by one. It was strange for us to see them so early.

The rumour was that something had happened, perhaps something tragic. The student the cleaner had found in the corridor next to the chemistry lab did not move when she talked to him. She thought he was asleep, took him by the arm and shook him. His whole body swung. The cleaner stepped back screaming and crossing herself. The body was hanging from the window's handle, the feet almost touching the ground. A waste-paper basket lay nearby. I immediately thought of Ion Pantea. His depression. His red-haired girlfriend leaving him. His father beating him. His stepmother hating him. His school companions mocking him. I broke formation and ran towards the teaching wing. I did not care about Comrade Dragnea running after me, yelling my name, telling me to get back. The janitor did not let me get in. I begged him to tell me what happened. He took pity on me – perhaps seeing Comrade Dragnea dragging me back to the formation, because he said that a boy had hanged himself on the first floor.

"Ion Pantea!" I shouted, struggling against my human restraints.

"They are bringing him down," he said.

Comrade Dragnea dragged me back – but I refused to stay there. The pain in my stomach was unbearable. I walked to the storage room and sat down crying with my head leaning against the wall. I pulled out of my pocket Ion Pantea's razor box, opened it, read the note again and again, crying to exhaustion.

After a while, some men quickly crossed the courtyard, carrying a stretcher covered with a white sheet. I never saw my friend again.

We were allowed to have breakfast but I couldn't eat, so I gave my portion to Ion Popa. There was silence in the refectory. Some girls were crying. After breakfast we were told to line up, year by year, in the courtyard and wait to be called to go to the classroom.

We had a surprise when we entered the classroom. Ion Pantea's last words were written on the blackboard in his familiar scrawl:

"Goodbye forever! If I did any wrong to any of you, please forgive me. Ion Pantea."

The whole class was stunned. The girls sobbed and some of the boys cried too.

I tried to imagine Ion Pantea and his state of mind as he wrote those words, knowing that he was going to be dead just a few minutes later. Did he cry, as we were doing? What were his last thoughts? He left me the razor and that was a great gesture. He certainly thought of me. I felt guilty. How could I not have seen it coming? The evening before he was doing his homework in geography, his favourite subject, and now he was dead. Was his an act of courage or one spurred on by unbearable desperation? Whatever it was, Comrade Caimac, the history teacher, was already erasing Pantea's last words from the blackboard, in spite of our protestations. He condemned the poor soul for having acted selfishly, contrary to the spirit of the new society with a luminous future, blah, blah, blah. None of the teachers was interested in what made Pantea resort to such a desperate act, because the new society, in progress, offered him everything and all he had to do was to accept that and say thank you. His spirit was just a projection of the material world that could be sliced up and put back together by a decision of the magnanimous Party or by the current laws which forged the new man. A person who took his own life was a person who refused to take advantage of the luminous future on offer. That was inconceivable and, most of all, obscene. It was his loss anyway, and our gain as a society. Just as with the enemies of the people, who were exterminated by the regime, acts like suicide proved the Darwinian law of the survival of the fittest. After all, how could the new society be built with weaklings? How could the new man be a weakling? There was no place for weaklings in our society. Hadn't we all seen the representations artists made of the new man in their work? Bold, proud, happy, fiery factory workers standing on pedestals with the hammers and sickles in their hands, fearlessly piercing the horizon with their eyes, all projected towards a future easy to attain, under the wise guidance of the Party.

Some of us wanted to go to Ion Pantea's funeral. There will be no class participation in the funeral, the order came. Instead we had a class meeting where Pantea's act was condemned, and the one who condemned it most vehemently was his own cousin, Vasalica. Pantea was always complaining about him, because Vasalica reported everything Pantea did to his father, who would sometimes beat him. Pantea had avoided Vasalica as much as he could. Now Vasalica was trampling on the dead body of his cousin. As a reward, he was again nominated as secretary of the school Youth Communist Organization.

Is There a Future Out There?

In a few months we would be free – well, as free as one could be in our tightly-controlled new society. Free from this type of school, which had become too stuffy for our fast-growing lungs. We needed fresh air and wondered what university would be like, what the working environment would be like, what just doing nothing would be like. These were our options.

Money for the final school leavers' class group photo was collected. Photos were taken by a professional photographer near the Patria Cinema, with students wearing ties and no matriculation numbers on our sleeves. Grown up men. Clean, fresh faces ready to go out and contribute to the glorious work of building our new society, led by the Party, which had an answer for everything and a place for everybody to do his or her bit.

We wanted Ion Pantea in the class photo.

No, we couldn't have him.

He didn't finish year eleven and he was a coward for having committed suicide.

The class photo was to be viewed as a celebration of youth, of life, of enthusiasm; a memento of our transition from adolescence into manhood, where we would prove our worth, facing the challenges our Party had planned for us.

My father came to visit me, and talked about a man from Calea Mare whose son was working in Foreign Trade. The son and his wife were coming home for a brief holiday in two weeks.

"We should go and see them," my father said. "You'll get more information about the Foreign Trade Faculty."

On the Sunday we thought the Foreign Trade man was going to be home, my father and I took the 4.30am train to Oradea and got out at Calea Mare. It was still dark when we walked down the long slope to the village, casting shadows on the lush fields as we took the paths running through them. We walked about until people started coming out of their houses to go to Sunday Mass. We soon found out where the family lived and knocked on the door of their modest house.

They were all up and eating fried lard, eggs and pickled cucumbers for breakfast. We were invited to join them but declined, as we had eaten our boiled eggs on the train. We couldn't refuse the coffee, as Ion, the Foreign Trade specialist, said he had brought it from Italy and Italy had the best coffee in the world. He was a short man with dark skin and a heap of curly hair. His blonde wife, Svetlana, was a Russian whom he had met as a student at Lomonosov University in Moscow. It was the first time in my life I had seen a Russian. She was tall, incredibly pretty and so kind, complimenting me on my Russian, which was not good – but I enjoyed hearing this from her charming mouth. She was so far from the stereotypical Russian.

Ion, her husband, told us that not everybody was allowed to sit the entrance exam for the Foreign Trade Faculty. The Securitate checked all the applications and put together a dossier on the candidate's family's past, his social origin – which had to be healthy – his behaviour in society and his school results.

When I asked him about the job itself, what he was doing in particular, he told us only that he was sent abroad with other colleagues in delegations of 4, 6 or 8 specialists to buy things we needed or to sell products to other countries, like our famous tractors.

I asked him why 8 people and not 2, for example. He said that the system worked like that, through delegations, each team member having his own specialization. This way they would not be individually responsible for any mistakes made, he said laughingly.

On our way back my father and I talked about the dossier – but only for a little while, for, in our enthusiasm, we dismissed its importance. Yes, my father had been declared a *chiabur*, but that was now history as the *chiabur* class had been dismantled in 1959. We were now in 1963 and the former *chiaburs*, those who had survived, were on their way to becoming new men, able to contribute to our society with a luminous future, like anybody else.

Even collectivization was behind us now.

No land in our name anymore.

No more excuses for me to be treated differently.

The Ball

When it came to the school leavers' end-of-year ball, Ion Pantea's memory was already fading.

I spent the night before the ball with Laura in the room above the gymnasium, until late. She knew I wanted to go to Bucharest and was crying because it was too far away. She asked me why I couldn't do what everybody else did and go to Cluj or Timișoara. She also knew that I had my heart set on the Foreign Trade Faculty, which was only available in Bucharest. For some reason, I just couldn't picture myself as a student anywhere else but in the capital. This was our last chance to see each other in school and, to mark the occasion, she had promised me a big going-away present, but after failing to persuade me to go to university in a city closer to home, though, she did not mention the present anymore. I asked her about it and she made me understand that she had wanted to seal our separation with what she called a permanent bond – she had wanted to give herself to me. I was very disappointed that she changed her mind and we separated on a rather dull note, each aware that our beautiful friendship, which had not made either a woman out of her or a man out of me, was going to become only the subject of letters from then on. For how long?

My parents came in the afternoon before the ball and I put on the new grey suit and blue tie they had had custom-made for me, for the occasion. I walked down the main street of Beiuș with my very proud Mama on my arm and my father walking beside me. Often, when Mama and I went into shops, they called me her brother, much to her amusement, and she told me that, in my suit, I looked more than ever like her younger brother.

The ball was in the gymnastics auditorium which was larger and lighter than most of the other rooms. The students were seated at a long table in the middle and the parents at tables by the walls. The food was prepared and served by our canteen cooks, perhaps as a reminder that we still depended on them. Our three course meal was simple: beef bones and vegetable soup, mashed potatoes soaked in gravy and pork steak – and a sweet rice pudding for desert. We were so excited by the party and the prospect of leaving the place, that we did not mind swallowing our last portion of bromide.

We were not allowed to hire a band for fear it would play corrupt, western music; but a small group of students were given permission to play for us, with Lucian on the saxophone, Horga on the drums, and Popa on the accordion. They played the western music we listened to on the radio anyway, and Comrade Vice Principal Berbec scolded them, telling them to play our music. They said yes, but continued to play what they wanted. There was nothing Comrade Berbec could do to us anymore. Teachers were on the lookout for troublemakers, ready to follow any couple getting into a dark corner or going up to the reading room.

We were not allowed alcoholic drinks but some parents, including my father, brought *pălinca* and many a school-leaver was seen running outside to vomit.

My ulcer was acting up, so I did not drink or dance. Instead, I ended up thinking of Laura, of Ion Pantea, remembering scenes, words, scents, sorrows and joys. I stared at Comrade Berbec, as he tried to impose his will on the band one last time and, in my mind, I called him Comrade Dickhead, telling him how glad I would be not to see him again.

Comrade Berbec left the band and smiled at me. Then, passing close, he said, "I know what you are thinking!"

"Better not, Comrade Principal."

"Let me see. You are thinking of going far away, becoming

somebody and coming back for your class reunion in ten years time. Am I right?"

"Only in one respect, Comrade."

"Which one is that?"

"About going far away."

As he moved away, he patted me on the back and laughed.

He was almost likable.

And yet, it was at this school that, for the first time in my life, I was given credit for my results, starting with year ten when I was awarded the first prize. Somehow, it came as an anticlimax, perhaps because I had to wait so long, or perhaps because having always been singled out as the *chiabur*'s son – and no matter how hard I tried I couldn't shake it off – had taken the joy out of my heart. I always thought of the Beiuş High School No. 1 as a tightly guarded cage, and of me, in my own even more tightly guarded little cage, inside it. I thought of myself as the sparrow my Grandpa Teodorea had caught for me when I was a child – with my legs tied to a string and my wings clipped at the whim of people like Comrade Berbec. I needed to move from my double cage to a bigger one, where my wings would be allowed to grow and I could roam, if not freely, at least like everybody else.

In a couple of months time, I was hoping to enrol in the Faculty of Foreign Trade in Bucharest, for two reasons: I liked foreign languages and I wanted to see the world. I was going to study English and Italian, the beautiful language I discovered by chance, only to find out that my Grandpa Teodorea had learned some while a prisoner of war, which made me love it even more.

The Faculty required a dossier from the Securitate about each candidate sitting for the entrance exams. In other words, if you had a healthy social origin and came from an unblemished proletarian family – automatons who responded blindly to any requests from the Party – that mattered more than what you knew or what you were able to offer society. However, at 17 years old, I was ready to face any challenge and tackle any obstacles blocking the road to my dreams. I was ready to take on the world. I was unstoppable. Bygones were bygones. The future, however uncertain it might be, awaited me. My brain was in a flying mood and I felt like the cranes I used to watch as a little boy in the evening skies of Dumbrava, going somewhere south in their 'V' formation to find more nourishment, to explore new lands and to build a new home. I often wondered about the cranes when I was little. I asked others around me but they didn't know much. I admired the cranes' regular formation, their joyous chant and their leader, who knew the long way to their mysterious destination. My destination, too, was mysterious but I knew there would be many new things for me to see, experience and learn.

Unhealthy Social Origin

My access to the bigger cage lay in the hands of Comrade Burete, a Party activist from Oradea with a friendly smile and without the menace of his peers. He entered the premises of the Lupoaia Municipal Council unannounced, soon after my final exams. He went up the few stairs on the left, just opposite the annexe where my father had been detained in the past, knocked on the first door, knocked on the second and got lucky when he knocked on the third door.

When the clean, well dressed Comrade entered the room, young Ilie got to his feet – almost military-style. Comrade Burete asked the whereabouts of the Council Secretary.

"You are looking at him, Comrade."

"Very nice to meet you. I didn't expect such a young person to be in charge here. You must be good," Comrade Burete said.

"One does what one is called on to do by the higher authorities," the scripted answer came.

"Yes, certainly. Oh, allow me to introduce myself. Petre Burete, from the Regional Party Headquarters."

"It's an honour for me, Comrade Burete. Please, make yourself comfortable. You must be tired from the trip. Had I known, I would have sent a cart to pick you up at the station. Did you walk all this way?"

"It's good exercise but I will take up your offer in the afternoon, if you don't mind. I have to catch the 4pm train to Oradea. Before that, I have to collect some information regarding Flonta Teodor, son of Pavel and Nuța."

"Anything wrong? He has just finished his high school exams."

"I know, I know. That's why I am here. He wants to sit for entrance exams to the Faculty of Foreign Trade in Bucharest. There are some restrictions. I wonder what you can tell me about the young man?"

"Well, he keeps to himself a lot but he is a studious kind of kid. His father is more active, if you know what I mean. He had a problem with the collectivization."

"Collectivization, yes, not a very spontaneous process. It's past now. We should understand our peasants' lifetime devotion to the land. What do you think?" Comrade Burete replied.

"Yes, Comrade."

Ilie picked up an old land and taxes register and opened it. He turned it towards Comrade Burete.

"Flonta Pavel. *Chiabur*," Comrade Burete read. He saw a future impeded, as he had seen so many over the years. He had seen a few things in his life; but he thought this young man went overboard. There were no *chiaburs* anymore. Why did he have to pull out this old register? Frowning and with a heavy heart, he had no choice but to mark it down in his report.

"Then I will record this," he said, with no enthusiasm in his voice.

"Please do," Ilie said, scripted and wooden once again, with no feeling at all for the future he had just damaged. My future.

Comrade Burete filled in a form. This was his last task on the case and the negative reference left a bitter taste in his mouth.

"Would you sign here, please?" he asked the young man.

"It's my duty, Comrade."

Comrade Burete watched him sign and his left eye twitched.

"I need another statement. Perhaps the Party secretary," he said.

"I'll take you to him," Ilie offered.

"Thank you, I'll manage. What's his name, please?"

"Vaida Victor. I can't let you go alone," Ilie insisted.

"You are very kind. These are delicate matters, you know."

"I understand. I'll have the cart ready on your return."

"I'd be grateful."

Vaida Victor told Comrade Burete that we were a good family. My father was a hard worker and, as far as he knew, I was always the best in my class.

Comrade Burete asked how my father was judged politically in the village.

"He is not a Party member, we are a small organization – only 25 members out of 600 villagers," he said.

"Does Flonta Pavel have a healthy social origin, you know what I mean, Comrade Vaida," Comrade Burete asked.

"Are you referring to his *chiabur* past?"

"So, he was a *chiabur*."

"Well, he was, and he suffered a lot for it. He didn't do anything wrong, forgive me for saying this."

"I see," Comrade Burete said.

"Is there anything wrong?"

"I only wish I had come to you first," the Comrade said. "The young Council Secretary signed a statement which will certainly do some damage."

"To think that they are close relatives," Vaida Victor reflected.

"Thank you, Comrade Vaida. Would you be so kind as to tell me where Flonta's house is?"

"You just go up to that high clay bank at the end of the road, follow the path up and, when you reach the top, it's the first house on the right. You can't miss it."

Comrade Burete climbed Hurupa and stopped in front of our beautiful, brick house. After a while he banged his fist on the entrance door. My father opened it. Comrade Burete introduced himself and told my father what he was doing there. He had no duty to come and visit my father but, at the last minute, he thought "why not?"

My father opened a bottle of *pălinca*, as he always did with guests. Comrade Burete told him he had gathered information about me from school teachers and from school companions and it was excellent. "You couldn't have better reports than that," he said. Then he suddenly asked my father, "Do you have enemies in the village?"

My father shrugged his shoulders. "Who knows? I haven't wronged anybody I know of, but in the past some of my friends became my enemies, writing anonymous letters, spying on my movements... Perhaps they still are..."

They drank more and Comrade Burete told him that his own son had just finished High School in Oradea and had decided to try his luck at the Faculty for Foreign Trade. He wished his son had the reports and the results I had. He also had the courage to tell my father about the encounter at the People's Council and he showed him the statement Ilie had signed. If that hadn't come up, I might well have had a chance of being a student there in the autumn, he said.

My father was dumbfounded and couldn't think straight, his face falling once again at the fact that his past would damage his son's future.

"Ilie... Ilie... what have I done to these people?" he managed to say after long moments of silence.

Ilie was my mother's cousin. His side of the family never looked favourably on my mother's marriage to my father. They had had somebody else in mind for her. My father knew that and ignored them. The fact that my father had, in spite of the difficulties he went through, done relatively well, made them envious. And the young Ilie acted in that spirit. A few years later, when I was in my last year of university, I asked him point blank why he had shown the activist the old register, where my father was listed as *chiabur*? He swore he had not. In the years that followed, Ilie became the president of the collective farm and continued tormenting my father over the few surplus square metres of land in his garden and did not allow my father to install his *cazan* – by then the *cazan* belonged to the State Wine and Spirits Company of Oradea – on the collective property. That meant my father had to go to other villages to do business. But Ilie never did anything directly himself, he only pulled the strings. From the safety of my home in Italy,

I wrote to Comrade Ceaușescu about my father's plight. While I did not receive an answer, my father told me that an activist came from Oradea and listened to him. From that moment on he was not bothered about the surplus land in his garden anymore, but still he was not allowed back in Lupoaia with his *cazan*.

My father poured out his sorrow to Comrade Burete, asking why should his son go through this sort of thing, why should his son be treated differently from others? He didn't do anybody any wrong, so why should imaginary sins of the father's fall on a son who did well in what society was asking of him? How could he be called a *chiabur* now when his land, his horses and his cart had all been taken by the collective, and even his little distillery had been nationalized by the State? Why should his son's life be ruined too? It was just too much for a human being to take. Comrade Burete drank a bit more. When my father accompanied him to the door, he put his hand on my father's arm. "Believe me, Pavel, I haven't felt so bad doing this job for a long time."

"It is hard to take it in, it is very hard indeed. There is no justice in this world, none at all."

"On the other hand, Pavel, consider yourself lucky to have a son who will certainly do something with himself. I am sure he'll be happy in the end. He will find a way."

Comrade Burete thanked my father for his hospitality, patted him on the shoulder and left him bleeding sorrow, anger, impotence and confusion through all his pores. Soon after Burete's departure, I received a dry letter which, in one sentence, ended my aspirations of a career as a foreign trade economist. As usual, no reason at all was given. You asked for something you thought you were entitled to and they said no, without feeling obliged to tell you the reason. That's how it worked. I knew that coming from a family with an unhealthy social origins, things would be harder for me. Nonetheless, in my heart, hope never died. However, over time, I had learned that trying never died either. Trying was one thing I always had to do more than others, because, in the self-proclaimed society of equals, we were made to be less equal than many of the families around us.

I consoled myself with the idea that perhaps I would not have passed the entrance exam anyway, and I would have had to look for other options. Apart from licking my wounds, I had one option left: relief teacher for a year and then try my luck at another faculty. The system was so short of qualified teachers that, once a person like me was accepted by a school, he kept the job for a whole year.

Teacher with Picu

I wrote a letter to Laura that summer and she did not reply, so one Sunday I borrowed my father's bike and went to Căpâlna to see her. It was almost noon and very hot when I arrived in her village. I asked a couple of old people sitting on the porch in their Sunday best where Laura's house was. They told me she had just gone with the girls to the river and pointed me in that direction. I found the group of girls but I did not find Laura. I sat on the bank of the river for quite a while, but no sign of Laura. I decided to return to her house. I entered the courtyard, went to the door, knocked, then circled the house and entered into the garden and found nobody. I asked a group of young boys if they had seen Laura somewhere and they shrugged their shoulders. It was getting dark and I decided to go home. The sadness in my heart was almost unbearable. The words of an Italian song, I had just heard in the last weeks, were making it worse:

> *Amore ritorna a casa* (My love come back home)
> *Ti prego, torna da me* (I beg you, come back to me)
> *Perchè mi vuoi lasciar* (Why do you want to leave me)
> *In un mondo così triste* (In a world so sad)
> *Per chi è solo* (For who is lonely)

I wrote a letter to her and I included the song with the translation. She did not reply.

Finding a job was easier than I thought. I went to the Salonta Education Department and put my application in. When the man saw my name, he said there was already a request for me by Comrade Picu Petroi, now the Principal of the recently formed middle-school of Hodiş, which also served Lupoaia and Forosig.

Not the Comrades Petroi again, I said to myself in disbelief, my mouth falling open. I had not expected our paths to cross again. On second thoughts, it was Hodiş and I would be able to live at home. No rent, no landlords, no hassle. As far as Comrade Picu Petroi went, well, I would be there for only a year and I could put up with him.

The comrade assigned me French, Russian, maths (grade seven only) and agricultural science to teach. He had three other young teachers like me: Nina from Lupoaia, Valentin from Holod and Filip from Vintere. A single mother, with a daughter in grade six, had been there for a couple of years. None of us had a university degree, including Comrade Picu Petroi himself. He had had some bad experiences with qualified teachers in the past and now he preferred to work with young, unqualified people like us whom he could control as he pleased.

He put us under pressure, asking us to submit a lesson plan for each class in advance. We did it for a week but it became a cumbersome task, given the amount of preparation and marking we had to do. We concocted a plan and decided to submit lesson plans only for Mondays and see what happened. Nothing happened for a day, two, three... Then, one evening, Comrade Picu Petroi went to Nina's house and asked her why nobody submitted their lesson plans anymore. She told him we had too much work. Seeing our solidarity, he never asked for lesson plans again. After all, he did not teach, despite the fact that he was supposed to do some minimal teaching a week. His important contribution to the school life was his trip to Salonta, once a month, to collect the bag of cash for our salaries. On payday, he would make us queue in front of his office and call us in, one by one, to sign the register. After that, he counted the notes of the pay-packet.

My first week as a teacher made me feel very strange indeed. Here I was, the big class register under my arm, aged 17 and ready to go into a class of students only 3 or 4 years younger than I was. The girls, already interested in boys, followed my every move with their languid eyes. Before entering the classroom, I quite often had to stop for a few seconds to hold back a smile and compose myself. It was both embarrassing and flattering. I had to learn to keep both my composure and the right pupil-teacher distance.

Having been freed from the cumbersome lesson plans, I had time to think about my future. My father said that the Communists didn't manage to make an engineer out of my uncle Gligorea, who failed his final project and was now working as a sub-engineer, therefore I should become a doctor. He believed I would be able to do it in spite of the odds. A doctor? Well, with Foreign Trade out of the way for good, why not try? So I pulled out my anatomy, physics, chemistry, and biology books and started getting up at 4am every day, to study for two hours before going to the school. I did this for a couple of months, but then I found out that, no matter how good you were at the entry exams, there was a chance you would not get in. First of all, candidates studied for these exams using university manuals – of a much higher standard than the Education Department textbooks. Second, places were prioritized to make room for Party apparatchiks' children. I did not give myself a chance under those conditions, more so after my attempts to obtain university course material failed. I gave up on medicine. My father was not pleased. What then? I had to get into the university or be drafted into the army for my compulsory military service.

Irene, My Hungarian Flame

I thought of going to Bucharest in September to sit for the entrance exams in Italian. The subjects required were Romanian language and literature, a foreign language and modern history. When I finished teaching in July, I went to Oradea to take some private lessons in Romanian grammar. Examiners had a fixation with long sentences, which had to be split into various clauses – causal, temporal, concessive, final – and built into a tree-diagram showing their dependence on the main clause and on each other. One evening, with my head bursting with exercises of this kind, I decided to go out to a summer garden restaurant with my roommate Viorel.

A young couple with a little boy and a beautiful teenage girl, with very pale skin and long hair, sat at the table next to ours. They were speaking Hungarian. The girl was talking to the older woman, but every now and then she turned her head towards our table. Viorel said she was giggling and looking at me. There was music coming from a recorder and he insisted I invite her to dance. I tried to dismiss the idea, but the girl nodded at me. I was somehow trapped into action, all the more so, when Viorel said that if I did not invite her, he would have a go.

My dancing skills were almost nil but, encouraged by the girl's look, I took the plunge. I got up and, as was customary, asked the man for permission to dance with the young lady. He said something in Hungarian to me, which seemed unfriendly from both his tone and demeanour, but the girl was already on her feet. We were the only ones on the little dance floor and the girl seemed so happy to be there. I excused myself for my poor dancing but she did not mind. Her name was Irene and the man was her brother-in-law. I asked her what he had said to me. He told me she was not allowed to dance with Romanians and that they were going home shortly. I asked her what she thought about dancing with Romanians and she said it was the same as dancing with Hungarians and Germans or other nationalities. If she liked the boy, she would dance with him.

I liked her attitude and the glimmer in her eyes and asked her if she could stay a bit longer – after her brother-in-law and his family left. She said she would try but he was such a mean bastard that it would be difficult for her to stay. When the music finished, I took her back to her table and said thank you to the man, but he did not even look at me, busying himself with his little boy. Irene started arguing with her brother-in-law, already up and ready to go. She remained seated and refused to go with them. I could see from their argument that Irene's sister was siding with her. In the end they left without her, the man giving me a grim look. I pretended nothing had happened but I couldn't help thinking of the stories of my childhood about the Hungarians and the Jews making salami out of the unaware Romanians going into their shops.

Irene told me that she had to be home in half an hour, otherwise she would be in big trouble. She lived with the couple because her parents had died in a truck accident a few years before. Her brother-in-law wanted her to date only Hungarian boys. I said I liked her and she said she liked me too – and when I took her hand, she did not withdraw it. I asked her if she liked Italian music and she said she loved it. Then, without any inhibition, she started singing for me in the sweetest voice:

I found my love in Portofino ...
perchè nei sogni credo ancor (Because I still believe in dreams)
lo strano gioco del destino (The strange game of destiny)
a Portofino m'ha preso il cuor. (Conquered my heart in Portofino.)

I was in awe of her. She knew more than I did of Fred Buscaglione, Domenico Modugno and Claudio Villa, because she listened to the Hungarian Radio and they played more Italian music than the Romanians, she said. She loved opera, to which I did not pay much attention. We walked hand-in-hand towards her home and I asked her if we could meet again the next day. She said yes and we agreed to meet on the bridge over the Crişul Repede at midday.

As we approached her house, we saw her brother-in-law waiting at the door, casting a long shadow with his back to the light. She told me it was better for me to go away, but I said that Romanians see their girlfriends at least to the door, if not into the house. They lived on the first floor, she said, and she would come to the window and wave goodbye to me. Her brother-in-law scolded her, indicating by his finger at me that I should go away. I pretended to leave but returned when he entered the main door; I saw Irene being pulled back from the window of her room before it opened, and the man started shouting at me in Hungarian.

The next day, five minutes before noon, I was strolling on the bridge over the Crişul Repede. At noon she wasn't there. I waited for another quarter of an hour. No trace of Irene. Still I waited, but she did not come. I had only four days left. That Saturday evening I went to Irene's house but all the lights were out. I threw a pebble at her window and there was no response. I threw another one, and another one. I went back on Sunday at noon and did the same. A neighbour told me in broken Romanian that Irene had left for the countryside with her family and he did not know when they would be back.

My short summer romance was over even before it started. My two-year relationship with Laura was over too. Three months after I started teaching, she had written to me saying that she was seeing my companion Adrian Popovici, now a part-time college tutor alongside Comrade Dragnea. A few months later she was expelled from school for a while, because she was caught petting with him in a dark classroom.

Although I did not know Irene's surname, I wrote to her address. She never replied.

Tatar Language

I went to Bucharest alone. My father called the now retired Captain Halca, for whom he had worked as an attendant during the war. I could stay with them for the duration of my entrance exams and I would make friends with his son, an engineering student, and daughter, a high school student, he said. My father was so pleased that he stuffed my suitcase with sausages, ham, eggs and *pălinca* for the Captain, just as he had done so often during his military service.

Nobody came to pick me up at the station. As it was early morning, I called the captain's house. Mrs Halca sounded bored or half asleep and, when I asked her the bus or tram number going their way, she just said, 'take a taxi' and put down the phone. I would have run away from the Halcas as fast as I could, but I had nowhere else to go.

Dragging my heavy suitcase out of the railway station, I was hit by a curtain of smog and had my first experience of the din of the city. For a moment I felt lost. A well-dressed gentleman pointed out the tram station, then I was on my way to the Halcas. I was tormented with apprehension every step of the way over the short distance from the station to their house, thinking of the cold reception Mrs Halca had given me on the phone.

I tried to enter the neglected courtyard, pushing open a rusty iron gate through which I could only squeeze sideways. The house in front looked like a shack with a flat roof that seemed to squash the already low building. Even our stables looked better, I thought. A coughing, skinny man came up from behind me and took the handle of my suitcase. Instinctively I pulled the suitcase away.

"Welcome," said Captain Halca. He apologised for not being able to come to the station. He'd had an appointment with the doctor, he said. Some of my apprehension dimmed but I was still nervous.

Mrs Halca smiled as she eyed my suitcase. All the stories my father told me about the war and about supplying the Halcas with food came flashing into my mind. She said her children were still in bed and I would meet them later. She made me empty my suitcase almost instantly. They seemed to be starving, with the captain's body so frail you could count the ribs through his shirt and the pale Mrs Halca looking like a ghost with a double dose of white powder on her face. That made me uncomfortable because, no matter how much we had been persecuted, my father always found a way of putting food on the table.

While the old people hardly ate, the two children stuffed themselves with everything they could get their hands on. The day after my arrival I heard Magda, the daughter, asking her mother for money. When Mrs Halca refused, Magda came and asked me to lend her 25 *lei*. I did and she made a habit of it. Every day she waited for me to come home to ask me for money. Then, after a week, Mrs Halca came and apologised, asking if I could lend her some money too, saying she would return it before I went home. I never got my money back and in the end it cost me more to stay at their place than at the students' hostel. When I told my father, he was lost for words. He made excuses for his captain, saying he certainly would not have been aware of what was happening. My father added that we would never do such a thing to our guests.

I did not sign up for the exams until the last day. There were ten places for Italian and five candidates for each one of them. The same happened with other languages except Tatar, where there were only two candidates for a place. I dreaded the military service and I did not think I would make it into Italian, so I enrolled in

Tatar.

I was surprised the next day when the final lists of candidates were pinned to the wall outside the Faculty Secretariat. Many candidates had thought along the same lines. Tatar had jumped to eleven candidates per place while the other languages had only seven.

Now I had to get high marks. I made a few mistakes with my French irregular verbs, but I did better in modern history, where the topic was the French Revolution. I must have been very convincing because I remembered the scarcity of food during that upheaval and that the French were chasing rats and eating them. For the Romanian language exam, I had to dissect a long sentence into ten clauses and name them according to their type, while in literature I had to write an essay on Eminescu's *3rd Letter*, in which he dealt with patriotism and the fate of leaders. He took his inspiration from the Turkish War of Independence and in the first part was concerned with patriotism, while the second was a powerful satire of the decaying present, swamped with politicians so corrupt, that only a radical intervention by Vlad the Impaler could rid society of them:

> "Why don't you come, Lord Impaler, to get your hands on them,
> And divide them in two groups: the mad and the corrupt,
> Then drive them by force into two large prisons,
> And set fire to both prison and madhouse."

Eminescu's angry question could be applied to our times, I thought, but I couldn't write that about the new society, which was preparing multilaterally developed, new men, and so I talked about the political situation of Eminescu's time at the end of the 19th century instead.

Six students were admitted to Tatar, because the last two had the same average mark. I was one of them, and a big weight was taken off my shoulders. The thought of being forced to do military service had haunted me for months. I saw military service as a complete waste of time for an educated young man and a means for the regime to drill their discipline, their slogans and their ideological nonsense into him. For me, it would have been a period of pain, depression and suffering.

I went back to Lupoaia until university started on October 1. I took our cow to the fields, carrying my radio in its red nylon net and listened to the beautiful sound of Italian, as I used to do in the past. Again I was mesmerized by the melody and harmony of the language that had kept me company in the solitary hours on Lupoaia's pastures. I devoured the music emanating from every Italian word, even from those I knew were Communist propaganda. Why had I let my fear of military service prevent me from trying for the Italian exam?

The Dean

My father decided to accompany me to Bucharest for the start of my university life. He got Mr Ardelean's phone number and told me that, while he was in Bucharest to settle me in, he planned to visit him. He said he wanted to see if Gicu Ardelean had become a snob, like many others who left the village and then pretended not to know you. I think my father was eager to introduce me to somebody who, in a time of need, would be there for me, because Lupoaia was 700km away. So, as usual, he packed a big suitcase with a demijohn of *pălinca*, half a pork, a few chickens, eggs, onions, and off we went.

Grandma Saveta and Mama cried again, just as they did when I left for Beiuş High School. For the past year they had become so used to my presence in the house, spoiling me with soups, cakes and whatever they could think of. They knew that this separation would be a lasting one, one that would eventually cut us off from each other. I was not their little boy, who would come home from high school every two or three weekends, anymore. Life was claiming me and taking me further and further away from them. It was hard for them to let go, thinking of all I had to face alone, in a world far away and full of strangers.

After twelve hours on the train, we arrived in Bucharest early in the morning and took a bus to the university, with my father wiping the suitcase now and then to remove the fluids seeping from the meat inside.

Luckily there was no queue at the Faculty Secretariat. I immediately received my bed allocation in a room that slept 8, in the college just across the road, in Academiei Street. Now we were free. The public phone in the hall was our first priority. Mrs Ardelean said Gicu was at the museum, but we could go to their place in Brezoianu Street. She was going to call him right away.

"You are very close," she said, "just turn left from Academiei Street, cross Calea Victoriei, pass the Army House and Brezoianu is at the end of the street."

As we passed the Army House, our suitcase oozing salty fluids on all sides, a slender figure, with long curly hair, waved to us with both hands.

"Pavelea!"

"Gicu!"

"Good to see you after so many years," Gicu said.

"You haven't changed a bit – you are still the old Gicu from Lupoaia," my father said. "I would have recognized you among a million faces."

Gicu helped my father with the suitcase, and took us to the communal courtyard of a low block of flats, buried among tall buildings.

"We are up there," Gicu said, pointing to a row of windows on the first floor.

Gicu had been adopted from a large family, at an early age, by the local pub owner who, when the Communists took power, was considered an exploiter. The smart Gicu decided to revert to his healthier social origin by having the adoption papers declared invalid. No sooner had he ended his formal schooling, than he took on the role of propagandist, first on behalf of the Communist youth organization, and later for the Party itself. As a reward for his efficiency, they had sent him to the university, with the intention of appointing him to an executive position. On completion of his studies, he had opted for a teaching post in preference to his promising political career. Now he was the director of a museum dedicated to a sculptor who, in 1948, had been quick to offer the new Communist regime all his works, to be displayed in a museum bearing his name.

Their apartment consisted of one large room, a tiny kitchen and a very small bathroom. There was a large, solid table in the middle of the large room, which comfortably seated twelve people but could be extended further if necessary. It was covered with a brilliant red oriental rug. Against the wall opposite the window, a solid antique cupboard stood beside a dark red terracotta stove where Marilena Ardelean kept her brushes. An unbleached linen curtain concealed a double bed. Behind it, piled in disarray, were wooden boxes of paints, brushes, pieces of fabric, pattern designs and metal strips. The walls were covered with numerous beautiful icons, rubbing shoulders, in cluttered confusion, with decorative ceramic plates collected by Marilena on long pilgrimages throughout the country. Here, Marilena, who had graduated in Fine Arts, could pursue her creativity. Daughter of a country priest, she had had difficulty getting into university until she had arranged to be adopted by a working class uncle.

Marilena received us as if we were members of her family. Her Turkish coffee was hot and her cakes exquisite. She created a corner in the room, moving the sofa there for my father to sleep on; because she had decided he was going to stay with them until he left Bucharest.

My father stayed for a week and wanted to visit his former captain. I told him that there was no point. He had a forgiving nature and he went alone. The captain was now a frail man and his wife was not as enthusiastic to see him as he had hoped. Their kids did not even bother to greet my father, but the thing which left the bitterest taste in his mouth was that they were rude to the captain. That displeased him most.

"I would not change my position for theirs," my father said.

When he left, he told me he was happy that the Ardeleans were so close to the university and that they were such good people.

There were supposed to be six of us in Tatar, but a fellow from Dobrudja gave up on the idea of studying. The one who stood out in our group was Suleiman, the son of an imam, he said. Being from the opposite side of the country, I barely knew what an imam was. Suleiman was tall and the curly mass of hair on his head, wide at the top and narrow at the bottom of the forehead, made him appear taller. The hair was cut in a shape that, from a distance, looked like the turban I had seen on Turkish sultans in the history books. He was older than I was and he made it clear, from the start, that his Tatar origin meant that he was stations above all the rest of us. He dismissed the other Tatar in the group, an even older girl called Nevrie, who was shy but cute and had an intelligent look about her. On top of that, she laughed easily and demonstrated a quick sense of humour. She said she had been a teacher and had decided to upgrade her qualifications.

I understood people like Suleiman, I thought, and did not bother feeding his ego. As my interest in him waned, I connected more with the three girls.

The two Romanian girls were Mia and Smaranda.

Mia, a tall, skinny girl with common sense, was the daughter of a factory worker. Smaranda lived with her mother, she said, and tried to hide the fact that her mother was also a factory worker. She wore beautiful coloured dresses, skirts, blouses you couldn't see in the shops, high heels that made her walk as if on walnuts. How could she afford those clothes? The answer came sooner than we expected. The next day she stepped out of a Mercedes; the few Mercedes in Bucharest belonged to the diplomatic corps or to highly placed Party apparatchicks, so our young Smaranda's clothes came from one of those shops where all goods were imported from the West, and were available only to the fat cats of the regime.

Suleiman immediatly named her a little whore and said she should be stoned in the public square. As a first retaliatory measure, he decided not to speak to her again.

A slim young lady entered the lecture room and said we were going to have our first Tatar tutorial. She had a doll-like face, perfect in every feature, from her little well-shaped nose to her discretely painted sensual lips, from her proportionate, white teeth to her velvety, olive skin that invited caresses. I liked her instantly, and during our first tutorial I stared at her more than normal. She rewarded me with gentle, charming smiles. As she walked out of the room, I couldn't resist turning my head to admire those long legs carrying her curvaceous, guitar-like figure.

Suleiman knew a lot about her and told me, with a grimace on his face, that she was a Tatar from Dobrudja, married to a Romanian lecturer in Physics. We were introduced to the language laboratory: a room with old reel-tape recorders which you had to handle carefully so that the reel did not come off. She had recorded a few exercises, mainly pronunciation, and wanted to drill them into our heads. She pointed out, from the beginning, that one of the most difficult sounds for us Romanians was the guttural Tatar "k".

Kara karga kanatlarîn kaga (The black crow flaps her wings)

Then she said that the sound î was going to be difficult, in spite of existing in Romanian, for we didn't have the sequences "n+î" and "sh+î".

Menîm basîmda bîr sîbîn otîra (There is a fly on my head)

When we finished practising with the recorders, she made us repeat the exercises and she would flatter me with her comments. For some reason, she couldn't stand Suleiman. The sentiment was mutual, as Suleiman hated her for having married a Romanian. Moreover, he thought a woman couldn't teach a man anything, particularly a woman, who showed her legs like that in nylon stockings and high heeled shoes. He was marked 8 and I was marked 9 out of 10 in our first paper, and Suleiman started hating me too. I was not going to put up with that, as he was hopeless in grammar and in all his other subjects. He just couldn't accept that it was not enough to speak the language; a future teacher had to master the rules and the grammar to help his students understand how the language worked.

The process of our transformation – into the new man with a luminous future – was slow or non-existent. Our dormitories in Academiei Street were on the upper floors, because the ground floor was home to a series of busy shops. Unfortunately, some of us got into the habit of throwing tomatoes, apple peels, breadcrumbs and the occasional splurt of milk and coffee onto the people walking on the pavement below. Within two months, we were out of there and into the more isolated Regnault dormitories, former stables for the king's horses.

Christmas was around the corner and my parents had killed the pig earlier, to send me a parcel. It was a big wooden box with the food they knew I liked, garlic sausages, blood and rice sausages, fried pork scotch fillet, cut into single portions and stored in melted lard in a big jar, stripes of fresh cured lard, fresh cheese – to be eaten quickly as it did not last long – *pancove*, walnut rolls and cheese buns. My father filled a 5 litres plastic container with *pălinca* for the Ardeleans. The parcel was so heavy that I had to go with Gicu to collect it. Luckily the post office was close to his house and we came prepared with a strong cord, tied the wooden box and made two handles on the sides, and carried it past the Army House like a trophy. This time there was no oozing... only a mixed smell of garlic, meat and *pălinca*, which blended well with the city smells.

It took some time to open the box. Gicu tried to lift the top board with a knife, which reminded me of my younger self when my father came from the mine with the jam box – but it wasn't enough, so he went downstairs to ask the neighbour for a hammer and a chisel. He inserted the chisel under the board and tapped on it with the hammer, just as my father had done with the knife that Christmas night.

On top of the wrapping paper I found a letter from Mama. She said that they thanked God they were reasonably well, although they missed me a lot, after having me in the house for the whole year. She said I should give the *pălinca* to the Ardeleans for being so good to me, and that I should share the rest of the food with them too. By Easter, the raw ham would be ready and I would receive another parcel like this and if the Ardeleans wanted something in particular they would be happy to do it for them. She had made a pullover for me from our sheep's wool over the last two years and I should wear it now that it was winter. The winters in Bucharest were heavier than those at home. She also said that, around the handle of the *pălinca* plastic container, there was a small roll of paper, tied with a string, and that I should be careful when I cut the string, because that was a present from Grandma Saveta. Grandma said that I should use it well.

I opened the present from Grandma and there was a good sum of money. She had the habit of keeping what little money she had in a secret pocket on the back of her apron and guarded it tightly. She was so sweet. I remembered how she would turn away from me and dip her hand into the apron pocket and give me a coin to buy lollies or a glass of raspberry syrup; but the sweetest memory of her was when I was 11 and she came to pick me up from the ditch where I lay sick after school, and offered to carry me home on her back.

Apart from a few sausages, I left everything at the Ardeleans.

I was doing well in Tatar but couldn't get Italian out of my mind. Although I had done Russian and French previously, I considered Italian my first love, if for no other reason than that I was never coerced into learning it. This language had been a great companion on the slopes of Lupoaia, and perhaps that added to its attraction. Crossing paths with the girls from the Italian section and seeing smiles and excitement on their faces as they came out of class, made me a bit envious. The thought of being stuck with the silly Suleiman and the guttural sounds of Tatar for five years made the situation worse, and my yearning to get out of it grew.

I found out that there was a People's University in Bulevardul Magheru, not far from my university. This was an institution for the masses, where various evening courses were offered, Italian among them. No sooner said than done I was in Bulevardul Magheru and, for a small fee, was accepted straight away. I found myself in a classroom of factory workers, teachers, dentists and artists of all ages. I was the only university student.

A young lady with a perfect body, from head to waist, and just the opposite from the waist down, as her thick tubular legs spoiled everything, introduced herself as Andreea and said she was going to be one of our teachers for the year. Her short hair and long neck made her look younger than she was. She got on to the pronunciation of Italian and praised some of us, although I had the impression she paid more attention to my answers.

I was disappointed not to see Andreea entering the classroom for the next session. Instead, our teacher was a relatively young but bald man. He introduced himself as Ovidiu and said he was the head of Italian courses at the People's University. He alternated with Andreea in teaching us Italian.

The following week, Andreea came back and I was very pleased. I had missed her already, in spite of her thick legs. I had prepared my vocabulary, reading and translation perfectly and she noticed it. During the break between the two hours, she asked me if I had taken Italian lessons before. How could I tell her that I had listened to Italian a lot, while taking the cows to pasture on the slopes of Lupoaia?

She said I was doing better than many of her Italian students at the university.

"I would love to study Italian at university," I said, "but I don't know how to go about it."

"Why don't you talk to the Dean?" she said. "I would be happy to give you a good reference."

The Dean! He was the one who had my destiny in his hands, I thought. The wheels of my future passed through his office.

The following day I was keen to visit the Ardeleans. Marilena made me a coffee and told me not to throw the dregs away. She was going to read my future in them, but first she had to take some work to the Artists' State Gallery. Gicu was on his way home, she said. I stayed and enjoyed my coffee, but after a few minutes I looked among their LP collection and pulled out a Beniamino Gigli disc of opera arias. I had not listened much to opera in the past, but when I heard him sing *Nessun Dorma* by Puccini I was mesmerized by the beauty. I listened to it again and again until I knew most of the words by heart. In my uneducated voice, I started singing with Gigli and tried to keep up with him in the final notes of *All'alba vincerò! Vincerò! Vincerò!* I was so transported that I did not see Gicu standing in the door until, at the end of my duet with Gigli, he applauded.

"Bravo! I must say, Gigli is no match for you," he said amused.

"Oh, yes, for noise," I said with a sheepish smile.

Then I told him about Andreea, the Dean and Italian. He listened but he gave me the impression his mind was somewhere else as his eyes seemed to be staring into space. When I finished he said, "So, you want to sing this aria to the Dean?"

"I'd love to, if that is what it takes," I answered jokingly.

"Let's hope that you'll be like the prince in the aria."

I did not know the story, so he told me about the unknown prince who falls in love, at first sight, with a beautiful but cold princess. Any man who wishes to marry the princess has to answer three riddles first; if he fails, he is beheaded. When the unknown prince has correctly answered the three riddles, she recoils at the thought of marrying him. The prince then offers her another chance. She has to guess his name by dawn. If she does so, she can execute him; but if she doesn't, then she has to marry him. The cruel and cold princess then decrees that, on pain of death, none of her subjects are to sleep that night until the prince's name is discovered. That's why the aria is called *Nessun dorma*, he said. In the end the prince kisses the princess who, knowing physical passion for the first time, weeps. The prince tells her his name but, when she goes before the emperor, she tells him that the prince's name is Love.

I was certainly impressed by the story. I saw myself as the unknown prince, doing everything in my power to conquer my princess. *Dilegua, o notte! Tramontate, stelle! Tramontate, stelle! All'alba vincerò! Vincerò! Vincerò!* (Vanish, o night! Set, stars! Set, stars! At dawn, I will win! I will win! I will win!)

Gicu knew the Dean, Professor Modrogan, from their university days. Modrogan was an excellent student in Classics then, while Gicu, older than the rest, was the Party Secretary for their year.

"We will go to see him," Gicu said.

Soon after, we were in Professor Modrogan's office. He was very expansive towards Gicu, which in itself I thought was a good sign. Then, as Gicu described my problem, Professor Modrogan's face became gloomier and gloomier. He said that I should have sat for Italian initially, and that by sitting for Tatar, which I was saying I did not like, I had stolen a place from a person who would be happy with Tatar.

"What marks do you have in Tatar?" he asked.

"Nine."

"Nine?" he almost shouted. "And you say you don't like Tatar?"

"I like Italian more," I said.

"Oh, yes, we are all trying to be smart. We create a problem for ourselves and expect others to solve it for us. That's smart, isn't it?"

Gicu told him I was taking Italian courses at the People's University and was doing very well. They were taught by university staff from the Italian Department.

The Dean seemed to listen but said that was irrelevant and that we all live with the consequences of our decisions. Then he dismissed us and I suddenly remembered *Nessun dorma*. None shall sleep. I wouldn't sleep, for sure, after my attempt had proved to be a failure. I might as well go home and sing with Beniamino Gigli of my desperation. *Non vincerò!* I shall not win. But what sort of prince would I be, if I did that?

"Perhaps I should have gone alone," Gicu said to me. "Perhaps not," he said after thinking a bit more.

Italian, *Amore Mio*

Mr Ardelean's involvement with the Dean, in relation to my transfer to Italian, had raised my expectations. I could easily see myself saying goodbye to Tatar and Suleiman. I also imagined a new life as a student of Italian, coming out of classes smiling and excited, just like the happy girls I encountered daily in the Faculty corridor. I had wanted it so much that the Dean's refusal shattered my world. It was worse than the refusal to sit the entrance exam in the Foreign Trade Faculty. Something inside me was dying. I felt like the young man killed by the wolves, when I was a little boy. He had been attacked by a pack of wolves as he walked alone through the forest in winter. After fighting valiantly and trying to use his axe, he had fallen, when the cunning wolves blinded him by kicking the fresh snow in his eyes with their hind legs. He was lost. When the snow melted with the onset of spring, his bones were found scattered near a black, bottomless waterhole in the depths of the forest. I had to try very hard to convince myself that I was in a better position than he was. Eventually, I found some consolation in the fact that Tatar was better than doing mandatory military service.

A few weeks after our meeting with the Dean, the Ardeleans presented me with a gift. No special occasion. I opened the packet and it was their Beniamino Gigli LP I was so fond of.

"This is your LP," I said with some concern.

"It's yours now," Marilena said.

"I can't take it," I said.

"Yes, you can," Gicu said.

"Why? What for?"

"For good luck," said Gicu.

"We know you like it," Marilena added.

A few days later, Andreea said that the Dean had asked her about my performance in Italian and that he had asked Ovidiu too.

I told Gicu and he said, "I know, I know." He had seen the Dean alone and pleaded with him about my future, telling him what a waste it was going to be, if I did Tatar instead of Italian.

The good Dean had agreed that I could put in an application for a transfer, in spite of his apprehension about being one student short in Tatar. Plans had to be met, and he was going against the grain. Little did he know how his decision would change my life.

I had his approval to go straight into second year Italian. This was due to the fact that Italian, Spanish and Oriental languages were offered only every second year and if you failed, you had to stay at home for a year waiting for the courses to catch up with you as happened to Corneliu, the son of the ambassador to Russia, who was my only male companion in Italian. My transfer approval was conditional on me passing all my winter exams, for the second year, and my first year Italian exams, in the February session. For the first time in my life, I felt my brain was going to explode. While all the other students had four days to a week between exams, I had barely one or two days. I sat for nine exams in just under three weeks. Fortunately, exhaustion set in only after I had finished. I ended up in hospital, though, as my ulcer was acting up under the stress.

I passed my exams with very good marks, particularly in Italian literature and Italian language, so I met the conditions set by the Dean and officially became a student of Italian.

I was sad to leave my beautiful Tatar tutor at the end of the year, but that sadness was soon overcome by the joy of qualifying in the most beautiful language in the world. My dreams, in the days when I took the radio in the red net to the pastures on the slopes of Lupoaia and listened to that unknown language, so melodic, harmonic and sublime, had become reality. I had become infatuated with it and, just like a persistent suitor who doesn't give up in spite of insurmountable obstacles, I had won my bride in the end. I deserved it, I thought. Although I knew my life would still be controlled by the regime, for the first time, I felt I might have some share in that control as well. I finally had a taste of freedom – the freedom to fight for the right to choose. The freedom to win sometimes. After all, one finds freedom in the most unexpected places, like my father when he found it in his hiding hole in the stable under the oxen's manger. My taste of freedom left me determined to fight for it, even if I had to *paint my hands and my face blue and be suddenly swept up by the wind and start to fly in the infinite sky*, like the lover in Modugno's famous song "Volare". It was a new feeling for me; a feeling that the outside world refused me in my childhood. Most of all I had learned that love – no matter if it be for a person, for an idea or for a cause – will always find a way. Sometimes it needed help from other people who were prepared to allow it to bring out the best in them. When that happened there was no way any regime, even the strictest of them all, could hinder it.

Postscriptum

By denying me access to the Foreign Trade Faculty, the regime thrust me into a world I loved and secretly yearned for – that of the Italian word. Soon afterwards I met my Italian wife-to-be, Ariella. She had come to the 12th International Congress of Romance Linguistics and Philology, hosted by my University. The Faculty had sent me and other Language students as guides, having trained us to help Congress participants with information about rooms and activities, sternly warning us not to go beyond that, in our dealings with the dangerous foreigners. Our work was assessed from the shadows – by the omnipresent Securitate.

On the last day of the Congress, Ariella and I spent the afternoon together on a guided tour of the Village Museum in Herăstrău Park. When our official guide was briefly distracted, we strayed from the set itinerary, to sit on a bench under the magnificent white crown of a plum tree. I broke off a flowering branch and handed it to Ariella who, blushing with pretty coquetry, pinned it in her hair.

It was April 20, 1968, the Orthodox Easter eve.

Ariella left me that evening, but the following year she came back. Since all my attempts to get a passport failed, she continued to visit me; and we discovered that we were made for each other and decided to get married. The whole world seemed to turn against us. Priests told us that, as a foreigner, Ariella couldn't marry me in Church, without our producing a civil marriage certificate first.

The civil marriage celebrants told us that Romanian citizens could not marry foreigners, without a special authorization from the State Council, headed by Ceauşescu himself. We learned that it took many months, or even years, to get the authorization; and it was often refused. The law went even further: Romanian citizens were not allowed to have any personal contact with foreigners.

It was too late for them to stop us. Three years after our first encounter, with the help of a courageous young priest, Ariella and I married secretly in a private home. All five people present – the priest, our two hosts, and the two of us – risked mandatory prison sentences. Four months later, after a series of dramatic events, we obtained our State Council authorization and had a civil marriage.

Life in Italy had its ups and downs, mostly the latter. Although I loved the Italian language, it was impossible for me to earn a decent living from it. Six months after my arrival, Ariella was operated on for breast cancer. However, she recovered and subsequently gave birth to our two beautiful, healthy children. Meanwhile, I had to cope with my fear of the *sorpasso* – the Communists were tipped to win the elections in 1976.

So in 1978 we migrated to Australia. This time Italian came to my rescue – it became my profession. But, then, after 15 years of being in charge of Italian at the University of Tasmania, I was made redundant at the age of 50. There had been threats of closure right from the beginning, but after a while I became used to them and did not take them seriously. After all, I had been given tenure along the way, and we had had monetary support from the Italian Cultural Institute for years. Only some months before we were closed, a fully paid lecturer had been assigned to us by the Italian government. Disbelief, dejection, confusion overcame me when it happened because, out of the six disciplines placed on the cuts-list, only Italian – which had clearly demonstrated its ability to help itself – was eventually scrapped. To me and those around me it seemed utterly unfair. I saw myself following in my father's footsteps, when he was declared a *chiabur*: redundant to the community he belonged to. Whatever he said and did to redeem himself did not count, just as in my case. The fact that Italian was run well and would have become the cheapest discipline in the Faculty did not matter. I started thinking that my father and I were both victims of politics: he of a tyrannical Communist regime and I of a poor capitalist administration. After a while I kept asking myself what would be the odds for a father and son, living in two different social systems, ideologically so far apart, to go through a similar experience again. In moments of inevitable self-pity, I remembered my father telling me, when I was a school boy, never to worry, because what I put up there, in my head, the Communists would not ever be able to take away from me. Well, what I had put in my head was still there, but it did not help me keep my job. And there were no Communists involved in my demise. That really hurt. Eventually, I adjusted to my new situation; but my father would have had a hard time understanding how it was possible for people with a PhD to lose their job. For him, doctorate holders were up there with the gods. Jobs ran after them, not the other way around.

I live now at that end of the world my Mama saw at my birth, where I am surrounded by children with beautiful, bright eyes and eager faces – who speak words unlike anything she'd ever heard – and yet have features resembling those of great-grandpa Pavelea and his Măriuța, of my grandparents Teodorea and Maria, Toderea and Saveta, and of my father and herself. I feel so comfortable around them and, while I count my blessings, I finally realise how far I've had to travel and how long I've had to wait to find a form of happiness.

Acknowledgments

My first two languages are Romanian and Italian, in that order. Then comes English, the language in which I wanted to write this book. Consequently, producing the first draft was rather a laborious task as I frequently had to consult dictionaries: Romanian-English or Italian-English, depending on the language in which words or expressions I was looking for, first came to me.

Then, as no man is an island, I am greatly indebted to many people whose support helped me bring this book to fruition.

First of all I am most grateful to my friend and former colleague, Dr Maria Flutsch, who, as my first editor, helped me purge the first draft of its many linguistic uncertainties.

My thanks go also to Louise Crowley and Leo Cini for going through the manuscript, or part of it; to Pat Bessell for early translations of material from Italian, and to Dr Edith Evenhuis for being there – in a very creative way – in the final stages.

My heartfelt thanks to three wonderful writer-friends from different continents, who read drafts and helped me improve them: Chris McLeod from Australia, whose initial advice set me on the right course, the late Jayne Pupek from the United States, who had the gift of unlocking my memory, and Helena Drysdale from England, who herself has written a wonderful book on Romania and who helped me shape the final draft.

Many thanks to my young friend, Jan Seiler, for formatting the book and designing a beautiful cover.

I owe a lot to my dear friends Roberto Carnevale and Giovanni Francesconi, with whom I have spent many a delightful night in the Australian bush, reminiscing about the time of our youth, helped in that way by their excellent wine, *prosciutto* and *pasta* – the flavoursome *grappa*, offered by our common friend, Toni Breda, kept reminding me of the *pălinca* my father made all his life. I would also like to thank Don Martelli, Ugo and Remo Carnevale, who contributed greatly to the convivial bush atmosphere. Through their tales and outdoor cooking I discovered that many traditions and customs, in their villages back home in Italy, were similar to those of Lupoaia. To my great bewilderment, I made another great discovery: a soldier in the Austro-Hungarian army, my Grandfather Teodorea had fought against Giovanni's father at the battle of Piave – they were born the same year. Instead of weakening our friendship, that discovery united us still more.

For our many often heated discussions of all things European during our daily walks around Taroona Beach, I am grateful to my former student and good friend Domenico Capece.

The proximity of my two sons, Francesco and Stefano, and my daughters-in-law, Rosalina and Ana – all born outside Australia – has often brought to mind my own family, when I was a child, and the crucial role it played in my life. Without my parents' sacrifices and their belief that education was the most important thing in one's life, I would, most probably, have gone nowhere.

I owe it all to my beautiful grandchildren, Matteo, Isabella and Lorenzo, for finishing this book. Their joyous presence in my life, these last years, has been a constant reminder that the story had to be told.

Last but not least, I am grateful to my lovely and patient wife, Ariella, who has made my life very different from what it could have been.

Printed in Great Britain
by Amazon

24875921R00195